BEGINNING YOUR JOURNEY

NASPA
Student Affairs Administrators
in Higher Education

MARILYN J. AMEY
& LORI M. REESOR

EDITORS

BEGINNING YOUR
JOURNEY

*A Guide for New Professionals
in Student Affairs*

NASPA
Student Affairs Administrators
in Higher Education

Beginning Your Journey: A Guide for New Professionals in Student Affairs

Additional copies may be purchased by contacting the NASPA publications department at 301-638-1749 or visiting http://www.naspa.org/pubs.

ISBN 978-0-931654-61-9

Contents

ACKNOWLEDGMENTS

The editors of this book are grateful to the contributing authors who shared their wisdom and experiences with the readers. These are leaders in our profession of student affairs, and we are appreciative of their participation in this book.

The contributing authors of this book wish to thank the many new professionals across the country who added their stories to this text. Their willingness to share experiences and insights made this a rich experience for us all.

Joy Blanchard expresses her appreciation to J. Douglas Toma, associate professor at the Institute of Higher Education at the University of Georgia, for his comments on drafts of chapter seven, and for allowing her to continue the work he started in previous editions of this book on the topic of reconciling life and work.

Florence Hamrick and Brian Hemphill wish to thank the following individuals who generously shared their expertise and words for use in chapter eight: Karl Brooks, Joan Claar, Patrick Day, Kristi Gimmel Becker, Dennis Golden, Sandra Gonzalez-Torres, Eric Hartman, James Holmen, Joi Lewis, Michelle Moore, Augustine Pounds, Dan Robinson, Mary Beth Snyder, and Mary Spellman. This chapter also reflects input from 14 new professionals who attended a focus group session at the Fall 1996 Iowa State Personnel Association Annual Conference. Their insights and concerns regarding career advancement issues helped structure the chapter.

Finally, the editors want to extend a special editorial thanks to Pamela Roy, doctoral student at Michigan State University, who worked tirelessly on the final edition.

INTRODUCTION

Marilyn J. Amey and Lori M. Reesor

"New professionals are the future of our profession." This is a common phrase heard when a seasoned staff member addresses a group of newcomers to the profession. Our graduate degree programs concentrate on providing students with the theoretical and practical experiences that will help them succeed in the student affairs profession. As we know, however, these programs are diverse in their teachings and emphases. It is crucial that NASPA be an active voice in the development of new professionals; this book is one way of demonstrating that commitment.

The purpose of the book is to help ease the transition from graduate student to full-time professional and to increase the retention of new professionals in the field. It is not intended as an administrative cookbook but rather as an examination of key issues facing new professionals and ways of thinking about the challenges and opportunities in careers in student affairs. The issues facing those entering the profession have a certain degree of comparability, whether one assumes a first professional position or moves into student affairs from a career in another field; and whether one is employed at a community college, a liberal arts college, or a research university. Understanding organizational culture and its impact on work, thinking through career configurations, reflecting on the aspects of collegiate life that affect the way work unfolds, exploring the values and belief systems of the field—all these issues confront new professionals. For more experienced professionals who are moving into the student affairs arena, past experience, knowledge, and expectations affect perspective and create a different set of needs and concerns. Because of the space limitations of the book, we assume a primary readership of entering professionals and try to capture experiences that those new to the field have in common. We use the term "new professional" throughout the text. We also assume that supervisors, graduate preparation faculty, and other supporters of new professionals constitute a secondary audience for the book, and that they will find the discussion of current issues as seen by new professionals useful.

To identify the most relevant issues, we begin with a brief discussion of the arena in which student affairs professionals work in the 21st century. We work in organizations that are both political and diverse. If new professionals are unaware of the nature of colleges and universities, or do not understand the competing priorities that cause institutional members to negotiate for resources, they can be adversely affected by organizational politics. In addition to its inherent political culture, the higher education system is struggling to achieve a truly multicultural orientation. Numerous authors believe that the future of colleges and universities lies in creating a multicultural environment (Chang, Denson, Saenz, & Misa, 2006; El-Khawas, 2003; Hurtado, Milem, Clayton-Pedersen, & Allen, 1998; Pope, Reynolds, & Mueller, 2004; Shaw, Valadez, and Rhoads, 1999; Stage & Manning, 1992). They call for changes in institutional climate and culture to accommodate an increasingly diverse student population; for increasing the cultural diversity of faculty and staff; for changing institutional directives, statutes, and policies to reflect the realities of a changing clientele; for increased technological expertise and instruction that accommodate a wider range of learning styles; and for leadership that can facilitate the transformation of the academy into a multicultural environment for the 21st century.

We also recognize the extent to which postsecondary institutions are struggling to redefine themselves in the midst of a technological and global revolution that is changing every aspect of academe—what it means to be an educator, to be a learner, to provide services for students, and even to be a college campus. Although we cannot foresee all the ways in which increased uses of technology will transform the practice of student affairs, it is clear that things are changing. New professionals face the press of politics, fundamental philosophic changes, seemingly unlimited innovation, and boundary redefinition. We have written this book with those environmental constructs in mind.

We believe, also, in the value of hearing from professionals themselves. Therefore, personal vignettes and the "talk" of new professionals are woven throughout the book to give voice to their concerns, strategies, and beliefs. Sometimes, these voices are those of individual professionals, included to illustrate a specific point; at other times, the voices represent amalgams of viewpoints expressed by many. Pseudonyms are used in all cases to protect confidentiality.

Kari Ellingson and Barbara Snyder start off by reflecting on the issues from the perspective of new professionals and senior-level student affairs officers. In dialogic fashion, Ellingson, Snyder, and several colleagues add their voices to the words of others included throughout the volume, speaking directly about the challenges facing new professionals and those who attempt to provide support and guidance. Marilyn Amey, Eric Jessup-Anger, and Connie Tingson-Gatuz discuss the organizational and political realities likely to confront new professionals as they take on full-time responsibilities in student affairs. They present a conceptual model of organizational culture as a framework for thinking through these critical issues. Anna Ortiz and Carla Martinez consider the implicit values that give form and nuance to administrative practice. They define professional and personal ethics, emphasizing the importance of ethics in all aspects of student affairs work. They describe the importance of having an ethical stance to deal with traditional issues such as excessive workloads and student conduct, as well as new issues such as those associated with social networking sites and social justice. Randi Schneider and Kevin Bailey examine the complexities of supervision and the role of the supervisor. Using organizational and leadership theories as guideposts, Schneider and Bailey describe how this relationship is manifested and offer insights for dealing with potential (often inevitable) dissonance.

Camille Consolvo and Michael Dannells help us think through the issues of collaboration between student affairs professionals and faculty. They highlight some of the challenges and opportunities, and provide useful strategies for cultivating the relationships that support student learning. Lori Reesor, Grace Bagunu, and Melissa Hazley discuss various approaches to professional involvement and networking, inter- and intra-institutionally. They describe avenues for participation and issues associated with cross-gender and cross-cultural support systems. Joy Blanchard tackles a key component of a successful career in student affairs work: finding life balance. New professionals need to find a healthy equilibrium as they strive to excel in their personal and professional lives. Blanchard offers insights and frameworks for thinking through these key decisions and choices. Florence Hamrick and Brian Hemphill take professional development and career planning in a different direction as they explore career paths and advancement opportunities. They discuss various scenarios, including the role of doctoral study, and present ways of envisioning one's future in the profession.

Eugene Zdziarski and Dawn Watkins look at the issue of campus crisis management, which has come to the forefront in recent years. Their matrix shows how a campus can prepare for and implement crisis management processes, and suggests a way of thinking about the small and large issues facing student affairs professionals that is planful rather than reactionary. Brent Paterson and Christa Coffey lay out strategies for the all-important first job search. Whether you are moving into student affairs from a graduate preparation program or making a switch in mid-career, Paterson and Coffey will help you think through your personal strengths, goals, preferred work environments, and so on. They offer helpful tools in an age of Facebook application portfolios and careers that span multiple jobs.

Finally, Shannon Ellis brings together the reflections of leaders in the profession. We honor the words of new professionals themselves throughout the book. In the same spirit, we find great value and wisdom in listening to the voices of the leaders who have come before, who helped shape the profession as we know it today, and whose commitment to student affairs remains as deep and unwavering as it was when they, too, were new professionals.

We are reminded of the words of one of these leaders. Although she wrote them almost two decades ago, Margaret Barr's (1993) advice about enjoying work and being an effective administrator is equally relevant today and serves as the foundation for our book. She said, "Enjoy the students"; "Become involved in the institution"; "Maintain perspective"; and "Take time to smell the roses" (pp. 525–526).

References

Barr, M. J. (1993). Becoming successful student affairs administrators. In M. J. Barr & Associates (Eds.), *The Handbook of Student Affairs Administration* (pp. 522–529). San Francisco: Jossey-Bass.

Chang, M. J., Denson, N., Saenz, V., & Misa, K. (2006). The educational benefits of sustaining cross-racial interaction among undergraduates. *Journal of Higher Education, 77*(3), 430–455.

El-Khawas, E. (2003). The many dimensions of student diversity. In S. R. Komives, D. B. Woodard, Jr., & Associates (Eds.), *Student services: A handbook for the profession* (4th ed., pp. 45–62). San Francisco: Jossey-Bass.

Hurtado, S., Milem, J. F., Clayton-Pedersen, A. R., & Allen, W. R. (1998). Enhancing campus climates for racial/ethnic diversity: Educational policy and practice. *Review of Higher Education, 21*(3), 279–302.

Pope, R. L., Reynolds, A. L., & Mueller, J. A. (2004). *Multicultural competence in student affairs*. San Francisco: Jossey-Bass.

Shaw, K. M., Valadez, J., and Rhoads, R. (Eds.). (1999). *Community colleges as cultural texts: Qualitative explorations of organizational and student culture*. Albany, NY: SUNY Press.

Stage, F. K., & Manning, K. (1992). *Enhancing the multicultural campus environment: A cultural brokering approach*. New Directions for Student Services, no. 60. San Francisco: Jossey-Bass.

VOICES OF EXPERIENCE

CHAPTER ONE

Kari Ellingson and Barbara Snyder

A ny new professional faces challenges in his or her role, regardless of the discipline or the organization. Student affairs professionals are no exception. To learn more about the transitional issues facing new professionals, Barbara Snyder, vice president for student affairs, and Kari Ellingson, associate vice president for student development, University of Utah, met with a group of seven colleagues who have been student affairs professionals for two to five years. These new professionals represent different ethnicities, sexual orientations, educational backgrounds, and life circumstances; however, common themes emerged among the group.

Choosing a Career in Student Affairs

Many new professionals select student affairs as a career after being identified by someone already in the profession as having potential. A student leader catches the eye of an advisor, who then serves as a vehicle for learning more about student affairs as a profession. Most students are pleasantly surprised to learn that the experiences they love as an undergraduate can be turned into a job.

Aramis, coordinator for leadership development, selection and training, housing and residential education: *I was approached while working on a homecoming event as a sophomore. My advisor said, "You enjoy being involved. Why don't you think about getting into higher education?" She talked to me about her experiences, and I spent the rest of my time there knowing that I was going to graduate school in the area.*

Michael, assistant director, housing and residential education: *My experiences were very similar. I got tapped on the shoulder by multiple people. In my sophomore year with Res Life (Residence Life), different advisors said, "Have you thought about student affairs?", but I didn't give it much thought until I graduated with a business degree. I realized I wanted to do something that was more my style and suited my personality.*

Jay, assistant dean of students: *I remember laughing at the person who tapped me on the shoulder, thinking, "Yeah, right, why would I work for a university? Isn't the whole point of coming here to eventually leave?" A few years later, I was at an ASJA (Association for Student Judicial Affairs) conference and my interests in law, conflict resolution, and student affairs all seemed to gel. I thought, "Wait a minute...I can do all these things in one place!"*

Aramis, Michael, and Jay followed a traditional path to student affairs. Although Jay completed law school while Aramis and Michael finished their master's degrees in a higher education program; all three were very involved as undergraduates and were steered toward student affairs by advisors. They came to the field with a theoretical knowledge base that many established student affairs professionals lack. Others, like Patrick, entered through other avenues.

Patrick, career counselor, career services: *My decision was really haphazard. I thought positions at institutions of higher education were for the class president, and I was never involved in college because I worked full time. So I was just randomly looking for a job four years ago and applied for a position with admissions at my alma mater. After I got the job, I realized that it was the best position I'd ever had, one that I can be passionate about.*

Regardless of how one enters the profession—from a traditional graduate preparation program or from a peripheral academic discipline—all new professionals bring valuable knowledge and skills they can use to enhance the student experience. Whether the new professional planned for this career since the first or second year in college or fell into the field while pursuing another goal, department managers can maximize experiences and build working teams by drawing from the strengths that individuals bring. New professionals will achieve the greatest success if they take time to learn from their colleagues and use their own skills to complement, rather than compete with, others. They should pay attention to the backgrounds and educational experiences of their co-workers, and team up with those who can help them approach problems or issues in innovative and creative ways. Senior student affairs administrators will appreciate and enhance the experience of those who work collaboratively with others. Effective student affairs programs are those that meld the institutional identity of more seasoned professionals with the enthusiasm and innovative ideas of new professionals.

> **Most students are pleasantly surprised to learn that the experiences they love as an undergraduate can be turned into a job.**

Identity

New professionals often struggle with the transition from student to professional. They might find themselves leaving a setting where they felt comfortable and competent, and moving into an environment where they are faced with a steep learning curve. And those who make the transition from student to professional at their undergraduate institution face a special set of challenges.

Tony, associate director, student recruitment: *I was involved in student leadership as an undergraduate and then, all of a sudden, I'm a professional at the same school and have a different role, a different schedule, and a different set of expectations. As a student senator, I was welcomed when I visited different deans and asked for things. Now, [as a professional] I'm treated differently. Instead of giving me money, they say, "Why are you asking our office for support when you have your own budget?" It's a little weird.*

Patrick: *My first job was with recruiting for my alma mater, and I knew everyone there from when I was a student. On the one hand, it's a really nice, positive experience, because you're the cool, young guy who gets to work with these 18-year-olds; but on the other hand, it was a difficult transition for me in terms of professionalism. I'll be the first to admit I don't think I handled it well, because I was still stuck in those two roles—how do I keep these students interested and excited while still having this professional persona? It was a huge learning curve for me that first year.*

Some found that making a clean break from their life as a student prepared them to take on the role of new professional.

Karla, enrollment management specialist: *My senior year, I quickly realized that if I was going to go into this profession, I needed to disassociate myself from my classmates. That was the most difficult thing I had to do, because I completely cut myself off to start focusing on my career. By the time I got into this position, it was a much easier transition.*

Jay: *Students would come up and start treating me like a student because I looked younger. They'd be swearing and telling me about the parties they went to—so it was a conscious choice for me to draw the boundaries and say, "Okay, you're not allowed into this space."*

The role of a supervisor during this early transition is critical. Two of the new professionals discussed having supervisors leave during their first several months on the job and floundering while they tried to establish their roles with no guidance. Whether new professionals are in a large or small student affairs division, many tasks are the same. While simultaneously discovering the nuances of a new job in a specific department, they are trying to learn the culture of student affairs and understand the big picture of how student affairs fits into the institutional mission. Supervisors should provide this link to the greater vision and introduce new professionals to colleagues who can help them complete their job successfully while providing additional opportunities to expand their experiences and competencies. New professionals must let their supervisors know what they need, so the supervisors can provide support and assistance. It is also a good idea to look outside the department for other perspectives and additional support. Volunteering for a committee in another department or outside student affairs can offer tremendous opportunities for growth.

> **The rewards of having chosen a professional career in student affairs are deep and life-changing.**

Experiencing Rewards

New professionals come to students affairs with expectations formed in their undergraduate and graduate experiences. As the person now responsible for helping create those opportunities for undergraduates, the new student affairs professional will reap many rewards—some unexpected.

Sara, service scholar coordinator, community service center: *One of my favorite things is seeing a student who may be struggling with what direction they should take, maybe needing to conceptualize their own service project as a scholar. I love to see them take on those leadership roles and guide other students. Helping them work through those issues without actually doing it for them and seeing them succeed is a really rewarding experience.*

Aramis: *I think one of the most rewarding experiences is seeing others whom you've helped choose this profession. Seeing them take those next steps to enter the field where you have chosen to devote your professional career and having had a role in that is great.*

Jay: *I think the bonus, as a new professional, is that you are closer to the age group so it seems students can trust you a little more. There is that little bit about being the "cool guy." If you are doing a good job, strokes to the ego are sort of gratifying, but it's important to know why that is—you're younger and you look like them. You can challenge them on issues that their peers won't challenge them on, yet you're almost a peer. It's almost like you're a big brother or sister they can look up to.*

Patrick: *For me personally, college was the greatest time of my life, so being involved with other people who are doing that thing I loved so much is just totally fulfilling. I can easily rattle off [the names of] 10 to 20 people who helped me as an undergraduate. It's sort of fulfilling to think that I might be one of those people for a student.*

The rewards of having chosen a professional career in student affairs are deep and life-changing. Because of these rewards, there is a tendency for new professionals to lose some balance in their lives. In seeking balance and experiencing occasional (but not frequent or permanent) burnout, it is important to keep in mind that the rewards will still be there. During the high-stress times, it is important for the new professional to remember the many reasons he or she chose student affairs as a career.

Meeting Challenges

Each new professional faces a unique set of challenges, depending on background, work setting, and specific job responsibilities. As new professionals embrace these challenges and use them as opportunities to learn about the profession, they can begin to identify their career paths. Some find that they enjoy developing innovative solutions to programmatic issues, while others enjoy budgetary and administrative puzzles.

Tony: *I guess I wasn't prepared for some of the issues involved in working with people from my own culture with Mexican backgrounds. I didn't know where to draw the line. I was getting calls on Sunday and going to dinners to talk about the [admissions] application process. I wasn't prepared for what different communities expected of me, and I didn't know how to meet all of the demands. Professionally, I knew what my director expected, but then there were cultural expectations and expectations from the high school guidance counselors and expectations from the students—and everyone wanted different things.*

Aramis: *I would say the most eye-opening aspect of being a professional is being a full-time person mentoring other full-time people. I don't think there's any amount of training that could prepare you for that mentoring piece, but I didn't really feel like a professional until I got that opportunity to be partly responsible for someone else's development.*

Sara: *I wasn't expecting to talk to parents very often, since I work with service learning scholars. I've had five or six parents call this year to talk about their students. I know it's a trend, but it hadn't been something on my radar until it actually happened.*

Michael: *One challenge for me was recognizing that, while my undergraduate experience was amazing, not everyone wants that. I came into the field because I wanted to replicate my experience, because it was a magical place. I now realize that students may have different experiences from mine and still enjoy college.*

Karla: *When I go to the high schools, I still get asked for my hall pass, and I have to explain that I'm not a student. I find with parents that, although they only half-trust me at first, after I talk to them, they are okay with me working with their students. And budgets—I wasn't trained in budgets, and there are some challenges in handling a budget. It's different and difficult.*

Tony: *Another challenge was realizing that I don't know as much as I thought I did. Reading the job description, interviewing, and being so confident, and then getting there and realizing that I needed to do a little bit of training. It was hard to realize that I wasn't able to hit the ground running and that there was going to be a learning curve.*

All professionals face issues of expectations and establishing a professional identity. Even seasoned professionals revisit these issues periodically throughout their careers as they move to new settings, advance their careers, or try to incorporate personal life changes into their jobs. But these tasks are never as salient as they are during the first several years in a field. Since most supervisors have been through these experiences, it is incumbent on them to help the new professional navigate these challenges. Each institution is unique, and being successful is not just about knowing the job but also about understanding the culture. Although challenges may be similar from one institution to another, expectations for new staff may differ, depending on whether the school is public or private, large or small, religiously affiliated or an historically black college or university (HBCU). It is critical for new professionals to ask what is expected of them or to check their perceptions of expectations with their supervisor or trusted colleagues. Also, they should be willing to admit mistakes and seek help. Taking advantage of opportunities or suggesting innovative ideas requires a certain amount of risk-taking, which often is uncomfortable for professionals at any level. As long as a new professional keeps his or her supervisor informed and asks for help as needed, new ways of seeing old problems are often among the most valuable contributions new professionals can make.

Achieving Balance

New professionals must develop a persona separate from their undergraduate or graduate role. They are often building a new life in a new place while starting a new job; this can be overwhelming. Knowing when to take time for themselves and establishing healthy behaviors are essential skills to learn early.

Karla: *I've always been an overachiever, and it's been hard for me to find balance, especially as a single parent. I've decided not to go for my doctorate until my daughter is older. I've decided to bring less stress home by delaying further education. I also used to have a PDA, but I decided against it. I was frantic when I was home, answering e-mails at all hours of the night.*

Michael: *I'd say I'm balanced about 75% of the time. Most of the time I'm balanced, but there are certain times of the year when work is your life, and that's just how I feel my job is. I'm sometimes working 10- to 12-hour days, but other times it's relaxing and we take long lunches. I'd say, "Enjoy those times!"*

Aramis: *The balance piece is harder to achieve when you live where you work. So many new professionals start out in the housing track and have to struggle with balance, because you can't leave your work space. Students knew where I lived and could track me down. At the same time, interactions with students at 2:00 a.m. were some of the fun times, and I know I'm going to miss that.*

Sara: *I make sure I go to the gym every day. I'm just a happier person. I can get pretty cranky if I sit at my desk all day. I also like meeting new people and getting to know personal things about them, even if it's just talking 15 minutes in the hallway. Also, I make it a point to leave work at work.*

Jay: *I think one of the great things about working in student affairs here is that it promotes balance. I feel like it's part of my job to talk about balance with student leaders. What I like about my job is that I have to stay centered to do my job well when it comes to difficult issues. There was a time a few years ago when I was in a rough spot and, when students came to me, I couldn't be that empathic person. Now I can be.*

Student affairs professionals tend to be passionate about their work. Helping students and leading exciting projects make the work stimulating and rewarding. The new professional may often have numerous equally attractive opportunities and, in an effort to learn more, agree to take on all of them. One of the greatest challenges for new professionals is finding balance in their work. Many enter the field because they want to work with students, so it is often difficult, if not impossible, to say "no" to student requests for late night, weekend, or even overnight commitments. Staff who develop good rapport with students will undoubtedly be asked to give more and more of their time. New professionals will benefit by establishing a work routine that shows that they value their health, their personal and family commitments, and their own sanity, as well as their professional commitments. Finding ways to have nonwork friendships, volunteering in the community, exercising, establishing a work routine, and developing hobbies and recreational outlets can help foster a healthy lifestyle.

Professional Development

New professionals have entered student affairs for many reasons: They loved their undergraduate experience; they are passionate about students; they are stimulated by the higher education environment. As they begin to master their job skills, understand the higher education culture and adjust to the role of professional, they must also find ways to make a personal commitment to their own development. This may mean developing a plan for career growth and working with supervisors to identify skill deficits, as well as determining appropriate (and affordable) professional opportunities such as conferences and trainings. Senior administrators who believe in professional development should support new professionals while balancing the needs of other staff and other fiscal priorities. All too often, seasoned staff can find the funds internally to finance their professional development, while new professionals, with small or nonexistent budgets, must pay the costs from their own pockets.

Tony: *I have turned to my supervisor, who is really good at giving me the appropriate amount of responsibility—not so much that I take over all the projects, but so that I can have a sense of his environment. It's been a really good thing for me—to have the appropriate number of programs to oversee with the appropriate number of staff and budgets to supervise.*

Jay: *When I think of professional development in our field, all my opportunities have been self-selected, things that I want to go to. I feel fortunate to be in a job where I really like learning about interesting things. If a conference pops up that really sounds great, it's neat that the university encourages that and provides support for it. I have friends in other lines of work where people say, "Argh…I have to go to this training in Albuquerque and it's going to be so boring." They are ordered to go and they hate it. We get to choose and we enjoy it.*

Patrick: *It's nice to have an outlet where I might address my deficits in terms of my own professional career. I feel I don't have enough presentation or publication experience. I've appreciated having the op-*

*portunity to see people who are just like me giving presentations that
are mind-blowing, and it gives me the desire to be like that. In higher
education, there's the opportunity to see people who do amazing things,
and it drives me to step up and do amazing things myself.*

Michael: *My supervisor wants each of her people to have their own professional development plan. It's part of our training for staff—you identify what you want to get out of the year and how you can achieve it.
She let me go to NASPA (conference) to interview alone. Now I'm able to
say I was in charge of the interviewing and selection process. She is very
intentional about her staff having those experiences so they can grow.*

When considering positions at different institutions, it is critical to ask
about the approach to professional development. How much support will the
institution offer? How intentional are supervisors about working with new professionals on their development? One way to determine institutional investment in professional development is to ascertain the activity level of the student
affairs leaders in professional organizations.

Professional development happens both at the home institution and at
conferences or workshops. Supervisors are often a good source of information
about opportunities on campus and beyond. In lieu of traveling to a conference, e-learning can be as close as the nearest computer. Student affairs staff
should take advantage of the opportunities that present themselves. With
so many online services and information sources, new professionals have
no excuse not to invest time and energy in their professional development.
Those who will advance most quickly and have the most rewarding careers
are those who stay abreast of issues, programs, people, and events on the
local, regional, and national levels. The new professional should probably
expect to pay for some of this involvement, at least initially. However, most
seasoned professionals agree that it is well worth the investment over the
course of a career.

Supervisors, Administrators, and Mentors

New professionals need help defining their jobs, seeking out responsibilities, and broadening expectations. They must feel comfortable making (and
admitting) mistakes and asking questions in order to develop the expertise required to advance in the field. They benefit from supervisors who help them
navigate the institution and explain the culture when it seems confusing. They

need assistance in assessing their career path, charting it, and preparing for future steps. They require both formal and informal feedback about their performance. And they often need someone to tell them to slow down, take a deep breath, and relax.

Aramis: *The most important thing a supervisor can give me is the freedom to put my ideas out there. I've had a lot of opportunities where I came to my former supervisor and said, "Here's what I want to do with my building—help me achieve this idea." It might not have been in the overall departmental picture, but everyone got behind my thought and that was because of my supervisor. What I need is support for my visions and thoughts, and help making it happen. And letting me have those ideas but not leading me down a path where I'll get shot down two seconds later.*

Patrick: *Having a supervisor who likes what I do makes me comfortable in challenging myself and thinking up new ideas. It's nice to have that support to try new things. Having supervisors who allow and encourage you to go beyond your comfort zone is great. They'll say, "Have you ever thought about trying this?" It gives me a sense of being recognized and makes my job totally awesome.*

Sara: *For me, a good supervisor is someone who gets to know me professionally but also has some personal knowledge of me and where I want to go. They think about what they can do to help me meet the next goal. I want someone who can push me a little bit and provide opportunities for growth.*

> **Just have fun doing what you do. I've always had the philosophy that when this stops being fun, I need to pick something else to do, but it hasn't stopped being fun yet.**

Karla: *I'm in a new position that I'm creating. My supervisor leaves me alone to decide what's going to be the next goal, which I take as a compliment. It's rewarding to have his trust and know that I can make a difference.*

For new professionals, access to student affairs leadership is also an important aspect in understanding their new environment. Diverse perspectives from supervisors, directors, deans, and senior student affairs officers can help the new employee understand his or her role in the department and where the department fits into the mission of student affairs and the university.

Michael: *I think accessibility to people in higher level positions is important. I want to know that people recognize me and that I can pick up the phone if I'm stuck and talk to someone about the issue.*

Patrick: *I also think it's important to realize that not all colleges are like that. I've worked at a campus where there isn't the same level of access between new professionals and upper level administration.*

Supervisors or administrators may become mentors, or mentors can be found outside the department, outside student affairs, or even outside the institution.

Jay: *I think finding a mentor is kind of like Greek recruitment—a mutual selection process. The strategy is for a new professional to put yourself around good people and let it happen. The mentors are usually the ones who are reaching out, saying, "Come on; let me show you the way."*

Michael: *Two of the people who helped me get into the field are my mentors. I think I've kept my mentors intentionally as people who aren't currently at my institution. Sometimes there are things going on where it is helpful to talk to someone objective from the outside.*

Patrick: *I even see peers as mentors. There are people in other offices—I just love what they do and I want to be involved with them. I see the impact they have on campus and I want to find out how they do it. I just shove myself in as a mentee to learn from them.*

Tony: *I think it's important that a mentor is someone you can open up and confide in. It's happened for me with people I've worked with on a project, where we begin to bond and they can give me that feedback.*

Senior student affairs administrators are responsible for setting the professional climate of the division and promoting a culture that brings new professionals along through support and encouragement. Just as the success of a university is determined by the accomplishments of its graduates, so, too, is the success of student affairs programs determined by staff at all levels and their ability to be effective in their work and their lives. Those just entering the field are often the ones who have the most direct contact with students. It is critical that both administrators and supervisors give them the tools they need to be successful as they learn to take their place at the student affairs table.

New professionals should look for leaders and mentors who are willing to answer questions and give advice, especially those who have successfully established themselves as respected members of the university community. Mentors can be found anywhere—often in unexpected places—and a mentoring relationship should not be limited to one specific supervisor. People from other institutions can be excellent sounding boards. With professional growth, mentors often become peers.

In interviewing for a job, it is important to learn what supervision is like and how comfortable staff feel with the leadership. Most senior administrators take great pleasure in working with new staff and helping them grow as professionals (and often move on to other institutions as they advance); this is one of the greatest rewards.

Voices of Experience

The new professionals involved in this discussion had several years to adjust to their roles, and yet they clearly felt that they were still finding their way. We asked them for one piece of advice they would give to those starting out in student affairs.

Sara: *Go in with an open mind, because your expectations are probably wrong.*

Patrick: *I think if you focus on being a professional, the actual job itself will fall into place. There's a tendency to jump in and focus on the work and not care as much about the professional persona. Thinking about those relationships early on is important.*

Karla: *Think about your lifelong goal and how student affairs plays into that.*

Jay: *I'd just say, "Do it." I've met very few people who go into student affairs and leave. They come into student affairs and stay forever.*

Michael: *My advice would be to talk to many people in the field before you start graduate school or pick your first job. Talking to a variety of people across the field about "fit" helps with your choices.*

Aramis: *Just have fun doing what you do. I've always had the philosophy that when this stops being fun, I need to pick something else to do, but it hasn't stopped being fun yet. I think it's clear when people don't enjoy what they do, particularly in our field, because it includes many long hours and requires energy. You can see when someone's hit their limit. And that's not what we should do to students, because they should get the best of us.*

Kari: *I'm a firm believer in the old adage "Don't sweat the small stuff." Our job can be stressful whether you are a new professional or a senior administrator. With multiple demands coming in from multiple sources, it's easy to be overwhelmed. Learn to recognize what is top priority, what is time-sensitive, what can be delegated, and what is inconsequential. Don't be afraid to ask for help when you need it.*

Barb: *From your start as a new professional until the end of your work path, you can and will have a very fulfilling career in student affairs. It is a privilege to be able to come to work with college students in an educational environment and to so profoundly affect their lives. We don't come into this profession to become wealthy, but we live rich and meaningful lives nonetheless. If this is where you find your passion, the challenges and the opportunities are endless.*

Conclusion

Welcoming new staff into a student affairs division is a challenge and an opportunity for senior student affairs administrators and supervisors. It is an exciting and wondrous time for most new professionals, who are eager to get started on a career and full of infectious energy. Most administrators and supervisors are ready and willing to share the wisdom gained in a career they love and do what they can to ensure the future of the field. New professionals should take advantage of opportunities for learning, mentoring, and support. They can get started in a positive manner, welcome new experiences, make mistakes and learn from them, and prepare for the future. New staff and seasoned professionals can learn from each other. This is the nature of student affairs: to continue to learn and grow in our work so that the students we serve receive the benefit. With this common goal, we are all destined for success.

> **From your start as a new professional until the end of your work path, you can and will have a very fulfilling career in student affairs.**

UNWRITTEN RULES:
ORGANIZATIONAL AND POLITICAL
REALITIES OF THE JOB

CHAPTER TWO

Marilyn J. Amey, Eric Jessup-Anger, and Connie Rose Tingson-Gatuz

H igher education is political. Experienced professionals will recognize the truth of this statement, but for new professionals in student affairs administration, the political nature of the world they have entered may feel like a cruel joke. They may have studied college adminis- tration and perhaps even administrative theory in their graduate programs, but translating textbook examples and theories to the real world can be challenging. This chapter provides some tools new professionals can use to assess their organizational culture and makes suggestions for managing this culture and the politics inherent in it. For the purposes of this discussion, we have used Kuh and Hall's (1993) definition of culture:

> [The] collective, mutually shaping patterns of institutional history, mission, physical settings, norms, traditions, values, practices, beliefs and assumptions which guide behavior of individuals and groups...

15

and which provide frames of reference for interpreting the meanings of events and actions on and off campus. (p. 2)

After briefly describing the political nature of today's higher education institutions, we present several common dilemmas facing new administrators; situations that might not conform to their expectations. Each dilemma is, in part, a product or function of the work environment and, as a result, can be ameliorated through a better understanding of organizational culture. Because new professionals are more likely to see themselves as counselors, programmers, or hall directors than as administrators, they do not always have a context for understanding and dealing with institutional challenges. Therefore, we present an approach to organizational analysis and relate it generally to student affairs work and specifically to the dilemmas confronting new professionals. This approach to understanding organizational culture is not intended as a panacea. We merely suggest that being an effective organizational analyst—that is, understanding the organizational and political realities of the job—is key to addressing essential professional issues that are generally not taught in graduate school.

> **Becoming a good organizational analyst... is key to survival and effective practice in a political organization.**

The Environment of Student Affairs Work

Compared with the corporate and private sectors, educational organizations are often touted as collegial institutions whose members are drawn together by a common mission to serve students and provide an educated citizenry. Lofty goals, rich traditions, ceremonies full of regalia and pomp and circumstance, and an air of elitism are stereotypical images of colleges and universities, and *family* is an often-used metaphor to describe their atmosphere (Bergquist & Pawlak, 2007; Birnbaum, 1988). In most cases, the vernacular definition of collegial (friendly) may accurately reflect colleges and universities today, but the organizational definition (small in size, shared goals, face-to-face interaction, consensus decision making, status differentials minimized) (Birnbaum, 1988) applies less often. Institutional growth or decline, diversification, technological advancement and online instruction, entrepreneurial spirit, and cultural diversification are just some of the factors that can affect the collegial atmosphere and change the way the college functions.

All colleges and universities are political organizations; they vary in how susceptible they are to political behavior and, therefore, how much new student affairs professionals might be affected (Hirt, 2006). In an era of declining resources, increasing competition for students, and conflicting demands, even small private liberal arts colleges—long held up as a model of the nonpolitical or at least less political (Birnbaum, 1988)—are becoming arenas for coalition building, win-lose games, ambiguous goals, and uneven power distribution, as noted by this new professional:

> *Before I started my first professional job, I had a preconceived notion that politics only took place in public universities. But I quickly learned that politics can even find its way to the religious college environment. We need to be aware of the role that politics plays in our work and, more important, how we choose to deal with it. We can't let it stifle our ability to put students first.* —First-year experience coordinator, private college

While the ideas of politics and political organizations tend to have negative connotations, there is nothing inherently negative about politics or its role in decision making and organizational behavior (Bolman & Deal, 2003). New professionals who are unaware of the nature of organizations or do not understand political functioning can be negatively affected quite easily. Becoming a good organizational analyst—a culturally competent student affairs practitioner, as Kuh, Siegel, and Thomas (2001) would say—is key to survival and effective practice in a political organization.

At the same time, new professionals need a clear personal identity to avoid being swept away by institutional gamesmanship that can occur when competition for scarce resources increases positioning and posturing. A strong sense of personal ethics, morality, and integrity is an important foundation for effective practice and is key to organizational leadership (Badaracco & Ellsworth, 1989; Bogue, 1994; Young, 2001; see chapter 3 in this book). However, these factors are not often discussed in graduate degree programs, in new member orientation, or even among colleagues. New practitioners must reconcile their personal expectations with the professional realities of the organization.

Issues of Dissonance Confronting New Professionals

No matter how carefully we prepare for a job interview, how thoroughly we question those employed at the institution, how competently we assume the responsibilities of a new job, inevitably, once the newness begins to wear off (and sometimes even sooner), we realize that our expectations do not match the job's realities. The nature of the administrative position, the college or university where one works, and the gap between expectations and realities vary from person to person, but new student affairs professionals consistently face similar challenges. Four broad issues of dissonance frequently appear in the literature: academic or experiential preparation; role conflict or ambiguity; lack of systematic evaluation and feedback; and professional opportunities or lack thereof. These issues can often be addressed or reconciled through a better understanding of organizational culture.

Academic or Experiential Preparation

The higher education/student affairs master's degree provides an orientation to the field and initial employment experiences, often in the form of paid assistantships and for-credit practicums. From a review of programs listed in NASPA's Graduate Program Directory (NASPA, 2008), it is clear that most entry-level graduate programs provide common course experiences for their students. The experiential component of degree programs varies significantly and is most noticeable with regard to how much classroom learning (including theory) connects to work experience and vice versa. It is not always clear whether the combination of in- and out-of-class experiences adequately prepares new professionals to hit the ground running in their first post-degree position and to succeed in the profession (Ambler, Amey, & Reesor, 1994; Renn & Jessup-Anger, 2008).

> *My classes in the master's program were fine; I learned a lot from my assistantship, too—a ton. But it was like living in two different worlds! The faculty hadn't been in practice for a long time, some of them not at all, and the supervisors, well, they just kept saying, "Don't give me theory. This is real life!" I wish we'd had more of an opportunity to bridge the gap. Sometimes it was hard to know which way to go.* —Recreation services director

> *The reality is that my coursework and field experience throughout graduate school prepared me for the profession to a certain extent. On many other dimensions, I had to learn so much on the job. But on the other hand, I value my graduate experience because it has informed my thinking about issues that I encounter every day.* —Service learning coordinator, private college

Because there is no specific undergraduate academic preparation (i.e., no undergraduate major in student affairs, although some institutions offer a single introductory class), people enter the field from many different disciplines. This is obviously true for positions requiring only a baccalaureate degree but also for those that require a master's degree. Previous work experience is almost as varied as academic major: an admissions recruiter may come from work in the private sector, and a financial aid counselor may come with a law degree. The mix is rich. The generalist nature of entry-level student affairs professionals helps institutions attract a diverse workforce. But for new professionals, the generalist approach often leads to insecurity, difficulty relating to peers, a sense that "others must know more than I do," and feeling overwhelmed with all there is to learn.

New professionals might also feel tension because they are trained at large institutions that award master's and doctoral degrees but often choose different kinds of employment settings. The extent to which their graduate preparation program addresses the needs and issues of student affairs work in smaller liberal arts colleges or community colleges, for example, may vary quite a lot.

It seems that higher education professionals are trained at universities, which is a night and day experience compared to the small private colleges where many of us work. In fact, most of my peers do not have training in higher education administration. This is often very frustrating for me, because I often feel that I am one of a select few people on campus who are familiar with student development theory, especially when I'm on institutional standing committees. —Academic advisor, private college

Role Conflict or Ambiguity

New student affairs professionals are often torn by conflicting job demands, differences of opinion with supervisors, or having to do things they do not want to do or are not very comfortable doing, such as terminating another's employment. Experiencing role conflict can be especially hard for those making the transition directly from senior year in college to the first position in student affairs. Although many entry-level positions today require or prefer a master's degree, many others require only a baccalaureate degree; as a result, in a matter of days, a person can go from being a student (i.e., one of the group) to being in charge (i.e., a leader). The dissonance caused by role conflicts can be especially overwhelming at this stage, when organizational understanding, influence, and power to resolve conflicts are often lacking. Two new professionals offer examples of this anxiety:

What was most difficult was having to separate from the group of Greek leaders. We thought we had developed such a very strong working relationship with them, and everything was going so well. We really thought this was the best group of leaders yet. But while we were at the conference, they all started drinking right there in front of us. We knew they weren't of legal age, and yet they did it right in front us. I'm not sure if they wanted us to do something or not, but we couldn't stay there with them. It would have been like sanctioning their behavior. I just couldn't believe they would put us in that kind of position. I thought we were friends, but they crossed the line that night, and I don't know how to go back now. —Greek advisor

As an academic advisor, I was the youngest professional in the entire division. Students often mistook me for a peer, and my colleagues often mistook me for a student. I was stuck in an awkward space of trying to assert my new identity. —Academic advisor, liberal arts college

Another aspect of dissonance is role ambiguity, which arises when the new professional is unsure of the scope and responsibilities of the job, job objectives, and colleague expectations (Rasch, Hutchison, & Tollefson, 1986). Positions may seem very clearly defined on paper, but so much of every student affairs administrative position falls into the "other" category that the true scope of a job seems ever-evolving and, sometimes, never-ending. Student, colleague, and supervisor expectations also play a role in defining the scope of a position, depending on the organizational culture. In small colleges, for instance, it may be understood that administrators are expected to attend various institutional events regardless of the relationship of the activities to their specific position. At both large and small institutions, committee work may be an unstated but important element of job responsibilities. As with other elements of culture, these expectations may not be clarified until they have been violated in some way.

And while organizational charts and position descriptions provide an interpretation of the reality of the job, many basic functions cut across organizational lines and formal reporting structures (Sandeen, 1996). In part because of the interrelated way offices work together to serve students and in part because of the inherently political nature of educational organizations, new professionals must understand the culture in their primary work unit and also the cultures of other units with which they work on behalf of students. Dissonance can arise as one straddles cultural boundaries, where norms, values, behaviors, jargon, and rewards differ.

Finally, many new professionals face role conflict between their expectations of being ready to take on the world of student affairs and their supervisor's perspective of what preparation entails. This might be particularly challenging for millennial students coming into work environments where most of their colleagues and supervisors are seasoned professionals. Expectations about the pace of change and a preference for immediate results and feedback are just two examples of issues that can cause frustration for new professionals. "Paying your dues" and "working your way up" are less relevant concepts for new professionals who feel they are more current with the use of technology, more closely connected with students, and more accustomed to assessment and evaluation tools than some of their more senior colleagues.

Lack of Systematic Evaluation and Feedback

> *Everything was going fine...or so I thought. The students liked me, we were doing some really exciting things, and we had come together as a team in a really short time. So I was shocked to get my six-month evaluation and find out that the supervisor didn't want to keep me; that she felt I wasn't "working out." I was very honest about myself when I interviewed; they said I was "just the kind of person they needed." I never saw it coming....* —Assistant activities director

Every setting has processes or sets of experiences through which newcomers learn norms, values, and behavioral expectations. During this early period of socialization, issues of role conflict are either lessened or heightened (Louis, 1980), as new professionals test their expectations against the realities of the work environment. If the gap is too great, the resulting dissonance may lead to the person leaving the position. Feedback, both positive and negative, can be very important during the first few months in closing the expectation gap and relieving dissonance. Most new professionals rely heavily, although not exclusively, on their immediate supervisor for feedback (Carpenter, 2001; Renn & Jessup-Anger, 2008). However, colleges and universities are notoriously weak in providing systematic, timely, and constructive feedback to employees.

> *As a new professional, I expected to get regular feedback from my supervisor. When that didn't happen, I quickly developed feelings of being unappreciated and undervalued. I had to figure out where my source of motivation would come from, since I was thirsty for recognition. My expectations that I would receive mentoring from my boss went unfilled*

until I started asking for feedback from my peers and from the students I worked with. I realized that evaluations and feedback can come from sources other than the top. —Student activities advisor

The socialization period may not even include training—or at least sufficient training for new professionals to feel that their questions have been resolved. Newcomers, especially those in their first post-degree professional position, may be unsure about the questions to ask or afraid of appearing insecure, and so may be particularly reluctant to seek feedback actively and early on, thereby increasing their sense of stress and transition dissonance. This is often the case for people of color (who may be underrepresented) and women in units dominated by white men—these people may feel more at risk.

Professional Opportunities or Lack Thereof

Most people accept a position because they believe opportunities will exist for personal and professional growth. Problems can arise, however, when such opportunities do not materialize.

During the interview, I didn't know enough to ask if there were opportunities for professional development. That was a mistake! I sorely needed to continue the opportunity to explore new knowledge and information that I received in my graduate school experience. Opportunities to attend national conferences weren't a priority. So I had to be creative.... —Career services advisor, faith-based college

Promotion often comes with an increase in decision-making authority, control of resources, and opportunities to affect the organization and effect change. Many associate directors, directors, and deans are actually quite constrained by demands on their time, increased responsibilities, increased administrivia, and the structure, values, and norms of their units (Mills, 1993). The aspects of student affairs work that appeal to many new professionals (i.e., working closely with students, programming) are engaged in less frequently or more narrowly by senior administrators.

Horizontal movement is a way of enhancing one's job and expanding one's skills before moving up in the organization (Young, 1990). This can be a good strategy. At the same time—depending on whether the move occurs within or across divisions, in the same or a different institution—opportunities may vary a lot. Previous comparable experience is not always seen as such, so lateral moves may lead to a "life at entry level" cycle rather than offering an opportunity to gain broader experience. Finally, opportunity is in large part a result of who is ahead of you on the ladder.

> *When I found out I was going to shift over full time to the advising center after having worked there part time for a year, I was thrilled. They told me my knowledge and expertise were going to be invaluable to the new team, and I couldn't wait to get started. What they didn't tell me was that, in the new structure, the director calls the shots...all of them. I may have expertise, but I'm not getting to use it. Most of the time, I'm just supposed to sit there and do what's handed to me....Now I'm looking to move out.* —Advising center counselor

As illustrated in this example, a supervisor who is unwilling to delegate important responsibilities or share plum assignments and committee activities limits the growth, development, and institutional exposure of fellow administrators (Amey, 1991). New professionals must be aware of the hierarchical and personnel structures of their organization as they consider their mobility and opportunities.

Each of those four dilemmas can cause dissonance for new student affairs professionals. At the same time, a person can curb the confusion, close the gap between expectations and reality, and learn to deal with the work environment by learning to understand the organizational culture. The degree of dissonance created by these dilemmas (and many others) is a function of the specific institution and unit, so the analytic tools presented are generic. Each new professional must identify the answers that fit his or her individual circumstances, career, and life goals.

Theory to Practice: A Cultural Framework for Professional Survival

New professionals are not likely to find quick fixes to eliminate the gap between expectation and reality as they go about the business of surviving in their organizations and thriving in student affairs. At the same time, many issues that hit new professionals head on, such as those described above, are a function of the organization itself and how it works. One strategy for managing these issues is understanding organizational culture and becoming a more effective organizational analyst. As one newer professional stated,

> *The best course I took in grad school was [on organizational governance], where we talked about decision making and politics, and why*

*things work the way they do, and how to figure it all out. This is what
I really needed to know to survive!*

In the framework presented in this chapter, we adapted Tierney's (1991)
six essential components of organizational culture: environment, mission, socialization, information, strategy, and leadership. Understanding the dynamics
of culture through analysis of these six organizational components can help
reduce the dissonance that results from a gap between expectations and the
organizational/political realities of the job. Familiarity with the values, norms,
rituals, symbols, myths, and impact of leadership helps a new professional recognize the behaviors and strategies that are most likely to succeed (or not succeed) in the unit.

*I quickly learned that there is an "institutional way" of doing things.
If I questioned why thing were the way they were, colleagues would tell
me, "Oh, you'll learn how we do things here." If I had a new idea, they
would tell me that it would never work here. It seemed like there were
insiders and outsiders. If you didn't participate in the indoctrination
process of learning the ins and outs, you would always be an outsider.*
—Admissions officer, private college

Understanding culture not only gives administrators a way to assess their
institutions and departments but helps them identify appropriate tasks and
roles for themselves, reducing some of the dissonance created by role conflict
and ambiguity. As Whitt (1993) suggests, "The potential reward [of discovering the culture of an organization] is greater understanding of both the visible
and the tacit elements—the furniture, scripts, and invisible props..." (p. 93).
But organizational analysis is not the answer for all the difficulties facing new
professionals. Making sense of things; being aware of ideologies, rituals, and
symbols that motivate and alienate members; identifying key supporters and
networks; and conceptualizing leadership as embodying these ideals are all important components of administrative effectiveness and success.

Environment

Student affairs divisions are not islands unto themselves; they exist within
many internal environments (e.g., departments within divisions, levels of directors within departments) and external environments that have an impact
on their effectiveness. Some of the external influences are located outside the
specific division but within the institution, such as academic affairs, business

affairs, and athletics. Others are external to the college or university altogether, such as national Greek organizations, the community, private sector suppliers, and state and federal laws. Not all internal and external environments have great influence, but in some ways these environments shape the context of work for new professionals, even in daily tasks and assignments. New professionals who believe that they only have to pay attention to their direct supervisor are very shortsighted and narrow in their thinking. Supervisors help define the most immediate environments, which is helpful, but new professionals can become so engrossed in performing the tasks for which they were hired that they fail to grasp the larger context. For example, changes in national accreditation standards in professional degree programs such as business or education might at first seem irrelevant to student affairs work; indeed, many new professionals might even be unaware that accrediting agencies exist. But those involved with recruitment, scholarships, educational support services, and cultural support services may see changes in their work as they help students adjust to new (usually higher) academic standards.

An example much closer to home is the importance of understanding what other units in the college or university, particularly faculty, think about student affairs. At some schools, for a variety of reasons, the professional staff and the faculty work closely together, especially in areas that affect students. Collegial relationships abound, faculty involvement in programming activities is the norm, and co-curricular activities are considered valuable contributions to the overall growth and development of students (Cook & Lewis, 2007; Hirt, 2006; Manning, Kinzie, & Schuh, 2006). At other institutions, academic and nonacademic units are more separate and even perceived as antagonistic (Cook & Lewis, 2007; Komives & Woodard, 1996). Individual interactions may be cooperative, but real collaboration is less likely. The interdependence of units and professionals in serving students is either less valued or less well understood. In these settings, new professionals are often dismayed when budgets are being discussed to hear their work described as "taking a load off faculty shoulders," "interfering with students' study time," or "not central to the institutional mission." Becoming an effective environmental scanner, both inside and outside one's immediate office, helps one understand which influ-

> **Understanding culture not only gives administrators a way to assess their institutions and departments but helps them identify appropriate tasks and roles for themselves, reducing some of the dissonance created by role conflict and ambiguity.**

ences matter most and how others' values and beliefs affect one's daily activities. This is a key to success in an institution.

Mission

At some point, every new professional comes in contact with a student handbook or a piece of recruitment material that contains the institution's mission statement. Usually a lengthy and lofty text, the mission supposedly describes what the institution does, how and for whom, and sometimes even provides a discussion of the social, ethical, and educational beliefs that shape the institutional context (Lyons, 1993). Divisions of student affairs often have their own mission statements that reflect the larger institutional mission but also describe more specifically the work of the division related to students. Individual units within a division may have their own versions as well. As guiding texts, these various mission statements provide a loose framework for organizing daily activities; as cultural artifacts, they often do not explain what really happens. This is especially true in colleges and universities, which are known for having multiple and competing missions (e.g., providing access for diverse students and increasing prestige by raising admission standards).

> *Don't be naïve to think that residence life is similar on all college campuses. I thought that my prior experiences working in residence halls on a large university campus prepared me for my current experience of working in a residence hall on a small private campus. I was wrong. The mission of the institution reflects the institution's priorities. Even in the residence hall, the policies are dictated by the values of the institution. As a new professional, I wish I had thought about whether my personal values were aligned with the institutional mission before I took the job. If these are not compatible, you will struggle.* —Kela, residence hall director, private college

Kuh and Schuh suggest, "The 'living mission' of a college is how students, faculty, administrators, graduates, and others describe what the college is and is trying to accomplish" (1991, p. 12). These descriptions of purpose help the new professional understand more fully what student affairs means in each institution (Sandeen, 2001). Looking for both agreement and disagreement in the way others think about the office's mission gives a clearer sense of what the office is about, for whom and how it will work. New professionals can find descriptions of purpose in the comments of the vice president for student affairs at the fall semester division gathering, in a director's design for professional training, in the staff evaluation criteria, and in the day-to-day talk around the office. The messages may not be the same. The most agreement may exist at smaller, private liberal arts colleges, where frequent interactions among faculty and staff reinforce a set of beliefs, values, and traditions (reflecting a stronger organizational culture). The greatest disparity may occur at a large research university, where multiple sets of beliefs, values, and traditions likely exist even within a division or department. Institutional and, therefore, student affairs unit missions can also be affected by history and heritage, organizational type and complexity of purpose, and type of student served.

Finding consistent messages is only part of the assessment; recognizing places where mission and belief statements conflict is also critical to succeed as a new professional. When what we say (i.e., the espoused mission) diverts from what we do (i.e., the mission in use) (adapted from Argyris & Schön, 1977), the new professional may find a lack of agreement about unit goals, little sense of common purpose driving or shaping decisions, less than strong support for work done within the unit by those external to it, and a clash between one's own value system and institutional or unit activity, or both. Remembering that missions exist both on paper and in the minds and actions of organization members should lead job candidates to ask more questions during the interview process and have a greater awareness of the culture during the early socialization period, when they might otherwise be preoccupied with learning specific tasks and buoyed by the euphoria of a new job.

Socialization

All organizations have rituals and ceremonies for welcoming new members. These activities may be as limited as having newcomers complete employment forms and purchase a parking permit, or as extensive as orientation programs and staff retreats. Just as we think of orienting students to campus or initiating inductees into student organizations, student affairs units should bring new members into the fold through planned activities that create a sense of shared meaning about work, the unit, the members of the unit, and the larger college or university. In addition to providing a sense of who's who and what's what, socialization, as Tierney (1991) describes it, is a process of becoming aware of and indoctrinated to the norms, beliefs, and values of the organization. This socialization process is related less to administrative functions than to the development of social consciousness; less concerned with short-term job tasks than with long-term direction and purpose. As the new professional develops an identity as a member of a department and the larger student affairs profession, socialization plays a key role in providing knowledge of what is required to succeed.

One factor of both early and ongoing socialization is the "professional anchoring" of a person's position in the department and the institution. Professional anchoring refers to the primary orientation and interaction patterns of a position. For example, does the position demand that you work most often with employees in the same office or unit (internal) or with those in other offices outside the unit (external)? Student affairs usually includes a very interactive, externally oriented set of positions, because members work with so many other people to get the job done. New professionals in advising or educational support services, for example, quickly realize the importance of building close relationships with faculty departments as well as with admissions and student orientation staffs (Amey, 1991). This external focus keeps the new professional aware of the college or university, its culture, and how it works, because attention is not primarily focused within the unit.

At the same time, many student affairs positions seem internally focused on a daily basis, either within the office or program itself or on students, rather than on interaction with other employees. Such positions tend to be fairly self-contained and emphasize more depth than breadth in professional growth. Advanced positions in student housing and financial aid, for example, may be very specialized and, therefore, will not encourage increased broad institutional knowledge. Individuals in more internally anchored positions may have to create their own opportunities, apart from job responsibilities, for developing relationships and interacting with the broader college community. The networks and support systems one develops help with this, especially as technology makes inter- and intra-institutional connecting easier. Institutional volunteerism, such as committee work, is another excellent way to stay connected outside the office (see chapters 6 and 8).

Information

Tierney's (1991) fourth essential component of organizational culture is information. In assessing the organizational and political realities, an early task of new professionals is to determine what constitutes information, who has it, and how it is disseminated. Even in a highly structured organization—where memos, written records, handbooks, and standard operating procedures are in great supply (Birnbaum, 1988)—information does not flow only hierarchically, from the top down. Certainly, this is the case in an institution characterized as more collegial or political (Birnbaum, 1988; Bolman & Deal, 2003). Listervs, instant messaging, online resources, and e-mail communication enhance the speed and volume of information flow; often making instantly accessible what traditionally was disseminated by an information gatekeeper. But communication explosion does not always mean information accuracy. New professionals must become skilled at gathering information from multiple sources and in multiple forms. Waiting for "official word" may mean missing an opportunity or not being able to avoid a crisis. You need to learn whom to ask for what and who is a reliable source for the information you need to be most effective and efficient. This is not something to figure out at the moment of crisis. In such situations, the relationships you have developed with key colleagues can be critical to getting the job done. Knowing whom to call for the right answer may have nothing to do with that person's position on the organizational chart.

New professionals quickly become aware of how many different points of view exist in a college or university. Gathering information from multiple sources allows for a kind of triangulation, through which one can draw conclusions on the basis of areas of agreement among sources (Patton, 1990). This can be critical in curbing rumors, creating coalitions, and seizing creative opportunities. Informal networks also provide important information, serve as critical sounding boards for ideas, and function as ways of gathering feedback for professional growth and development. Learning whom to work closely with and developing those relationships is not often a conscious activity, although research on academic leaders suggests that it should be more intentional (Winship, 1991). As one new professional explained,

> *Rich and I have a standing lunch the third Thursday of every month. He's been here two years longer than me and works in [another unit], so I'm always looking to him for advice, to figure out what's really going on. He's been great to talk with, and introduces me to lots of folks he knows.* —Hall director

We all sometimes feel as though we do not have enough information or the right facts on which to base decisions and take action. The better we understand the department and institution in which we work, the more we can see what is "enough" and not feel as though we are being excluded or left to our own devices. New professionals must realize that, in addition to being purposeful in developing good contacts and networks, when they do not receive the kind of information they seek, it is not necessarily because someone is withholding it. Asking questions, listening carefully, seeking perspective outside one's office, and building a strong informal network helps new professionals learn how to gather and broker information more effectively.

Strategy

Many new professionals believe that most decisions are straightforward, that the designated leader has the final say-so, and that their own authority is very limited. Others seek or are hired into an institution that touts a team or participative approach to management, in which everyone is involved in decisions and discussions of mission, goal setting, and evaluation. Still others believe they are being hired into one kind of environment and discover that the reality is very different. It is important to recognize the difference between talk and action, between espoused theory and theory in use related to decision making (Argyris & Schon, 1977), and to learn as quickly as possible how things actually get done. It is not helpful to bemoan the fact that the organization is not the way you hoped it would be; instead, focus on figuring out how it really operates so you can operate effectively within it. How the institution makes decisions and enacts them is what Tierney (1991) calls "organizational strategy."

> There are many unwritten "rules" in institutions, divisions, and departments. Find a trusted supervisor and mentor to help you process and navigate the invisible politics and culture of the institution.

Becoming familiar with the obvious and subtle ways in which decisions are made—who is involved and at what level, and what the penalties are for ineffective decisions and the rewards for effective ones—is part of understanding your unit. Unfortunately, these things are often learned by trial and error and by observing rather than questioning others. New professionals can begin understanding the strategies used in their own office early in the socialization period by asking some basic questions. Is this the kind of unit where the director signs off on everything before you are allowed to move ahead? Are symbols and symbolic meaning (including something as simple as event T-shirts) prevalent and effectively used throughout the office? At department meetings, is everything discussed, from what to give the administrative assistant on his birthday to next year's budget proposal? If the supervisor casually mentions an upcoming event, do you really have a choice about attending? Does an invitation to be creative and innovative and to take the lead mean only within limits that are not well known? A clear sense of proper procedures, cliques, active countercultures, and informal networks that are common in every organization helps a new professional work more effectively and efficiently, build supportive connections, capitalize on opportunities, and succeed more consistently on behalf of students.

> *There are many unwritten "rules" in institutions, divisions, and departments. Find a trusted supervisor and mentor to help you process and navigate the invisible politics and culture of the institution.* —Hall director; large, private university

Leadership

Organizational charts ostensibly show who the campus leaders are; what they really show is who is in a position of authority, not who is necessarily a leader. An institution has many leaders, and they are not obvious by title or position; you find out who they are by paying attention to who gets things done. These informal leaders are everywhere, at every level, including new professionals. Often, the informal leaders wield a lot of power and influence over daily activities in student affairs. A long-standing mid-level director may not appear as strong as her senior-level supervisor, judged on the basis of title and position, but her institutional knowledge and well-established reputation as a team player may allow her to exercise significant leadership throughout the division. Another person may live or work next door to the college president and often can raise important issues and concerns without an appointment, even though he holds an "assistant to" position, which a theorist would perceive as low status. Good practice, organizational intuition, and a willingness to get involved are key to informal leadership—more so than title and place on the organizational chart.

People who choose careers in student affairs tend to look for ways to develop and exercise their own leadership early on rather than assuming that they have to wait until they are senior leaders before they can make a difference. If a leadership culture exists at the institution, you will see leaders who are and are not in positions of formal authority. You will also see staff who are lifelong learners, participating in ongoing professional development and organizational learning (Meyerson, 2002; Senge, 1990). They inspire confidence in others and will work collectively to create new answers and identify new issues (Lewis, 1994; Meyerson, 2002). In many ways, this is similar to the learning imperative that we articulate when we are working with students. In a culture of leadership and lifelong learning, one's job title is less important than the fact that one chooses to exercise personal leadership. This can be an important lesson for new professionals.

> *I never saw myself as a leader before—that really sounded so "out there" to me. I'm a helper, and I guess being the leader always seemed less important. And then I sat on two committees, and there were things to be done, so of course I just jumped in to help get the work done, and all of a sudden everyone is calling me the leader, looking to me for leadership. It was weird! I guess that's what I was doing, but I also kept saying to myself, "Who am I? I don't have that fancy office or a long title." No one seemed to be worried about that but me....*
> —Multicultural affairs counselor

As this practitioner learned, there is a close connection between effective leaders and effective followers. The literature primarily focuses on the leadership side of the equation. The bookshelves of senior administrators are full of works by leadership strategists promoting seven steps or five keys or eight things to remember. While these books have their place, the work of those who promote effective followers (De Pree, 1993; Kelley, 1993; Lee, 1993); team leadership (Bensimon & Neumann, 1993; Heider, 1989); and servant leaders (Bogue, 1994; Pollard, 1996; Wheatley, 2002) is equally important and perhaps more vital to the diverse higher education institution of the future. In addition, because the face of leadership in student affairs is changing slowly, it is important for new professionals to see themselves in leadership roles where role models may not yet exist. Aguirre and Martinez (2002); Astin and Astin (2000); Curry (2000); Hackney (2003); Ideta (1996); and Johnson, Benham, and Van Alstine (2003) are only a few of the writers who are presenting new lenses for identifying leadership that is different from the traditional images and narrow ranges of acceptable behavior (Nidiffer, 2001; Tedrow & Rhoads, 1999). Whether through readings, conference participation, networking, or insightful supervisors and role models, new professionals should seek opportunities to engage in leadership/followership development and start seeing themselves as potential leaders in their organizations and in the student affairs profession.

Conclusion

Many of the dilemmas facing new professionals present difficult challenges not easily resolved through cookbook philosophies or how-to lists. Becoming an effective organizational analyst changes the nature of the questions one asks during job interviews, which can lead to finding a better initial institutional fit.

This kind of analysis also offers a different way of making sense of and interacting with the college or university, the student affairs division, the department, its members, and even the job itself.

During the first few months on the job, new professionals are busy learning the specific tasks required of their position, adjusting to the new environment, and going through numerous balancing exercises, many of which are addressed in subsequent chapters of this book. At the same time, they need to quickly become culturally competent educators, managers, and leaders who regularly engage in ongoing discovery and rediscovery of their organizational context, its evolving situations, and their own actions (Kuh, Siegel, & Thomas, 2001). If new professionals take an organizational analysis approach to their professional transition, they will pay attention to issues such as these: What are the important offices with which I will interact? What are the agreed-upon values and beliefs of my unit, and where is there disagreement? How will I get connected within and apart from my office? How is information communicated? Who are the key people to know, and why? Where will my support systems be? How do decisions get made, and by whom? Who are the informal leaders? Using this approach encourages new professionals to ask questions and be aware of certain aspects of their work environment during the first few months on the job and throughout their career. Realizing the importance of understanding the culture of the work setting will also help lessen frustration during the socialization period, when gaps between expectations and job realities are common, and provide some guidance on how the new professional can successfully address these tensions.

References

Aguirre, A. Jr., & Martinez, R. (2002). Leadership Practices and Diversity in Higher Education. *Journal of Leadership Studies, 8*(3), 53–62.

Ambler, D. A., Amey, M. J., & Reesor, L. M. (1994). *Strategies for improving collaboration between faculty and practitioners*. Paper presented at the meeting of the National Association for Student Personnel Association. Dallas, March 24–27.

Amey, M. J. (1991). Bridging the gap between expectations and reality. In K. M. Moore & S. B. Twombly (Eds.), *Administrative careers and the marketplace.* New Directions for Higher Education, no. 72 (pp. 78–88). San Francisco: Jossey-Bass.

Argyris, C., & Schon, D. A. (1977). *Organizational learning: A theory of action perspective.* Reading, MA: Addison-Wesley.

Astin, A. W., & Astin, H. S. (2000). Principles of transformative leadership. In A. W. Astin & H. S. Astin (Eds.), *Leadership reconsidered: Engaging higher education in social change* (pp. 8–17). W. K. Kellogg Foundation. Retrieved August 1, 2008, from www.wkkf.org/pubs/CCT/Leadership/Pub3368.pdf.

Badaracco, J. L., & Ellsworth, R. R. (1989). *Leadership and the quest for integrity.* Boston: Harvard Business School Press.

Bensimon, E. M., & Neumann, A. (1993). *Redesigning collegiate leadership: Teams and teamwork in higher education.* Baltimore: The Johns Hopkins Press.

Bergquist, W. H., & Pawlak, K. (2007). *Engaging the six cultures of the academy: Revised and expanded edition of the Four Cultures of the Academy.* San Francisco: Jossey-Bass.

Birnbaum, R. (1988). *How colleges work.* San Francisco: Jossey-Bass.

Bogue, E. G. (1994). *Leadership by design.* San Francisco: Jossey-Bass.

Bolman, L. G., & Deal, T. E. (2003). *Reframing organizations: Artistry, choice, and leadership.* San Francisco: Jossey-Bass.

Carpenter, D. S. (2001). Staffing student affairs divisions. In R. B. Winston, D. G. Creamer, & T. K. Miller (Eds.), *The professional student affairs administrator: Educator, leader, and manager* (pp. 211–244). Philadelphia: Accelerated Development.

Cook, J. H., & Lewis, C. A. (Eds.). (2007). *Student and academic affairs collaboration: The divine comity.* Washington, DC: National Association of Student Personnel Administrators (NASPA).

Curry, B. (2000). *Women in power: Pathways to leadership in education.* New York: Teachers College Press.

De Pree, M. (1993). Followership. In W. E. Rosenbach & R. L. Taylor

(Eds.), *Contemporary issues in leadership* (3rd ed., pp. 137–140). Boulder: Westview Press.

Hackney, C. E. (2003). Struggling for authentic human synergy and a robust democratic culture: The wellspring community for women in educational leadership. *Advancing Women in Leadership Journal.* Retrieved June 1, 2007, from www.advancingwomen.com/awl/spring2003/HACKNE~1.html.

Heider, R. (1989). The leader who knows how things happen. In W. E. Rosenbach & R. L. Taylor (Eds.), *Contemporary issues in leadership* (2nd ed., pp. 161–167). Boulder: Westview Press.

Hirt, J. B. (2006). *Where you work matters: Student affairs administrators at different types of institutions.* Lanham, MD: University Press of America.

Ideta, L. M. (1996). *Asian women leaders of higher education: Inclusionary empowerment in pursuit of excellence.* Paper presented at the meeting of the Association for the Study of Higher Education, November 2, Memphis, TN.

Johnson, V., Benham, M. P. K., & Van Alstine, M. (2003). Native leadership: Advocacy for transformation, culture, community, and sovereignty. In M. P. K. Benham & W. J. Stein (Eds.), *The renaissance of American Indian higher education: Capturing the dream* (pp. 149–166). Mahwah, NJ: Lawrence Erlbaum Associates.

Kelley, R. (1993). How followers weave a web of relationships. In W. E. Rosenbach & R. L. Taylor (Eds.), *Contemporary issues in leadership* (3rd ed., pp. 122–133). Boulder: Westview Press.

Komives, S. R., & Woodard, D. B. Jr. (1996). Building on the past, shaping the future. In S. R. Komives, D. B. Woodard Jr., & Associates (Eds.), *Student services: A handbook for the profession* (3rd ed., pp. 536–555). San Francisco: Jossey-Bass.

Kuh, G. D., & Hall, J. E. (1993). Clinical perspectives in student affairs. In G. D. Kuh (Ed.), *Cultural perspectives in student affairs work* (pp.1–20). Lanham, MD: ACPA/University Press of America.

Kuh, G. D., & Schuh, J. (1991). *The role and contribution of student affairs in involving colleges.* Washington, DC: NASPA.

Kuh, G. D., Siegel, M. J., & Thomas, A. D. (2001). Higher education: Values and cultures. In R. B. Winston Jr., D. G. Creamer, T. K. Miller, & Associates (Eds.), *The professional student affairs administrator: Educator, leader, and manager* (pp. 39–64). New York: Brunner-Routledge.

Lee, C. (1993). Followership: The essence of leadership. In W. E. Rosenbach & R. L. Taylor (Eds.), *Contemporary issues in leadership* (3rd ed., pp. 113–121). Boulder: Westview Press.

Lewis, P. H. (1994). Implementing the culture of leadership. In S. A. McDade & P. H. Lewis (Eds.), *Developing administrative excellence: Creating a culture of leadership*. New Directions for Higher Education, no. 87 (pp. 93–100). San Francisco: Jossey-Bass.

Louis, M. (1980). Surprise and sense making: What newcomers experience entering unfamiliar organizational settings. *Administrative Science Quarterly, 25,* 226–251.

Lyons, J. W. (1993). The importance of institutional mission. In M. J. Barr & Associates (Eds.), *The handbook of student affairs administration* (pp. 3–15). San Francisco: Jossey-Bass.

Manning, K., Kinzie, J., & Schuh, J. (2006). *One size does not fit all: Traditional and innovative models of student affairs practice*. New York: Routledge.

Meyerson, D. (2002). Everyday leaders: The power of difference. *Leader to Leader,* No. 23. Peter F. Drucker Foundation for Nonprofit Management. Retrieved June 30, 2007, from http://leadertoleader.org/knowledgecenter/journal.aspx?ArticleID=116.

Mills, D. B. (1993). The role of the middle manager. In M. J. Barr & Associates (Eds.), *The handbook of student affairs administration* (pp. 121–134). San Francisco: Jossey-Bass.

NASPA. (2008). Graduate program directory. Retrieved October 1, 2008, from http://www.naspa.org/gradprograms.

Nidiffer, J. (2001). New leadership for a new century: Women's contribution to leadership in higher education. In J. Nidiffer & C. T. Bashaw (Eds.), *Women administrators in higher education: Historical and contemporary perspectives* (pp. 101–134). Albany, NY: SUNY Press.

Pollard, C. W. (1996). The leader who serves. In Drucker Foundation (Ed.), *The leaders of the future* (pp. 241–248). San Francisco: Jossey-Bass, Inc.

Patton, M. (1990). *Qualitative evaluation and research methods* (2nd ed.). Newbury Park, CA: Sage.

Rasch, C., Hutchison, J., & Tollefson, N. (1986). Sources of stress among administrators at research universities. *Review of Higher Education, 9*(4), 419–434.

Renn, K. A., & Jessup-Anger, E. R. (2008). Learning about graduate preparation curriculum through the experiences of new professionals in student affairs. *Journal of College Student Development, 49*(4), 319–335.

Sandeen, A. (2001). Organization, functions, and standards of practice. In S. R. Komives, D. B. Woodard Jr., & Associates (Eds.), *Student services: A handbook for the profession* (3rd ed., pp. 435–457). San Francisco: Jossey-Bass.

Senge, P. M. (1990).*The fifth discipline: The art and practice of the learning organization.* New York: Doubleday.

Tedrow, B., & Rhoads, R. A. (1999). A qualitative study of women's experiences in community college leadership positions. *Community College Review, 27*(3), 1–18.

Tierney, W. G. (1991). Organizational culture in higher education: Defining the essentials. In M. Peterson (Ed.), *ASHE reader in organization and governance in higher education* (pp. 126–139). Lexington, MA: Ginn Press.

Wheatley, M. (2002). The work of the servant-leader. In L. C. Spears & M. Lawrence (Eds.), *Focus on leadership: Servant-leadership for the Twenty-first Century* (pp. 349–362). New York: John Wiley & Sons.

Whitt, E. J. (1993). Making the familiar strange: Discovering culture. In G. D. Kuh (Ed.), *Cultural perspectives in student affairs work* (pp.81–94). Lanham, MD: ACPA/University Press of America.

Winship, S. (1991). *An analysis of gender differences in position paths of community college presidents.* Unpublished dissertation. Lawrence, KS: University of Kansas

Young, R. B. (Ed.) (1990). *The invisible leaders: Student affairs mid-managers.* Washington, DC: NASPA.

Young, R. B. (2001). Ethics and professional practice. In R. B. Winston Jr., D. G. Creamer, T. K. Miller, & Associates (Eds.), *The professional student affairs administrator: Educator, leader, and manager* (pp. 153–178). New York: Brunner-Routledge.

DEVELOPING A PROFESSIONAL ETHIC

CHAPTER THREE

Anna M. Ortiz and Carla R. Martinez

N ew professionals encounter ethical dilemmas in their work on a near-daily basis. These range from micro-decisions as they balance personal values, professional ethical codes, and institutional expectations in virtually every independent decision they make in the early days of the job to major incidents or crises that involve student safety, job security, or criminal or civil law. Decisions and dilemmas arise as new administrators develop a professional identity and the confidence and experience necessary to function in a coherent, authentic way. Unfortunately, for many new professionals, this negotiation takes place in isolation. The daily workload and rapidly unfolding crises seldom allow time to discuss the ethical dimensions of practice. Even when a debriefing follows a decision or crisis, competing interests (e.g., job security and institutional liability) can inhibit candid discussion of ethical lapses and important learning for future events. Lingering ethical issues can require dialogue with peers, supervisors, and institutions that is beyond the new professionals' skill and comfort level, so they are drawn into compromises of their own ethical codes without outlets for relief. Developmental issues that are part of being a new professional can also compound the execution of a professional ethic when personal needs and desires conflict with the work student affairs professionals do.

In this chapter, we attempt to guide new professionals in the development of a professional ethic, by which we mean the integration of personal values, professional ethics, and institutional expectations and cultures. This integration informs how new professionals deconstruct experiences, incidents, and crises that arise in their daily work, and the actions they take. The congruence that results from integration can give new professionals the integrity and confidence to execute their professional ethic in various settings, to defend their professional ethic in the face of competing demands and interests, and to become ethical leaders in their institutions.

> Cardinal rule number one: Know thyself first....I'm forced to take a daily assessment of who I am and what I value, not only as a person, but as a professional challenging students to do the same.

To assist in the development of a professional ethic, we offer an overview of the ethical foundations of the profession and research on the development and execution of ethics in student affairs practice. We also describe common ethical dilemmas that new professionals encounter in the first years of practice. These dilemmas are from our work with new professionals, our own experiences as new professionals, and current ethical issues. We list some key principles new professionals should consider in developing a professional ethic; these encompass current issues and emergent values in student affairs. Finally, we offer two scenarios and a processing model to use in class discussions and professional development.

A new residence life professional said this about his development of a professional ethic:

> *Cardinal rule number one: Know thyself first. This environment, more than any other, has me in a constant state of reflection. I'm forced to take a daily assessment of who I am and what I value, not only as a person, but as a professional challenging students to do the same. Self-reflection is the pathway to making a real connection with students. How can I expect students to dig deeper and search for purpose in life if I'm not willing to do the same? Every day is an opportunity. Every day is a journey.*

The Nature of Ethics

The word *ethics* comes from the Greek word *ethos*, "which relates to customs, conduct, or character. It is concerned with the values and morals that a particular society finds appropriate" (Wallin, 2007, p. 34). The study of ethics is "much more complex than merely making decisions about the right or wrong way to act in a given situation" (Rebore, 2001, p .6). It is concerned with matters that are often ambiguous and with no clear answers. According to Rebore (2001), the study of ethics is a complex area because it is concerned not only with human behavior but with human conduct, which requires not just action but a conscious choice and the use of rational inquiry when faced with an ethical dilemma; "...the underlying assumption is that conduct is rational because it is intentional" (Rebore, 2001, p.6). Ethical decision making requires rational thought and critical analysis.

Integral to ethics are its effects on individuals and society. Costa (1998) proposes that while ethics are personal in nature, ethical commitments are made when people acknowledge and accept their effects on others and on the community. This point is critical: Ethics are often assumed to be a personal choice, but the true value in ethics stems from the effect on others, and a person's willingness to accept the consequences of living and working ethically. As a new professional develops a personal ethic, he or she makes choices based on deeply held values, embraces behavioral congruence, and understands the effects of one's choices on others. As one new professional said,

> *If you end up at a place where you are asked to do things that "make you feel funny inside," it's probably not the right place for you.*

Culturally Bounded Ethics and the Development of a Professional Ethic

Ethics are culture-based. Different cultures hold unique values and may act in a variety of ways when faced with similar situations (Komives, Lucas, & McMahon, 1998). What is acceptable behavior in one culture may not be in another; therefore, it is important to be cognizant of cultural dimensions in ethical situations (Benjamin, 2006). According to Rebore (2001), "How human beings should treat one another is thus predicated on certain notions about humanity. Those notions are significantly influenced by the culture and traditions of each society" (p .6). In the higher education context, culture also plays a role in the ethical standards we hold as a profession. Fried (2000) says,

The ethical beliefs of the student affairs profession are grounded in Anglo-American culture. This culture believes in scientific material- ism, individual autonomy, achievement and responsibility, a belief in the necessity of progress, and a strong emphasis on the future, rather than the present or past. (p. 411)

The emphasis on individual autonomy is different from that of many collec- tivistic cultures and may contradict familial and cultural values that our students or colleagues hold. This makes ethical dilemmas complex, because no universal principles exist that can guide our behavior in all situations (Benjamin, 2006).

The culture of the institution also has an effect on ethical values and standards. "Culture is a quality inherent within an organization that creates an atmosphere setting it apart from other organizations with similar purpos- es" (Rebore, 2001, p. 62). Higher education institutions have various cultural norms based on institutional mission, history, student population, geographi- cal location, and so on. These cultural norms can be observed across campus through interactions among faculty, staff, and students, or they can be seen in campus publications and websites (Hellmich, 2007). According to Vaughan (1992), "...culture consists of those things that make an institution distinct: its history, traditions and values, interaction with the larger environment, ceremo- nies, renewal process—including recruitment and selection of personnel—and evaluation process, including assessment of its ethical values" (p. 21).

The culture of an institution can be very powerful. When these cultural norms promote ethical behavior, "...a functional as well as successful organiza- tion emerges—one that not only achieves its mission and approaches its vision, but that is also a rewarding place to be a student, employee, and visitor...." (Hellmich, 2007 p. 23). As student affairs professionals, we have the power to contribute to the institutional culture and promote ethical behavior that, over time, preserves or promotes the institution's commitment to ethical standards (Hellmich, 2007; Vaughan, 1992).

New professionals may encounter conflict between long-held personal val- ues and those of the student affairs profession and the institution where they are employed. The question is how they will reconcile those conflicts. Handels- man, Gottlieb, and Knapp (2005) base their concept of professional ethical identity development on the psychological acculturation work of Berry (1980, 2003; Berry and Sam, 1997). Handelsman and colleagues (2005) contend that new professionals become a part of and adapt to an organization or profession, and adjust to its ethical culture much as new immigrants acculturate to the host culture The four strategies of professional identity development are assimilation, separation, marginalization, and integration. In *assimilation*, new professionals abandon their personal ethics and adopt the profession's ethical code without question or critical analysis. A person using a *separation* strategy will adhere to his or her personal values and dismiss the profession's values. In *marginalization*, new professionals have no commitment to personal values or the profession's values. They make decisions based on short-term concerns. New professionals using the *integration* strategy will find a way to meld their own values and ethics with those of the new profession. They will likely encounter conflicts between personal values and those of the profession, but they will be able to critically examine the conflict and find solutions to make better ethical decisions (Anderson, Harbour, & Davies, 2007). According to Rebore (2001), "...the educational leader becomes a person who melds together the personal and professional dimensions of his or her life. The educational leader recognizes that ethics springs from his or her personal perspective of what is contained in authoritative documents" (p. 13).

Ethical Decision Making

Ethical situations or dilemmas involve situations in which there may be no clear answer or course of action. In fact, they often involve situations in which one must choose between outcomes that all have negative aspects (Beckner, 2004). According to Beckner, "...the difficulties in making ethical decisions often revolve around the fact that many aspects of human interaction are ambiguous—the surrounding circumstances are not clear, they may be subject to interpretation or cultural perspective, or their meaning many be uncertain (p. 91)." A review of the literature reveals many models and concepts to aid in the ethical decision making process (Benjamin, 2006; Humphrey, Janosik, & Creamer, 2004; Kitchner, 1985; Komives et al., 1998; Mattchet, 2008). Rebore (2001) suggests that higher education professionals need to use ethical analysis in their daily work because it "...provides a framework for decision making...[and it] addresses issues through a disciplined way of thinking" (p. 8). According to Mattchet (2008), ethical deliberation is an open-ended process that should follow three principles. First, Mattchet says that ethics is more than just following a set of rules; we must be able to understand how the rules can be applied to different situations. Second, every choice we make has an ethical dimension; therefore, "ethical deliberation is inherently practical. Its point is never simply to figure out what we should think or believe...rather, its point is to figure out *what we should do*" (Mattchet, 2008, p. 31). Finally, ethical deliberation is not solely personal. Mattchet says that "ethics at least requires us to give some explanation of our conduct" (p.31).

Benjamin suggests discussing ethical concerns with supervisors and reviewing professional ethical standards. He also notes that part of the discovery process involves confronting persons who act unethically. Humphrey and colleagues (2004) outline a four-step model for ethical decision-making specific to student affairs practitioners. The steps are: (1) identify the problem; (2) frame the problem in ethical terms; (3) consider the relevant ethical principles, character traits, and professional values related to the problem; and (4) make an ethical decision.

Ethics in Higher Education

The history and purpose of higher education is closely tied to the development of moral and ethical leaders. "Since the founding of Harvard in 1636, higher education has been a major force in the nation's struggle to establish and maintain high ethical standards in all aspects of society....Much like the major religions, higher education has been responsible for establishing and interpreting ethical standards as well as for maintaining them" (Vaughan, 1992, p. xv). Even today, higher education is held responsible for producing graduates who are not only competent in their fields of study but also ethical, contributing members of society (Mattchet, 2008). According to Woody (2008), higher education has a large responsibility for teaching ethical behavior: "...across fields, ethical teaching reaches beyond classrooms; ethical teachers reinforce these ideas by modeling appropriate behavior, and ethical teachers seek to extend ethical behaviors beyond their students and into society at large" (p. 39).

Our professional associations assume leadership on this issue by providing ethical and professional standards that student affairs professionals can use to address ethical situations. The National Association of Student Personnel Administrators (NASPA) does not have a specific ethical statement; however, it offers 18 Standards of Professional Practice (1990):

☞ Professional Services

☞ Agreement with Institutional Mission and Goals

☞ Management of Institutional Resources

☞ Employment Relationship

☞ Conflict of Interest

☞ Legal Authority

☞ Equal Consideration and Treatment of Others

☞ Student Behavior

☞ Integrity of Information and Research

☞ Confidentiality

☞ Research Involving Human Subjects

☞ Representation of Professional Competence

☞ Selection and Promotion Practices

☞ References

☞ Job Definitions and Performance Evaluation

☞ Campus Community

☞ Professional Development

☞ Assessment

Overall, NASPA's Standards of Professional Practice require "…personal integrity, belief in the dignity and worth of individuals, respect for individual differences and diversity, a commitment to service, and dedication to the development of individuals and the college community through education."

The American College Personnel Association (ACPA) Statement of Ethical Principles and Standards (2006) outlines four standards to help student affairs professionals make ethical decisions: (1) Professional Responsibility and Competence; (2) Student Learning and Development; (3) Responsibility to the Institution; and (4) Responsibility to Society. According to ACPA, student affairs professionals must be competent and accept responsibility for their actions. Student learning must be at the core of student affairs work, and professionals must be cognizant and sensitive to the various backgrounds, cultures, experiences, and abilities of student populations. ACPA's standards also require professionals to be committed to the institution and to seek a balance between supporting student development and the institution's policies and interests. ACPA's ethical standards take a global perspective in including a responsibility to the community.

The Council for the Advancement of Standards in Higher Education (CAS) has developed its own Statement of Shared Ethical Principles (2006) that encompasses the commonalities among its member organizations' ethical codes. The CAS Statement focuses on seven principles: (1) Autonomy; (2) Non-Malfeasance; (3) Beneficence; (4) Justice; (5) Fidelity; (6) Veracity; and (7) Affiliation.

The ethical codes of these three professional organizations promote common standards of doing no harm, justice and equality, and responsibility. According to Wallin (2007), "...at best, these codes serve as guideposts, and they model the ideals of the profession" (p. 41). To truly make a difference and be effective, student affairs professionals must model these behaviors on a daily basis and integrate them into their professional ethic.

Ethics in Action

A new residential life professional shared an ethical dilemma he encountered:

My director had me gather my male staff members at midnight; they were told to walk around in pairs, without a police escort, and knock on every apartment in my complex until someone answered the door and hand out a flyer that explained that there was an attempted rape three hours earlier. The rapist had a gun, and we had no idea who he was or where he lived. For all we knew, he lived in our complex, and here we were, sending our student staff out without protection of any kind to knock on his door with a flyer telling everyone about the crime he just committed. I should have resigned right then but found ways to rationalize the decision. Now, many months and a new job later, I am still struggling with the fact that I just stood by while the leaders of my department put my student staffs' lives in danger. —Residence life professional

Despite the responsibility to educate future leaders and maintain high ethical standards, a search of newspaper headlines reveals that higher education is not immune to unethical behavior. Witness the plethora of stories about scandals involving athletics, sexual harassment, misuse of funds, and violations of laws (Hellmich, 2007; Humphrey et al., 2004; Janosik, 2007). New student affairs professionals encounter many significant ethical situations (Janosik, 2007). In fact, Humphrey and colleagues (2004) emphasize that "ethics is at the core [of student affairs]...putting the practitioner center stage to serve as both role model and moral conscience for the campus" (p. 676).

A study by Janosik (2007) sought to identify the most common professional behavior concerns of student affairs practitioners. A total of 303 student affairs professionals from a variety of institution types and organizational levels, and with various amounts of experience, participated in a six-item electronic survey. The most common ethical problems cited involved "an obligation to act." Respondents had difficulty deciding when to intervene or share information with others. Respect for privacy was another common ethical theme from the study. Respondents struggled with how the Family Educational Rights Privacy Act (FERPA) was being interpreted. Another issue was loyalty. For the survey participants, the issue of loyalty centered primarily on when to tell supervisors about future employment plans. Finally, "misstatement of facts" ranked as a top ethical concern. Respondents reported that a misstatement of facts often occurred to cover up mistakes or to improve one's position. The study revealed that ethical dilemmas are an everyday part of work in student affairs and that professionals at all levels grapple with similar issues. We agree that new professionals encounter ethical concerns similar to those reported by the participants in Janosik's study. We review these and other common ethical concerns that professionals face early in their careers.

Use of Social Networking Sites

We will discuss two ethical issues regarding social networking sites such as Facebook and MySpace. Because students are essentially creating communities in these virtual spaces, new professionals should use the same judgment they use in making decisions about the role of student friendships in their professional lives when they consider entering virtual student communities. For example, is it appropriate for a staff member to accept an invitation to be a student's "friend?" Likewise, is it appropriate for students to be "friends" on staff members' pages? These questions are important to consider, as they relate to levels of trust and familiarity, the development of dual relationships, and the risk of perceptions of favoritism among students. A related dilemma arises when a staff member discovers violations of codes of conduct on students' community pages. Students erroneously believe these to be private spaces and treat them as such. They post information and photos that expose policy violations or present themselves in less than desirable ways. Purposefully seeking out student pages to gather evidence for student conduct cases or to evaluate employment suitability may be a breach of one's professional ethic; at minimum, the practice is worthy of critical discussion.

Assisting Students in Difficulty

Assisting students who are facing difficulties presents a number of ethical concerns. New professionals must be keenly aware of their skill level in crisis management and counseling, and must be comfortable making referrals to colleagues who are trained and experienced in managing specific issues. They also need to be cautious in agreements with students that may prevent them from sharing necessary information with coworkers and supervisors. If a new professional breaches a student's trust by sharing sensitive information, that student and others may not confide in him or her again. However, new professionals need to consider the institutional liability in failure to report as well as the delivery of needed services to a student in crisis.

Job Searching While Employed

Many student affairs professionals conduct their first job search at the end of their master's degree, and the process is widely shared with mentors, peers, and potential employers. However, subsequent job searches can be fraught with ethical concerns for new professionals. They may feel that there will be repercussions in the work environment if coworkers or supervisors find out that the new professional is looking for another job. New professionals should consider all elements of the job search consequences for self and institutions. If you stick to the primary ethic "Do no harm," you will make decisions based on the impact of leaving your current job. How much time will it take to replace you? Have you already made commitments for the next academic year? If you have considered the needs of the institution, you should feel confident that news of your job search will be met with support. Regardless of the circumstances that might lead to a job search, once you become a finalist for a position (i.e., invited for a campus interview), you should inform your direct supervisor.

Dual Relationships with Students

Student affairs professionals work closely with students, so it is likely that close personal relationships will develop. An ethical dilemma occurs when new professionals decide to expand those relationships. For example, a student advisee or student staff member invites you to attend her 21st birthday party. You work closely with this student and enjoy her company, and would like to celebrate her special occasion. However, the ethical implications are great. What if you see underage students drinking at the party? Will the dynamics of your relationship with the student change if she starts to consider you a friend? Other dilemmas can occur if a new professional enters into a romantic relationship with a student. Will there be a perception of favoritism? What happens if the relationship ends? As a new professional, you need to be student-centered, which may mean putting your responsibility to promote student growth and development above your need to spend time with students as friends.

Negotiating Ethical Decision Making with Superiors

New professionals can also face ethical situations resulting from inequities in power positions. When new professionals have the opportunity to work with senior level staff and faculty, they may find themselves in the awkward position of witnessing unethical behavior by superiors. The ethical dilemma occurs as new professionals must decide whether or not to voice concern about the behavior. New professionals may want to prove themselves, especially to senior staff at the institution, or they may fear negative consequences for their career if they speak out against a superior.

Another ethical dilemma may occur if new professionals are asked by superiors to personally engage in unethical behavior. Once again, new professionals must weigh the obligation to fulfill job requirements as directed and thus disregard their own professional ethic. In both situations, new professionals should consult professional associations' ethical statements and consider speaking to a mentor about the situation and about possible courses of action. Overall, new professionals must remember that they can be agents for change to help move the institution toward more ethical practice. One new professional said,

> *Trust your instincts in ethical situations. It's easy to make excuses for why people violate ethics, but by making excuses you are colluding in unethical practices as well. It can be easy to be idealistic, or to want to believe the best in people, but it's important to take a stand when you first notice ethical issues.*

Bending Rules

There are multiple opportunities for bending rules in a work setting, and new professionals are bound to face this ethical dilemma. Students, families, and campus colleagues often make requests for slight accommodations or exceptions to institutional policies and procedures. For example, what if applications for student staff positions are due at 4:00 p.m., and a student rushes in at 4:30? The student would be an asset to the team, and no one else would know that the application came in late. In this situation, it would be very easy to bend the rules. However, what if other students were interested in the position but did not apply because they missed the 4:00 p.m. deadline? It would be wise to consider issues of equality and fairness in this situation. Application deadlines are set to help standardize the recruitment process and create equal opportunities for students to be selected for positions. Bending the rules for one student may put the integrity of the process in jeopardy. New professionals should consider their position as a role model for students and should adhere to the highest ethical standards when dealing with student issues, no matter how trivial the matter may seem.

Excessive Workload

Student affairs professionals often work many more hours than they are paid for, which can create an imbalance between personal and professional lives. Working late and on weekends if often par for entry-level positions; however, employers need to acknowledge this workload and make accommodations in terms of additional compensation or provisions for comp time. Here the ethical responsibility rests with the supervisor, unit, or division—or perhaps even the institution.

> New professionals should consider their position as a role model for students and should adhere to the highest ethical standards when dealing with student issues, no matter how trivial the matter may seem.

New professionals should feel supported in their quest for a balanced life and justified in claiming their rights as employees. Despite a strong desire to prove competence and demonstrate team spirit, new professionals should protect themselves from chronic unreasonable work demands by talking assertively and respectfully with supervisors and by offering strategies for improvement and other solutions. New professionals should also consider constructing explicit boundaries with their students regarding their availability via cell phone, text messaging, or instant messaging. In a world where students (and, increasingly, employers) expect an instant response, setting reasonable boundaries is prudent.

Essential Ethical Principles for Student Affairs Professionals

In the 21st century, student affairs professionals have the opportunity to take a position of leadership in the academy regarding ethical practices in an increasingly complex environment. As our institutions include greater numbers of people from very diverse educational, cultural, and socioeconomic backgrounds, our essential ethical principles may need to change, but absolutely need to be reconsidered so that they best serve contemporary students and institutions. One new professional shared the conflict she experienced when her personal ethic did not match that of her department:

> *When I interviewed, I didn't realize the true and practical implications of this and how different my philosophy would be from [that of] my department director...If you end up at a place where you are asked to do things that "make you feel funny inside," it's probably not the right place for you. Even if it's your first professional position; even if you've only been there several months; if you regularly don't feel good about the job you're going to every day, you're going to the wrong job.*
> —Anna, coordinator of new student orientation, regional university

New professionals should consider the following essential ethical principles as they develop their professional ethic.

Place Students at the Center

Placing students at the center of one's work seems like an obvious component of a professional ethic. However, new professionals might have to hold their own needs for affirmation, affiliation, and acceptance at bay when they are working with students. Decisions should always be made in the best interest of students, not in the best interest of the new professional. Of course, meeting the needs of both is ideal but often difficult to orchestrate. New professionals also must negotiate institutional cultures, policies, and practices that may not be student-centered, and they must do this in ways that allow that element of their professional ethic to remain intact, while at the same time working to be a change agent in their institutions.

Act to Promote Social Justice

Higher education has long been considered a place where societal injustice can be transformed to enhance individual opportunities. However, much in the academy replicates the social structures that result in injustice. New professionals can work to eliminate barriers in the academy that prevent students and groups from achieving their academic and life goals. This requires creativity, critical thinking, use of networks, and the ability to respectfully challenge institutional values and practices that disenfranchise some students while privileging others.

Consider Culture

Integrating one's culture into a professional ethic is essential to maintain authenticity and congruence. This requires reflection to discover how culture influences ethics and ethical behavior. New professionals need not abandon their culture to execute ethics in a subjective way. This is not only undesirable, but largely impossible. Rather, new professionals must understand the impact of culture so they know when they are overlaying their own cultural values and expectations on the values and behaviors of students or the institution. It is helpful if the new professional can articulate this interaction, as a way of modeling how institutional culture and ethics can become more pluralistic.

Become Stewards of the Profession

A steward of the profession is someone who advances the profession's goals and good standing within the academy and in society at large. New professionals should understand that their decisions and behaviors reflect on the profession at the institutional level and in the broader context of higher education. They need to integrate the ethical statements and standards adopted by our leading professional associations into their own professional ethic.

Be an Agent of Change

New professionals should take every opportunity to learn more about the change process and to participate in training and other educational programs that help them effect change in their environments. Promoting and guiding change requires us to be expert relationship managers, political strategists, and problem solvers. Successful change agents know how to approach people and issues respectfully, using the best negotiation and conflict management skills. Student affairs professionals who can cross institutional boundaries effectively will be able to work on behalf of students and advance social justice agendas. One new professional shared her need to be authentic in ethical decision making:

I strive to be authentic in everything that I do, and that alone helps with so many ethical decisions. I always take a deep breath and focus on what my soul is saying, and that usually guides me in the right direction. It may not always be the popular (or right, eeek) decision, but I always feel good about what I've done.

Strive Toward Congruence

The essence of a professional ethic is congruence between a person's personal and professional ethics—commonality between what we do in our personal and community lives and in our professional lives.

Your ethics are yours to own. As a field, we have the overarching values and ethics, but how you practice these is yours to decide. Stay true to how you live out your ethics. —Kirsten; hall director; large, private, four-year institution

Living and Working the Professional Ethic

As new professionals build and implement a professional ethic, they will encounter challenges along the way. Congruence requires a finely tuned balance of self, institution, and profession. Lapses in congruence will cause dissonance and consternation, but careful reflection and consultation will help the new professional get through. New professionals will make mistakes as they make ethical decisions and take action. They need to be kind to themselves as they recover from mistakes, and their supervisors need to show empathy and offer guidance as they coach new professionals to become more effective ethical practitioners. It is helpful for many reasons to create and maintain a network of peers, trusted colleagues, and mentors; but it is especially important for consultation about ethical dilemmas. A network of caring "outsiders" can help a new professional consider

> As our institutions include greater numbers of people from very diverse educational, cultural, and socioeconomic backgrounds, our essential ethical principles may need to change, but absolutely need to be reconsidered so that they best serve contemporary students and institutions.

ethical decisions and actions without worrying about institutional credibility, and they are more likely to provide authentic and critical feedback. Nash (1997) suggests using these 10 essential questions to analyze ethical situations and issues:

1. What are the major moral themes in the case?

2. What are the conflicts in the case that make it an ethical dilemma?

3. Who are the major stakeholders in the case?

4. What are some foreseeable consequences of the possible choices in the case? What are some foreseeable principles?

5. What are some viable alternatives to the possible courses of action in the case?

6. What are some important background beliefs you ought to consider in the case?

7. What are some of your initial intuitions and feelings regarding the case?

8. What choices would you make if you were to act in character in the case?

9. What does your profession's code of ethics say regarding key moral principles in the case?

10. What is your decision in the case? (pp. 2–6)

The following scenarios have multiple dimensions of ethical concerns. They can be used to stimulate discussion in small groups or classrooms. We do not offer solutions to the dilemmas, reinforcing the idea that ethics have cultural and context elements, and are not black and white.

Scenario #1

Tim is a new student activities advisor at a suburban community college. His responsibilities include leadership development, program planning, and advising various student government committees. He works closely with the student leaders and has developed strong working relationships with them. Recently, he noticed that one of his student leaders, Greg, has been behaving differently. Greg appears withdrawn and uninterested in his leadership position. He looks tired and disheveled, and his eyes are always bloodshot. Tim has also witnessed Greg in the middle of a recent conflict within the student leader organization. After Greg misses a number of meetings, Tim becomes concerned and attempts to contact him by phone and e-mail but is unable to reach him. He asks Greg's friends if they have seen or heard from him. His friends report that Greg is not returning their phone calls either. Tim is unsure what to do, so he asks Greg's friends if they can try to contact him on Facebook. Late one Friday afternoon, Greg finally stops by Tim's office. He reveals that he has been suffering from insomnia and has been going days without sleeping. Tim asks how he is managing his classes, and Greg says that he has missed most of his classes that week. He says his inability to sleep at night is causing him stress, because he needs to find a part-time job but cannot stay awake during the day to look for one. Greg says that his home life is in turmoil—he is fighting with his parents and wants to move out on his own.

As Greg's advisor, Tim is worried about him. He seems to be failing not only in his leadership position but also in his coursework and personal life. Tim wonders if Greg is depressed or taking drugs. He is concerned about Greg's lack of sleep and his demeanor. Tim knows that this situation requires more training than he has, so he refers Greg to the student health center to inquire about counseling sessions. However, given his lack of attendance at classes, Tim is not sure whether Greg would even follow through with counseling appointments. He wonders what else he can or should do to help Greg. He considers calling the director of the student health center to alert her that Greg will be visiting the clinic. Tim also knows one of Greg's professors and contemplates calling her to see if she has any information about Greg's situation and to ask her to keep an eye on him. Tim worries about FERPA regulations—he doesn't want to violate Greg's privacy rights; however, he is concerned about Greg's mental health and well-being, and wants to make sure that he gets the help he needs.

Scenario #2

Sylvia is a career counselor at a large public university in the Southwest. She works with students in one-on-one career counseling sessions and in career planning and development workshops. The career center also conducts outreach to student organizations to connect with underserved populations at the university. Sylvia is responsible for reaching out to the Latino/a student organizations. As the first person in her Mexican immigrant family to go to college, she is well aware of the unique career planning issues that affect some Latino/a students. She has developed a strong rapport with students; they readily invite her to conduct workshops and seek her out for individual counseling.

Last year, Daniel, an undocumented Latino student, came to her for individual career counseling. He was trying to get an internship in a local school district (a requirement of his academic program in elementary education), but the application process included providing a state-issued ID and a social security number for the background check. Although Daniel had been in the United States since he was seven years old and graduated from high school with high honors, he was not a U.S. citizen. Sylvia was perplexed about how to help Daniel meet his educational and career goals. She told him that the same problem would resurface when he needed to student teach and later when he looked for full-time work. Daniel was devastated that he might never achieve his dream of being a teacher. Using creativity and her professional network, she recommended that Daniel pursue his goals through private schools, many of which have more flexible rules and procedures, especially parochial schools in areas with high concentrations of immigrant families. Through her work with Daniel, Sylvia began to develop expertise in helping undocumented students in their career development process.

Daniel found Sylvia to be so helpful that he referred other undocumented students to her for career counseling. She teaches these students how to build networks and use them to achieve their goals. She experiences a conflict between following her professional ethic of placing students at the center of her work and offering advice that is questionable in terms of state and federal laws. When she connects students with individuals or companies that will illegally employ them or waive ID requirements for internships, she wonders if she is doing the right thing. She's concerned that if someone higher up in the university finds out how she helps these students, she may have to discontinue her work. She has developed strong empathy for the plight of these students and is actively working to promote the passage of the Dream Act, which would improve the situation of undocumented students in higher education. She feels an ethical responsibility to work to pass this legislation and believes that it would be unethical to do otherwise.

Tim's ethical dilemma concerns how much contact he should have with members of the college community who are close to Greg. In a community college, students tend to be more mobile and have uneven attendance patterns from course to course and semester to semester. Tim's need to approach friends, the health center, and professors demonstrates the webs of connection that may be required to get students the help they need. But his concern about sharing confidential information makes him wonder whether he should put this web to use or not.

Sylvia's dilemma concerns the conflict between her desire to work on behalf of her students and the illegal nature of some of the advice she might wish to give them, as well as the conflict her work with undocumented students may create for the public university where she is employed. She has to weigh what students need and the services she should be providing for them in the context of federal and state laws. She considers herself a private citizen when it comes to her activism in the political arena.

Both Tim and Sylvia are experiencing tension in developing their professional ethic. These two scenarios illustrate the difficulty of this task, which is required to become a mature professional in student affairs. New professionals must consider their personal values, institutional norms and cultures, and the profession's ethics. Paying attention to intuition, lessons learned from mistakes made, and the advice of trusted mentors and colleagues will help new professionals navigate the difficulties in this task and lead them to a place where they begin to trust their own professional ethic as a guide to practice. Adopting a lifelong learning perspective and a willingness to forgive themselves for mistakes will make the journey more productive and tranquil.

References

American College Personnel Association (ACPA). (2006). ACPA statement of ethical principles and standards. Retrieved August 30, 2008, from www.myacpa.org/ethics/statement.cfm.

Anderson, S. K., Harbour, C. P., & Davies, T. G. (2007). Professional ethical identity development and community college leadership. In D. M. Hellmich (Ed.), *Ethical leadership in the community college: Bridging theory and daily practice* (pp. 61–76). Bolton, MA: Anker.

Beckner, W. (2004). *Ethics for educational leaders*. Boston: Pearson.

Benjamin, M. (2006). Everyday ethics. *NetResults*. Retrieved August 30, 2008, from www.naspa.org.

Berry, J. W. (1980). Acculturation as varieties of adaptation. In A. M. Padilla (Ed.), *Acculturation: Theory, models, and some new findings* (pp. 9–25). Boulder, CO: Westview Press.

Berry, J. W. (2003). Conceptual approaches to acculturation. In K. M. Chun, P. B. Organista, & G. Marin (Eds.), *Acculturation: Advances in theory, measurement, and applied research* (pp. 17–37). Washington, DC: American Psychological Association.

Berry, J. W., & Sam, D. L. (1997). Acculturation and adaptation. In J. W. Berry, M. H. Segall, & C. Kagitcibasi (Eds.), *Handbook of cross-cultural psychology: Vol. 3. Social behavior and applications* (2nd ed., pp. 291–326). Boston: Allyn and Bacon.

Costa, J. D. (1998). *The ethical imperative: Why moral leadership is good business.* Reading, MA: Addison-Wesley.

Council for the Advancement of Standards in Higher Education (CAS). (2006). *CAS statement of shared ethical principles.* Washington, DC: Author.

Fried, J. M. (2000). Maintaining high ethical standards. In M. J. Barr, M. K. Desler, and Associates (Eds.), *The handbook of student affairs administration* (pp. 410–424). San Francisco: Jossey-Bass.

Handelsman, M. M., Gottlieb, M. C., & Knapp, S. (2005, February). Training ethical psychologists: An acculturation model. *Professional Psychology: Research and Practice, 36*(1), 59–65.

Hellmich, D. M. (2007). Considerations of power, influence, and cultural norms for the ethical community college leader. In D. M. Hellmich (Ed.), *Ethical leadership in the community college: Bridging theory and daily practice* (pp. 23–32). Bolton, MA: Anker.

Humphrey, E., Janosik, S. M., & Creamer, D. G. (2004). The role of principles, character, and professional values in ethical-decision-making. *NASPA Journal, 41*(4), 675–692.

Kitchner, K. S. (1985). Ethical principles and ethical decisions in student affairs. In H. J. Canon & R. D. Brown (Eds.), *Applied ethics in student services.* New Directions for Student Services, no. 30 (pp. 17–29). San Francisco: Jossey-Bass.

Janosik, S. M. (2007). Common issues in professional behavior. *NASPA Journal, 44*(2), 285–306. Retrieved August 30, 2008, from www.naspa.org.

Komives, S. R., Lucas, N., & McMahon, T. R. (1998). *Exploring leadership.* San Francisco: Jossey-Bass.

Mattchet, N. J. (2008). Ethics across the curriculum. In S. L. Moore (Ed.), *Practical approaches to ethics for colleges and universities.* New Directions for Higher Education, no. 142 (pp. 25–38). San Francisco: Jossey-Bass.

Nash, R. J. (1997). Teaching ethics in the student affairs classroom. *NASPA Journal, 35*(1), 3–19.

National Association of Student Personnel Administrators (NASPA). (1990). *NASPA standards of professional practice.* Retrieved August 30, 2008, from www.naspa.org.

Rebore, R. W. (2001). *The ethics of educational leadership.* Upper Saddle River, NJ: Merrill Prentice Hall.

Vaughan, G. B. (1992). Preface. In G. B. Vaughan and Associates (Eds.), *Dilemmas of leadership: Decision making and ethics in the community college* (pp. 3–29). San Francisco: Jossey-Bass.

Wallin, D. L. (2007). Ethical leadership: The role of the president. In D. M. Hellmich (Ed.), *Ethical leadership in the community college: Bridging theory and daily practice* (pp. 33–45). Bolton, MA: Anker.

Woody, W. D. (2008). In S. L. Moore (Ed.), *Practical approaches to ethics for colleges and universities.* New Directions for Higher Education, no. 142 (pp. 39–54). San Francisco: Jossey-Bass.

SUPERVISORY STYLE: THE PHOTOGRAPHER WITHIN

CHAPTER FOUR

Randi S. Schneider and Kevin W. Bailey

S upervision is an exciting component of student affairs administration. It is also a challenging responsibility. Helping shape the professional and personal growth of another person is not a responsibility to be taken lightly. For many people, the supervisory role is the most rewarding facet of their professional career. As exciting and rewarding as this role can be, it can also be a source of anxiety for a new professional. The feelings of this recent master's graduate are virtually universal for new supervisors:

> *As I leave here (mid-sized public university), I am mindful that I am heading to a position where my supervisor is going to trust me to take responsibility for 15 undergraduate students who are both resident assistants and peer advisors. I interviewed for the position as a confident new graduate of a well-regarded master's program. As I pack my truck*

and head east, I cannot help but be a little nervous about what lies ahead. What if I'm not as good as they think I should be?

Making the transition into a role that involves supervising others can—and probably should—give us reason to think about our readiness for the challenge. Rest assured that this sense of readiness does not begin or end with our first professional position. We may be responsible for a wide variety of personnel. We may supervise someone new to the profession who needs a great deal of attention or personnel who are very experienced and either need little supervision or perhaps resist any efforts to provide supervisory guidance (Dalton, 2003). Although this book primarily addresses the issues associated with being a new professional, even student affairs officers farther up the career ladder may have concerns about supervising veteran personnel.

There is no one-size-fits-all approach to supervision. Scores of books have been written about the best approaches, and each one is likely to have some nuggets of invaluable guidance that in a given situation on a given day could be the key to success in a difficult situation. "Student affairs leaders no longer manage their organizations in any single fashion but, instead, borrow from a variety of management and leadership styles, suited for their organization and institution" (Dalton, 2003, p. 398).

In this chapter, we rely on Bolman and Deal's (2008) four-frame organizational model. Like the lens of a camera, each frame offers a new set of ideas, values, and emphases from which to view the many issues a supervisor faces. The *structural frame* looks at formal roles and responsibilities, including rules, policies, and management hierarchies. Although some people believe that highly bureaucratic systems are out of sync with today's primary leadership paradigm, understanding them can help new professionals succeed in their organization. The *human resources frame* focuses on the needs of individuals within the organization. (This chapter focuses on human resource priorities.) The *political frame* examines how people and groups interact and compete in the organization for scarce resources. The *symbolic frame* analyzes the symbols, myths, and rituals that provide the roots for much of what happens in an organization. The four frames can be discussed separately, but it is the combination of the four perspectives that constitutes the dynamics of the workplace.

Supervisors as Architects

The leader who sees the organization primarily through a *structural frame* is considered an architect. This type of leader focuses on the design and analysis of the organizational infrastructure (Bolman & Deal, 2008). In organizations, responsibilities are allocated to participants (division of labor); and rules, policies, and management hierarchies are created to coordinate diverse activities. Structures are the organizational elements that can be seen (such as an operations manual), the things that are measured (such as quantitative data), and the things that can be defined (such as a policy or the chain of command). All effective supervisors must be architects to some extent.

> **There is no one-size-fits-all approach to supervision.**

Whether you supervise peer educators, resident assistants, orientation leaders, support staff, graduate assistants, or seasoned professionals, your obligation is to provide and use the structures that support success. This is apparent in the words of one new professional whose first job was in a large research university's career services center:

> *Two years ago, I started a job at a school that had a primary focus on data, such as learning outcomes and alumni and employer satisfaction. At my first performance evaluation meeting, my supervisor told me I placed too much emphasis on the "fluffy" aspects of my job. I realized that in order to meet her needs and the demands of the university, I needed guidance in how to refocus my energy. I needed to give the university and my supervisor the data they craved in order for my skills as a counselor to be appreciated. I never want to hear the word "fluffy" in a performance evaluation again. My supervisor was willing to work with me on the skills I needed to improve her perception of my performance. I don't know that I will ever particularly like that some people see my counseling skills as "fluff" and data skills as "essential." I do think, given what I have learned, that this may be a fact of life for anyone who works in a data-driven organization.*

To reduce ambiguity, organizational structures often provide a fixed division of labor (Kuh, 1996). Distributing a position description and an organizational chart helps staff members understand their roles in the organization and how those roles fit into the department. A supervisor must also articulate basic expectations for successfully accomplishing a particular job (Career Press, 1993). Employees want to know how a job description translates into the day-to-day performance of their job (Andersen, 2006). Performance guidelines help reduce the ambiguity that staff members feel in a new job or with a new supervisor. The supervision issues of documentation, working with unionized employees, and hiring staff require many skills, including those that are embedded in the role of the architect.

Documentation

An essential element of structure is documenting organizational and supervisory activity. Documentation plays many roles in an organization, from maintaining records of important conversations to providing needed information for program planning. While a supervisor's emerging style and the organization's history will dictate when documenting personnel concerns is appropriate, a new professional should avoid underestimating the role that documentation plays in performance reviews. Maintaining adequate documentation and completing required forms can help avoid misunderstandings in personnel decisions. In extreme cases—when performance leads a supervisor to consider disciplinary action—proper documentation saves time and frustration. Without documentation, supervisors must recreate history and may be unable to take disciplinary action because of the lack of a proper paper trail. Documentation also provides an excellent written record of support for salary increases and promotions. Sending a letter to document a behavioral problem or simply to say thanks is also part of good supervision.

If the department's tradition does not include documentation, emphasizing it may be seen as untrusting or overzealous. Likewise, a supervisor who has a low need for documentation may be perceived as lazy or irresponsible in an organization where it is expected. If the organizational motto is "If it's not in writing, it didn't happen," supervisors who rely on informal verbal communication may experience frustration.

Professionals should distinguish between *personnel files* and *personal files*. Personnel files are usually the university's formal repository for documents and information about an employee, including hire letter, performance appraisals, merit letters, disciplinary actions, and salary information. Employees are free to inspect their personnel file, which is usually kept in the human resources department.

Personal files, on the other hand, are usually kept in a secure location in the supervisor's office. They may contain private notes about an employee, including behaviors to monitor, leadership roles held on and off campus, involvement in professional associations, a list of presentations, awards received, and vacation or sick days taken. Some of this information can be used as part of the narrative in the performance evaluation, which gives meaning to the numerical score. A personal file may also contain copies of documents contained in the personnel file, such as disciplinary action and merit letters.

One of the most interesting documentation issues to emerge in recent decades is management of electronic communication. E-mail can be a documentation and communication tool, or it can be a nuisance. Organizations that rely heavily on documentation may overuse electronic communication. Learning how to archive messages and sort them in folders can help prove that you complied with a specific request or objected to a particular course of action. With the volume of e-mail, the trick is to know which messages to keep among those you send and receive, as this residence hall staff member shares.

> *As a complex director, I receive approximately 70 e-mails per day. The central office staff, my RDs (resident directors), and my colleagues send me anything anyone believes may have some value. My supervisor feels strongly that we should read and respond to e-mail at least three times per day. I spend many hours at my computer and following up on e-mail-related issues. It is an efficient way to communicate, but hardly an effective use of my time. I estimate that 50% of the e-mail I receive is the professional equivalent of spam. In the days of telephones and paper, I would have lived without the information with no consequence.*

Labor Unions

Among the most structured supervisory relationships are those involving members of labor unions. Even for supervisors trained in labor relations, the potential for conflict is significant. Some new supervisors resist the structures that are firmly in place for union-affiliated employees, but it is incumbent upon them to become educated about the collective bargaining agreements involving their staff. Supervisors of unionized employees must understand that the policies and procedures negotiated into the labor contract are designed to protect those covered by the agreements. Two of the most basic values underlying labor agreements are due process and individual rights (Carnevale & Stone, 1995); both are also values underpinning higher education (Carnegie Foundation, 1990). Contracts are often strictly enforced; ignorance of the rules is not an excuse for noncompliance. There is little room for ambiguity in the interpretation of a labor contract. This scenario is common:

> *I supervise 10 staff members who are from a collective bargaining unit. I have many years of experience in my profession, but this is the first*

time I have supervised unionized staff. In the beginning I found it very difficult to hold staff accountable to my expectations and blamed the labor agreement specifications. However, I quickly learned the importance of the content of the labor agreement. I needed to learn that if accountability was a goal for me, I would need to be unfailing in my approach to establishing and documenting expectations, being consistent in my management of issues, never take anything personally, and document, document, document. —Health center director

To avoid grievances, supervisors should understand union contracts, promote good relationships with the union steward and staff, maintain a fair work environment, keep an open mind when conflicts arise, and use appropriate investigation skills in resolving conflicts (Career Press, 1993). When a unionized employee is not performing up to expected standards, it can seem difficult to work within the labor contract to hold the employee accountable. A supervisor with just cause to confront a unionized staff member must be ready to deal with the bureaucracy and the conflict. It is easy to fall into an "us versus them" mentality when dealing with unionized staff, particularly in times of conflict, but that just creates another barrier. Unions exist to protect their employees, and professionals must work with them accordingly.

Hiring Practices and Policies

Hiring new staff is the most important way to shape the future of an organization. Part of supervision is participating in search and selection procedures; part of hiring is knowing the expectations and practices outlined by law, organizational policy, and our profession's ethical standards. A new professional must be aware of the laws and policies related to hiring. For instance, supervisors must consider institution- and unit-specific hiring policies. If a department has a personnel officer, that person often will have a working knowledge of how the hiring procedures fit into the framework of legal practice. This person is important to know, especially for a new professional who is involved in hiring for the first time in a particular organization. If there is no human resources officer or supervisor with knowledge of proper practice and the new supervisor has questions about the hiring process (time lines, forms, documentation, letters, etc.), the campus human resources or affirmative action office can help by reviewing hiring plans. On some campuses, the hiring and firing of student staff are considered of minor importance compared with issues related to professional staff and faculty, but new professionals who supervise student staff must ensure that the practices they follow align with the ethical standards of the field. (See chapter 3 for a discussion of ethics.)

Supervisor as Catalyst

Bolman and Deal's (2008) second organizational frame is *human resources*. Supervisors who are good managers of human resources are seen as catalysts, because they promote high performance among staff members. The human resource frame, based on the concepts and research of organizational and social psychology, starts with the premise that organizations are made up of individuals who have needs, feelings, prejudices, skills, and limitations. From a human resource perspective, the key to effectiveness is to tailor organizations to people while addressing these underlying issues (Bolman & Deal, 2008). The effective supervisor empowers and supports people so they can reach the highest levels of personal and professional achievement. An effective catalyst knows how to lead and serve people within the framework of expectations, procedures, and policies established by the organizational architects.

While the architect's metaphor for an effective organization is that of the well-oiled machine, the catalyst sees the organization as organic—alive and growing. In student affairs, building effective teams is a process of bringing out the best in the people who work in the organization. Effective supervisors know that the individual personalities of their staff members are as important as their job descriptions. The catalyst recognizes that when there is a good fit between the person and the organization, both benefit. A supervisor who leads from this metaphor may be perceived as someone who cares very much about employees. Consider this quote from a new professional:

> *Care about your staff, not just as employees but as people. Make sure they know from the very beginning that you care about them – when you have them set goals at the beginning of the year, have the big session where they discuss what they want to accomplish as a team in their jobs, but then have another session where they set personal goals, in work, school, finances, wellness, spiritual life, etc. Make a copy of their goals for you to keep and periodically (maybe once a month) pull out their goal sheet and ask them how they're coming along with each of those goals and what they're specifically doing to reach them, and then cheer them on when they do reach them.*

An effective relationship between supervisor and supervisee is crucial to the success of both professionals. The relationship exists on a continuum between directive and laissez faire approaches; the supervisee should have space to demonstrate competence, ask questions, discuss expectations, and receive feedback about performance. Supervision is one of the most complex activities in the organization, and it requires certain skills and knowledge about staff development (Tull, 2006). In the end, "employees need to feel, regardless of their differences, that their supervisor is fair, consistent, and concerned about them" (Dalton, 2003, p. 413).

Communication

Effective communication skills are among the greatest assets of a supervisor—or any employee. Paying attention to and effectively communicating with staff members is a foundational skill in supervision. Staff members have important things to say, may know more about what is happening in the organization (or with students) than their supervisor, and may feel much better about their role in the organization if they know their supervisor is listening. Communication, when carried out effectively, is a two-way street.

All supervisors face various difficult conversations with staff, whether they relate to disciplining an employee or sharing information that will make the employee unhappy. Rather than avoid the fear, anger, or hurt of the interpersonal interaction by sending an e-mail message, a supervisor needs to be confident and direct.

In their book *Difficult Conversations: How to Discuss What Matters Most*, Stone, Patton, and Heen (1999) suggest that these conversations have a certain structure. The authors say that each conversation is really three conversations in one. The first conversation is the "What happened?" conversation, which is about determining the interpretations and perceptions of how the parties arrived at the current situation. It is not about getting the facts right or who is right or wrong. The second conversation is about understanding and sharing feelings. Each of us has developed an "emotional footprint" "whose shape is determined by which feelings we believe are okay to have and express and which are not" (p. 91). This manifests itself in several ways, including the idea that we should not hurt someone's feelings or that we should not disagree or question our senior colleagues. If we change the way we think about those things, it will change our feelings and enable us to say what is on our mind. The third conversation is the identity conversation—it is about how we see ourselves. What self doubts do we harbor? What is the narrative or story that plays in our heads when we are about to enter a difficult conversation? In the example of terminating an employee, the tendency may be to question our own competence or goodness because we bear news that hurts other people. There is no quick way to resolve the identity conversation; you must pay attention to the self-talk and try to keep the negativity from affecting your sense of self-worth.

Synergistic Supervision

Synergistic supervision is a holistic approach that emphasizes two-way communication and a mutual investment in organizational goals, in which supervisees are actively involved in the process (Dalton, 2003; Tull, 2006; Winston & Creamer, 1997). As a concept, synergistic supervision falls into the organizational frame of the catalyst. Because of its collaborative approach, synergistic supervision positively correlates with greater job satisfaction in new professionals (Tull, 2006); however, this style is time-intensive because of the ongoing dialogue and feedback between supervisor and supervisee (Dalton, 2003). The synergistic supervision scale (Saunders, Cooper, Winston, & Chernow, 2000) can help determine the extent to which a supervisor exhibits the traits described.

With a synergistic framework as the foundation for the supervisory relationship, performance expectations can be mutually shaped to match organizational goals and staff professional development plans. Issues such as granting compensatory time (whether formal or informal), vacation time, or flex time during the workday for physician appointments or to balance out late night meetings and events with students are clearly articulated and understood. Appropriate communication methods between supervisor and supervisee should be discussed and agreed upon, and not just assumed in today's e-mail, text messaging, and instant messaging world. The method may have less to do with available technology and more to do with the nature of the information that needs to be communicated. One-on-one and departmental meetings are sometimes best for sharing information, resolving problems, and charting a direction. They also avoid the problems of inadvertently hitting "reply all" when you really only need to communicate with one person, or having to read from the bottom up to understand the flow of conversation that precedes your input.

Delegation As Staff Development

Most professionals want their jobs to provide autonomy, variety, challenge, and enjoyment. Supervisors must learn how to delegate interesting projects to staff members who are ready for new challenges. Often, the only way to find out who is ready is to ask, or to provide the challenge and monitor the results.

Delegating a project is particularly difficult for supervisors who like to maintain a high level of control. Providing appropriate guidance on a project based on the skill level of the staff without being too controlling is a difficult balance to achieve but an important skill to learn. Supervisors should remember that the more people they have doing innovative and interesting work, the more productive their staff and department will be, which reflects positively on the supervisor and provides excellent experience for the staff. If the supervisor is the only person doing innovative projects, the whole team suffers.

Staff Training and Development

Kaufman (1994) views the human resources of an organization as *human capital*. This idea parallels traditional notions of organizational capital—the financial resources available to corporations and other organizations. Kaufman (1994) says that investing in human capital is important in order to have a high-quality labor force and an effective organization. When supervisors invest in their employees—including helping them gain greater skills, increase their knowledge, and maintain good health—the result is a happier, more highly skilled, more motivated, and more effective workforce. Investment involves allocating time for education and training (Kaufman, 1994). For new supervisors, this means that staff training programs should include helping people improve their job performance (e.g., how to program, how to advise a student group, how to handle a disciplinary referral) and grow in areas outside their jobs (e.g., personal wellness, career advancement). Good training and development programs take into consideration the needs of the organization and the needs of the individuals. Training and development can occur in group settings (e.g., formal time for staff development in the weekly schedule) or individually. Allow time during one-on-one supervision meetings to discuss ways that you, as a supervisor, can enhance the professional development of each staff member by creating individualized learning opportunities.

Performance Review

Investing in human capital means more than providing training and development opportunities for staff members; a supervisor must also find ways to assess employees' ongoing performance. The ability to review performance fairly is an important skill to develop. Student affairs professionals who plan a career path that includes supervision must learn the key skill of giving both positive and constructive feedback to staff.

Performance review does not mean the same thing to everyone. A student affairs professional who once worked in a corporate setting said she was evaluated there on purely measurable criteria: "If I made my goals, I was a good employee." In student affairs, a performance review is often less quantifiable; at its best, it blends qualitative and quantitative measures. A numerical score—even with a description of what the numbers indicate—does not sufficiently describe an employee's strengths, accomplishments or challenges, and the little comment box underneath each rating does not provide adequate space to be thoughtful about your narrative. It is frustrating to be new to the institution and review an employee's past performance appraisals only to see numbers circled on the page with no context. A narrative description that supports the numerical ratings enhances the overall evaluation by providing greater understanding of an employee's performance, noting improvements from previous years, and articulating employee strengths on which the supervisor can build.

> **Supervisors should remember that the more people they have doing innovative and interesting work, the more productive their staff and department will be.**

Different supervisors use evaluation as a tool to achieve different ends. A supervisor can use the performance review to exercise power in appropriate (to influence) or inappropriate (to manipulate) ways. A review can be an important yearly ritual or a requirement that supervisors (and staff) learn to dread. The supervisor must communicate the purpose of performance review and the criteria used to evaluate performance to staff members. What staff members believe about evaluation is very important. Even the simple rating scale used in a performance review process can cause stress. Supervisors should provide staff members with the knowledge they need to understand the "grading" scale. For example, on a scale of 1 to 5, it is important to define what a 3 represents. Of course, it is imperative that supervisors use the grading scale in a consistent manner with all members of the staff.

Evaluating performance should be part of an ongoing feedback loop. The loop does not begin at the performance review. In a synergistic supervisory style, the loop begins on the day staff tasks are defined and expectations are mutually negotiated, continues at every supervisory meeting, leads to the formal performance review, and culminates with the articulation of new staff expectations. Staff members should be given an opportunity to provide feedback on the expectations of the organization and to appraise their own performance through a self-evaluation.

The annual performance appraisal may be a time to review previous feedback discussions, but it should not be a time for surprises. If the staff member is surprised by the evaluation, it means that the supervisor has not given enough ongoing feedback. And, while supervisors are busy providing constructive ways for staff members to improve performance, they should also be providing appropriate positive feedback. If giving constructive criticism is difficult, supervisors should consider finding at least one positive for each constructive issue presented. If there is nothing positive to say in a performance review, supervisors should ask themselves: "Why is this person still working for me?" The answer could be political (e.g., a person cannot be fired because he or she is related to a senior administrator), but it could just as easily be that the supervisor is not providing sufficient structure and feedback.

New professionals should determine whether their departments provide opportunities for staff members to evaluate them as supervisors. Giving staff members a process through which they can provide feedback to the supervisor is invaluable. If there is no formal mechanism for this type of feedback, one should be created. Few people know the skills, foibles, and vulnerabilities of supervisors quite like their own staffs. This type of evaluation also sets a positive example for ongoing evaluation and self-development.

One mechanism that allows supervisor feedback is 360-degree feedback. In this process, supervisors receive feedback from staff members at various levels: their supervisor, staff who report to them, and peers with whom they work. For example, a hall director would receive feedback from an immediate supervisor, RAs and desk staff, and peers such as other hall directors and staff in other departments where the hall director has significant peer relationships because of job responsibilities. The feedback is usually anonymous and is given to the supervisor in the aggregate from each of these groups. Usually coordinated by the person's supervisor, 360-degree feedback can be a time-consuming process because of the dissemination, collection, sorting, and aggregating of data; however, it provides a holistic view of the person's impact on multiple constituencies in his or her sphere of influence.

Supervisor as Advocate

A new supervisor who views organizational activity through the *political frame* realizes that all action is not dictated by policy and all decisions are not made in formal meetings, as would be assumed by someone viewing the world strictly through the structural frame. Seeing the organization through the political frame encourages a focus on how different people and interest groups compete for power and for scarce resources to influence action and focus energy in an organization. The advocate, or the political supervisor, builds coalitions, serves as spokesperson for staff, and works the formal and informal systems for the benefit of the staff and the whole institution (Bolman & Deal, 2008). All members of an organization interact as political beings. Being apolitical or choosing to remain outside the political arena is practically impossible and professionally irresponsible given the multiple obligations of a supervisor. The political frame encourages recognition of informal ways of influencing action in the organization, in contrast to the structural frame, which focuses on formal means to ends and goals (e.g., through written policies).

In the political frame, supervisors work within systems composed of different interest groups that are constantly involved in bargaining, negotiating, compromising, and, occasionally, coercing. Virtually all decisions of consequence offer many possibilities for the dynamic interplay of organizational politics. Professionals in the supervisory role for the first time may be uncomfortable with conflict. Wanting to be liked and to feel good about one's environment and relationships may exacerbate the discomfort; when conflict arises, the new supervisor may wonder, "What have I done wrong?" In the political frame, however, conflict is seen as inevitable, a natural and necessary element in the growth of the organization. When conflict is faced openly and honestly, relationships can build on trust, and individual and organizational performance can be enhanced. The following quote is from the coordinator of new student orientation, a former residence hall director at a regional university.

> *Particularly when working with student staff for the first time, it's easy to feel uneasy about where the lines are drawn. Trust that you can make good decisions about boundaries, and then follow through, prepared to defend your actions to yourself, your peers, and your staff. I went through several stages, from "Oh, no! They'll never take me seriously because I'm too young" to "Oh, no! They'll never take me seriously because I'm too (insert personal adjective here)" all the way to "Oh, no! They'll never take me seriously because I'm too old." In the end, there is always a reason to feel uneasy. You just have to trust that you know how to make good leadership decisions.*

The Advocate and Power

Some professionals dislike the word, but *power* can be good or bad, used or abused. Power is the ability to perform or act effectively, to exercise influence or control. Supervisors need to be aware of the various types of power they have or have access to, and the power that others have, so they can enhance their ability to influence organizational action and obtain necessary resources.

The most obvious power available to an organizational member is the power of position; that is, the formal authority associated with a position in an organizational hierarchy. Even persons higher in the hierarchy—such as directors, deans, and vice presidents—recognize that this type of power is limited and that other forms of power are necessary to influence the staff members they supervise. These include the powers associated with rewards, information, and access.

The power of rewards

In some organizations, supervisors do not control formal rewards, such as salary and benefits; but other types of rewards are available to the supervisor, such as positive feedback, public recognition, professional development opportunities, job enrichment, and advancement. Some rewards, however, are not under the supervisor's control. Consider this new professional's experience:

> *Where I work, the funds for attending conferences are controlled by a central office administrator other than my supervisor. The person controlling the funds is notorious for approving funds for some staff members, while making others virtually beg for conference funding. It is clear that the best way to get funds for conference travel is to "play up" to the person with the travel budget. I'm not sure if the funds are allocated with a consistent eye for equity. However, most of us feel like the decisions are arbitrary.*

The power of information

Information is the lifeblood of an organization and of the people in it— information about resources, budgets, expectations, perceptions, outcomes, goals, changes, organizational history, and priorities. Having, controlling, and filtering information are inevitable aspects of organizational life. Supervisors are conduits for information flowing through an organization. While flow may be seen as a structural matter—information flows up and down the hierarchy—all information is filtered in the process of communication. When information is selectively disseminated to influence decisions, it becomes a political tool. New professional supervisors must seek out information if they expect to enhance their performance and the performance of their staff. When supervisors recognize that all information is, inevitably, filtered and incomplete, they become more proactive in clarifying the data they receive and seeking the data they do not have. Supervisors are better able to do their jobs when they obtain and pass on necessary information to their staff members.

Consider the plight of the complex director (CD) who is concerned about the volume of e-mail. Some of that mail, in the eyes of the CD, is a documentation nightmare, while central office staff sees it as the fastest way to empower staff with knowledge. Here are some thoughts to consider when making choices about electronic communication:

☞ E-mail is not confidential or private. E-mail is never truly deleted from your files. Electronic correspondence can be requested through sunshine laws, subpoenaed, or used as official university documentation in the same way any other document can be used.

☞ Electronic communication sent and received from a personal e-mail account can be subpoenaed or produced in a sunshine law request if the information is work-related.

☞ Be concise. Be mindful of the receiver's time.

☞ Use e-mail subject lines that help the reader prioritize and organize—as if you were providing a hint about which file folder the e-mail should be stored in.

☞ Do not overuse "reply all" or mass mailings when a targeted e-mail would suffice.

☞ Respond to e-mail in a timely fashion. If you need time to provide adequate information, offer a quick response that includes a time line for getting the requested information.

☞ Request delivery receipts only if documentation is essential. Use the "high priority" option in your e-mail program sparingly.

☞ Civility is as important in electronic communication as it is in face-to-face communication. If you are angry, frustrated, or hurt, reconsider your impulse to send an e-mail.

☞ E-mail can be a reflection of professional writing skills. Be careful to differentiate between circumstances that permit informality and those that are more formal or that require attention to detail.

☞ Be mindful of the chain of command in the organization when sending e-mail. Political issues are the same in any form of communication when you use the carbon copy (CC) or the blind carbon copy (BCC) function on a memo.

☞ Communicate supervisory expectations about e-mail, instant messaging, or text messaging to staff members.

☞ Attend training or read policies associated with how the legal council/human resources personnel at your institution view electronic correspondence, particularly with regard to supervisory documentation.

The power of access

Having access to individuals and groups with power is one way new supervisors can influence the effectiveness of their staff and garner the resources they need. The first step is to determine which persons and groups in the organization wield influence in a particular area of interest (e.g., budgeting, policymaking). Access can be formal (e.g., getting appointed to the budget planning committee) or informal (e.g., establishing a relationship with the chair of the policy and procedures committee).

In addition to information, rewards, and access, power may include personality (charisma) and expertise. Viewing the supervisory role through the political frame means being aware of the bases of power in the organization (including one's own) and learning how to use them effectively.

Team Development

Regardless of where we work—whether in the private or public sector—the value of working collaboratively is well documented. Corbin (2000) said, "The power of teamwork remains true today. Multiple people working in unity are so much more powerful than the same number of people working independently" (p. 133). According to Dalton (2003), student affairs organizations are notorious for assembling teams. "Teams are used for advisory and planning purposes, appellate decisions, assessment and accreditation, and selection committees..." (p. 412).

Supervisors are often in the position to select staff members to participate on or lead a team. In selecting someone for a team, supervisors should match the needs or purpose of the team with the skills or interest of the staff member. A team assembled to select a new student conduct database requires different skills and expertise than a team assembled to plan the division's holiday party. In leading a team, a supervisor must manage the team dynamics, which includes understanding and dealing with multiple personality traits, various levels of skill and experience, and different levels of willingness to work collaboratively. Conflicts in the group over power and resources can make the role of team leader and supervisor particularly challenging. Some groups are easier to mold into teams than others. Corbin (2000) offers this caution regarding supervising groups of people:

> Because of the power of teamwork in organizational success...leaders must arrange workspace for collaborative efforts and arrange the work itself so that each person, when making his or her most expert contribution, produces a necessary part of the whole. Additionally, rewards are given for the team's projects at completion. Ideally, competition is fostered between organizations, not within organizations, which is why rewards are given for individual improvement and not on the basis of comparative performance. The greater reward, however, must be given on a team level—something that can be achieved only through cooperation. (p. 120)

Supervisor as Interpreter

The fourth frame of reference is that of *organizational culture or symbolism*. Probably the most elusive of the four frames, it is a significant influence in campus and personnel issues (see chapter 2). While organizations can be viewed as machinelike (structural frame), they also have qualities of a culture similar to those of the cultures of racial, ethnic, or religious backgrounds; that is, patterns of shared values, beliefs, assumptions, and symbols. Every organization develops distinctive patterns of beliefs and behaviors over time. Many of them are subconscious—reflected in myths, stories, rituals, ceremonies, and other symbolic forms. Managers who can interpret and make use of the meaning of symbols have a better chance of influencing their organizations than those who focus only on the other three frames (Bolman & Deal, 2008).

Institutions of higher education are loaded with very powerful messages about who their members are and what they believe. Consider why people cry when they sing the alma mater or why they paint their faces at football games. They do not do this because there is a campus policy mandating emotion at football games, but because rituals, heroes, and myths are powerful ways to share common meaning and experience within a culture. Faculty, students, alumni, donors, staff, legislators, administrators, parents, and others compete to have their voices heard on campus, but on Saturday afternoon, the crowd—composed of all these groups—cheers for the football team. It is not accidental that college athletics has symbolic power in higher education.

The cultural frame takes the focus away from what the organization does and how, and places emphasis on why we do the things we do; that is, on the meaning of organizational and individual action. The culture of the organization and institution often dictate how supervisors should behave—the "shoulds" that begin as part of the formal structure become part of the culture. For example, the issue of documentation discussed in the structural frame will vary in emphasis and meaning depending on the culture of the particular organization. To the new assistant dean, following up a meeting with a memo meant that he was ensuring accurate communication; to his supervisor, it meant that the assistant dean did not trust him to do what he said he would. Formally documenting meetings and agreements was just not part of that organization's culture.

As a supervisor, interpreting and understanding the culture as soon as possible increases the new person's chances of success. Time in the position helps, but so does careful and sensitive observation of practices, reactions, language, and priorities. A new supervisor should observe what people do and listen to the stories they tell about the organization. Who are the departmental heroes, and what did they do to gain such fame? On any campus, one can look around and identify the department or staff groups that seem to be the tightest knit teams.

What are the department's special rituals? What are the inside jokes and special stories that make the team seem cohesive? Skilled supervisors learn how to manage and shape the culture of their staff and of the organization. Practical examples of culture management are special banquets, award ceremonies, regular social gatherings, slogans, T-shirts, songs, and mission statements. One must, however, go beyond the surface meaning of activities to their underlying, more powerful, subconscious meanings. Note the implicit messages in an organizational culture described by this financial aid officer:

> *Our new supervisor was flabbergasted by the lack of communication in the office. We didn't talk to each other. We went about our business and got the job done. The office was quiet. There was no laughter, and certainly there was no conversation about anything unrelated to our work. One day, she practically did a cartwheel to try to get someone to smile. She called me into her office and said, "Tell me about the silence." I told her that our previous supervisor didn't tolerate anything other than obvious work-related interaction. Interaction with personnel other than our own department was to be kept to a minimum and only if necessary for the accomplishment of the task at hand. Over time, it was clear that her number one goal was to change our culture and establish a sense of teamwork and joy in the office.*

In the office culture described above, two supervisors had distinctly different points of view on the culture of the office. On further discussion with the professional who provided this quote, it became clear that both the old and the new supervisor were capable of accomplishing the work of the department. The difference was in the office culture created by the style and priorities of the two supervisors.

Supervisors work within the context of a historically based institutional culture. Supervision does not occur in a vacuum. Supervisors need to be aware of the culture of the department, of the overall organization, and of the various constituency groups within the organization.

Integrating the Frames

It is unlikely that a new supervisor will be a skilled architect, catalyst, advocate, and interpreter in his or her first position. He or she will probably be most comfortable and effective with one, perhaps two, of the four frames. And the organizational setting will have a significant impact on the emphasis the supervisor can or will place on one or more of the frames.

One supervisor may be structure-oriented and thrive on budgets, operational calendars, and development of policy and procedures; another may be oriented toward the people in the organization and thrive on collaborative projects, relationships, and committee work. Regardless of how the supervisor is most comfortable, it is wise to view the organization and a supervisor's role in it through multiple perspectives. The supervisory role requires some skills from each of these perspectives; focusing on one frame will mean missing out on important information or actions.

As an example of the need to integrate perspectives, an analysis of the typical RA (resident assistant) staff meeting provides a useful scenario. You can raise questions about structure (e.g., purpose, agenda, outcomes, degree of formality, required attendance); human resources (e.g., role of RAs, degree of collaboration); and politics (e.g., working together to influence departmental policy). From a cultural perspective, you can ask, Why are staff meetings important? Are they weekly rituals that enhance the performance of the group as a whole? Are they weekly requirements to pass along memos from the central administration? Does the group's culture support change, or does the status quo usually prevail? Considering all four of Bolman and Deal's (2008) frames not only raises different questions but also may lead to different outcomes and more effective decisions.

Another common example of the integration of the four frames is the role of the live-in staff member. One professional shared this story:

When I was a resident director [RD], one of the first items on my training agenda was "Please do not contact me in the evening unless there is a building emergency." Well, as it turned out, the previous RD in my building gave his RAs 24-hour access to the key to his apartment, so they could drop by and use the kitchen, watch TV, or just chat. Well, you would not believe how upset my staff became. They really felt as if I had taken away quite a major perk of being an RA. And they questioned whether I really cared about them because I didn't want them to call me after hours.

This RD was not obligated to allow her RA staff to have access to her apartment 24 hours a day. There were, however, ramifications from this change. The students associated the apartment and RD access as a reward for being an RA. The veteran RAs passed along to new RAs folklore about late-evening conversations with the RD while in the apartment in the late evening hours. The new RD took away the reward and, therefore, was perceived as using the power of her position in a negative manner. The RAs translated the removal of the key from the desk as meaning that the RD did not care about them or what was happening on the floors. One seemingly reasonable decision quickly became a political and organizational culture issue.

Integrating the Frames to Build a Coherent Style

Many different concepts have been presented in this chapter, representing the different perspectives, or frames, with which we can approach a topic. In any given organization or situation, different approaches or different perspectives can be brought to bear and, in all likelihood, none of them would be incorrect. That is the crux of the complexity of being a leader and a supervisor: One situation can be dealt with using many different approaches. The discussions in this section take a few issues and approach them from different frames of reference.

Generational Issues

Defining a generation is controversial in and of itself. The defining characteristics attributed to a "boomer" or an "X-er" may or may not be appreciated by a member of the labeled group. Boomers think X-ers lack loyalty, work ethic, and commitment. Nexters think boomers are stuck in the past. "Like death and taxes, defining characteristics are assumed to be immutable and irreparable, and consequently, they are never openly addressed. In the 'old' rigid, highly regimented organization, that may not have mattered. In the 'new' organization, they can be devastating. They nonetheless fester, cause tension, and lead to unnecessary, at times disabling, personal, departmental, and organizational conflict" (Zenke, Raines, & Filipczak, 2000). An example of a generational conflict is embedded in this quote from a residence director at a large, research institution in the Midwest:

> *The senior student affairs officer on our campus participated in a panel discussion about strategies for getting ahead in our profession. Among the messages was his clear disdain for professionals who seek balance between their professional and home life. He worked 100 hours a week as a young professional and was promoted to the vice presidency as a result of hard work. If I make a choice to hold my family in higher regard than my university, I will not succeed. Fortunately, I am pretty sure he is a breed of professional that is out of touch with the realty of my generation. I intend to be successful both at home and at work. I do not intend to work myself to death.*

Strategies for facing generational issues cannot just be given lip service; we encourage reading on this topic. *Generations at Work* (Zenke et al., 2000) includes a cross-generational workplace assessment within which are many embedded concepts regarding how you and your organization relate to generational differences. Consider these examples, taken directly from the assessment:

☞ There is no one successful type in this organization. Managers, leaders, and those in the most desirable jobs are a mix of ages, sexes, and ethnicities.

☞ When a project team is put together, employees with different backgrounds, experiences, skills, and viewpoints are consciously included.

☞ There is lots of conversation, even some humor, about differing viewpoints and perspectives.

☞ Our atmosphere and policies are based on the work being done, the customers being served, and the preferences of the people who work here.

☞ There is behind-the-back complaining, passive-aggressive behavior, and open hostility among groups of employees.

☞ There is an element of fun and playfulness about most endeavors here.

☞ Managers adjust policies and procedures to fit the needs of individuals and the team.

☞ We are concerned and focused, on a daily basis, with retention.

☞ Work assignments here are broad, providing variety and challenge, and allowing each employee to develop a range of skills.

☞ We market internally, "selling" the company to employees and continually looking for ways to be the employer of choice.

This list represents 10 of the 20 items on the assessment; it shows the types of organizational and supervisory priorities that get to the heart of cross-generational issues. Each item offers a clue to the theoretical framework that is the bedrock of the assumption. For instance, in this group of 10 items, some issues are associated with the organizational architect (policy, procedure, hiring policy); the catalyst (variety, challenge, playfulness); the advocate (selling, employee behaviors); and the interpreter (development of organizational culture through retention of employees).

Discipline

One of the most agonizing and difficult tasks for a student affairs professional is disciplining an employee, because we are trained as helpers, are collegial by nature, and believe in the development approach to modifying staff behavior (Dalton, 2003). But even with synergistic supervision, ongoing feedback, and opportunities to improve, sometimes there is no alternative but to terminate an employee. Some people believe that terminating an employee is a recognition that both the supervisor and the employee have failed, but the reality is that good supervision does not always work. "Some employees lack and cannot gain the necessary skills to perform their jobs. Some seek to obfuscate and deny any responsibility for failure. Worse, some engage in personal diatribe and denial in which they adopt a vitriolic attitude toward the supervisor and the organization" (Zenke et al., 2000, p. 416).

Your direct supervisor should be in the loop on your plan to terminate an employee, to make sure the documentation supports the outcome. The human resources department should also support your decision in case legal action is taken against the university. The process should be done humanely, with attention to the employee's dignity. The employee is not a bad person, just not a good fit for the job. The conversation should be brief but direct, stating the opportunities you gave the employee to improve, the fact that the employee did not act on those opportunities, and that the next step is termination. You should be absolutely clear in your mind that the termination is the direct result of the employee's lack of performance and that you did not contribute in any way to getting him or her fired. The termination should occur with a witness in the room; the employee should be given a time frame for vacating the office and turning in keys and ID card, and for when access to e-mail and other systems will be deactivated. Issues of last paycheck and unused vacation hours can be referred to the human resources department or explained in a letter that you hand the employee. Do not set yourself up for a hostile exchange with the employee by debating the issue, devaluing contributions made to date, or making the termination personal. As Dalton (2003) says, "[M]ost people respond to termination with greater resourcefulness than we are inclined to think, especially if the termination process is handled in a professional, respectful, and transparent manner" (p. 416).

Less severe disciplinary measures include a formal letter of warning or reprimand, a performance action plan, or a reduction in merit pay. In each instance, you should refer back to job expectations, provide specific examples of expectations that were not met, give the reason for the corrective action, and state what both parties need to do in the future so that the employee can be successful in the job. If you write a letter or develop an action plan, review it carefully to ensure that the feedback is clear and concise and that improvement can be easily measured.

Multicultural Issues

Cross-cultural supervision can be challenging. If a supervisor is uncomfortable because of a cultural (e.g., racial, ethnic, international) or other (e.g., gender, disability, sexual orientation) difference, it is the supervisor's responsibility to identify the root of the discomfort and take appropriate steps to address it. Being selected to supervise others does not eliminate a person's experience, biases, or stereotypes. In fact, to assume that one does not have biases is perhaps the greatest obstacle to self-learning and effective cross-cultural supervision. Pope, Reynolds, and Mueller (2004) challenge practitioners to achieve competence in three distinct categories in student affairs: exemplary multicultural awareness, exemplary multicultural knowledge, and exemplary multicultural skills. The combination of self-awareness, knowledge, and practical skills enables us to serve at the highest levels of our profession with regard to multicultural competence. While having an intellectual command of multicultural issues may be a good attribute, knowledge alone will not provide the basis of good supervision in a multicultural environment. Being aware of our own biases and issues associated with oppression is helpful, but awareness alone is not enough.

> The combination of self-awareness, knowledge, and practical skills enables us to serve at the highest levels of our profession with regard to multicultural competence.

In recognizing the need to learn more about a particular difference (e.g., supervising a deaf staff member for the first time), the supervisor should not place responsibility solely on the staff member but must take the initiative to learn about those who are different. New professionals—both members of majority groups and those who are marginalized in the institution—should reflect on their experiences and assumptions regarding supervision of people they perceive as culturally or otherwise different. "By reexamining the core competencies of student affairs professionals and infusing the multicultural attitudes, knowledge, and skills that are needed to create a more multiculturally sensitive campus, both practitioners and scholars provide more ethical and effective programs and services. Multicultural awareness, knowledge, and skills are core competencies that all student affairs professionals need regardless of their job responsibilities and level of training" (Pope et al., 2004, p. 28).

Turning the Table: Supervisor As Supervisee

Strengths, areas for development, and major skill deficiencies exist in most supervisors, regardless of how many years of experience they have in the profession. What if we find ourselves working with a "bad boss"? First, we should understand that, for example, an extraordinary architect who is not a strong catalyst is probably not a bad boss. Nor is the supervisor who is a skilled catalyst but a weak architect necessarily a bad boss.

A laundry list of traits that describe a bad boss should not just be traits that are the opposite of our preferred style of leadership. It is essential to look for ways to capitalize on our similarities with our supervisors for the betterment of the organization. Coming from opposite perspectives? Learn how to incorporate the supervisor's perspective to enhance your personal skills and job effectiveness. Even when differences are extreme, try to develop a relationship grounded in mutual respect. Once respect is established between two people, possibilities arise for sharing concerns about weaknesses and areas for improvement. Accept differences and learn from them.

> **Remember that supervision is a two-way street, not just a top-down structure.**

There are times when a supervisor's lack of skill or inappropriate behavior warrants concern. A supervisor may be unable to manage job responsibilities or may exhibit uncivil or unethical behavior. The subordinate must make some choices when a supervisor's behavior goes beyond a few underdeveloped skills and starts to seriously and negatively affect the professional or personal environment on the job. The sensitive nature of any relationship that has a power and authority differential calls for case-by-case analysis.

The ideal course of action to deal with conflict is to directly address the problem. If appropriate, confront the supervisor with specific issues and requests for behavior change. Use civil language and behavior. If the behavior changes and the outcomes are satisfactory, the story has reached an ideal ending. If the behavior is so extreme that a one-on-one confrontation is not possible, or if the behavior does not change after an initial confrontation, seek assistance. If mentors are available to help develop a strategy, talk with them. Additional campus resources include human resources personnel, an ombuds officer, harassment officers, and the direct supervisor of the person causing concern. Coworkers with more experience can offer perspective and suggest strategies to work through difficult situations.

But, again, always look first for ways to capitalize on similarities and differences with supervisors for the betterment of the organization.

Being a Good Supervisee

Although this chapter's focus is on supervision, being a good supervisee also requires certain skills. A program advisor from a large public institution offers this perspective:

Remember that supervision is a two-way street, not just a top-down structure. I think new professionals often find themselves waiting for a supervisor to initiate a conversation or take the reins on a project. Be assertive and communicate regularly with your supervisor regarding challenges you may face and goals you wish to attain.

We must all remember that we are a part of larger systems. The choices we make as supervisees are as important as those we make as supervisors. There is much discussion on college campuses about civility. Perhaps the lessons of civility statements are among the most important we can bring to our supervisory relationship. A strong work ethic and a commitment to civility are a winning combination for both supervisor and supervisee.

Conclusion

Understanding and integrating the four frames does not mean that all supervisory decisions will be popular and perfect; however, supervisors increase the probability of making a good decision when they tap a deep understanding of the organization. Additionally, supervisors may have more empathy with persons who are opposed to a decision if they can see that the opposition is based in a particular way of viewing the situation. Improved decision making, working relationships, and performance provide ample justification for trying to understand and view the organization through multiple lenses. A veteran supervisor talked about supervision this way:

> *There is no question that the most rewarding part of my job is supervision of staff. With each passing year, I learn as much about myself through the role of being a supervisor as I do about the people I supervise. I have always believed that supervision is a two-way street. There was a time when I tried to make everyone happy. I have learned through experience that making people happy isn't always the best path. It may be the path of least resistance, but it is often not the path that will maximize my team or the individual. The joy in supervision often comes many years later at a conference, when someone you may have butted heads with says thank you for caring enough to be critical or being bold enough to face conflict. As I have gotten older, I admit that I still do enjoy those supervisory relationships that fit like a glove. However, I am genuinely grateful for the supervisory relationships that force me to be a little uncomfortable.*

It is one thing to read about supervision and quite another to actually do it. Each new professional has a unique style that, initially, will be a good fit for some individuals, staffs, and organizations and not such a great fit for others. Strive to weave the principles of lifelong learning and civility, and the perspectives of the architect, catalyst, advocate, and interpreter into your skills as a practitioner.

References

Andersen, E. (2006). *Growing great employees: Turning ordinary people into extraordinary performers*. New York: Penguin Group.

Bolman, L. G., & Deal, T. E. (2008). *Reframing organizations: Artistry, choice, and leadership* (2nd ed.). San Francisco: Jossey-Bass.

Career Press (1993). *The supervisor's handbook* (2nd ed.). New York: Author.

Carnegie Foundation for the Advancement of Teaching. (1990). *Campus life: In search of community*. Princeton, NJ: Author.

Carnevale, A. P., & Stone, C. S. (1995). *The American mosaic: An in-depth report on the future of diversity at work.* New York: McGraw Hill.

Corbin, C. (2000). *Great leaders see the future first: Taking your organization to the top in five revolutionary steps.* Chicago: Dearborn, A Kaplan Professional Company.

Dalton, J. C. (2003). Managing human resources. In S. R. Komives & D. B. Woodard, Jr. (Eds.), *Student Services: A handbook for the profession* (4th ed., pp. 397–419). San Francisco: Jossey-Bass.

Kaufman, B. E. (1994). *The economics of labor markets.* Fort Worth, TX: The Dryden Press.

Kuh, G. D. (1996). Organizational theory. In S. R. Komives & D. B. Woodard, Jr. (Eds.), *Student services: A handbook for the profession* (pp. 269–294). San Francisco: Jossey-Bass.

Pope, R. L., Reynolds, A. L., & Mueller, J. A. (2004). *Multicultural competence in student affairs.* San Francisco, CA: Jossey-Bass.

Saunders, S.A., Cooper, D.L., Winston, R. B., Jr., & Chernow, E. (2000). Supervising in student affairs: Exploration of the synergistic approach. *Journal of College Student Development, 41,* 181–192.

Schuh, J. H., & Carlisle, W. (1991). Supervision and evaluation: Selected topics for emerging professionals. In T. K. Miller & R. B. Winston (Eds.), *Administration and leadership in student affairs* (pp. 495–532). Muncie, IN: Accelerated Development.

Stone, D., Patton, B. and Heen, S. (1999). *Difficult conversations: How to discuss what matters most.* New York: Penguin Books, Inc.

Tull, A. (2006). Synergistic supervision, job satisfaction and intention to turnover of new professionals in student affairs. *Journal of College Student Development, 47,* 465–480.

Winston, R. B., & Creamer, D. G. (1997). *Improving staffing practices in student affairs.* San Francisco: Jossey-Bass.

Zemke, R., Raines, C., & Filipczak, B. (2000). *Generations at work: Managing the clash of veterans, boomers, xers, and nexters in your workplace,* Toronto: Amacom.

COLLABORATION WITH
ACADEMIC AFFAIRS AND FACULTY

CHAPTER FIVE

Camille Consolvo and Michael Dannells

The organizational and functional gap between academic affairs and student affairs is generally distinct and often problematic for student affairs professionals who endeavor to navigate the institution with the ultimate goal of student learning. Collaboration between student affairs professionals and the faculty is one logical and oft-prescribed solution (AAHE, ACPA, & NASPA, 1998; ACPA, 1994, 1999; ACPA & NASPA, 1997).

Collaboration has been defined as working jointly with others in an intellectual endeavor and cooperating with someone with whom one is not immediately connected (*Merriam Webster's*, 2008). Our intellectual endeavor with faculty is the design and delivery of learning environments and opportunities for students. Because we are not immediately connected with faculty in most institutions, and because faculty tend to perceive the formal curriculum as the core of education, we must cross organizational lines and work with faculty to develop a shared vision—a common agenda—for student learning. Working toward this common agenda requires faculty and student affairs professionals to identify and recognize their different assumptions. Colleges and universities must work as a single system (especially academic affairs and student affairs) to successfully educate students in the 21st century (Cook, Ghering, & Lewis, 2007, p. 6). As interest in assessment of learning outcomes increases, faculty and student affairs staff can work together both in and outside the classroom to create systems that promote these learning outcomes.

Understanding Both Cultures

To build bridges between students' in- and out-of-class experiences, new professionals must first understand and appreciate the cultures of both the faculty and student affairs. Although faculty may work at the same institution, they may not necessarily communicate regularly, have common goals, or value undergraduate education in the same way (Eimers, 1999). Faculty tend to identify more with their discipline than their institution (Love, Kuh, MacKay, & Hardy, 1993). A faculty member's closest colleague may work at another institution. Faculty members are not a homogeneous group, and student affairs professionals must view each faculty member as an individual. To understand the faculty at a particular institution, one must consider the type of institution, the history, traditions, and culture of that institution, and the socialization process for faculty (Hirt, 2006).

> To build bridges between students' in- and out-of-class experiences, new professionals must first understand and appreciate the cultures of both the faculty and student affairs.

Despite institutional differences, faculty tend to share four values: (1) pursuit and dissemination of knowledge; (2) professional autonomy, including academic freedom; (3) collegiality through self-governance; and (4) a preference for thinking and reflecting over doing. In contrast, student affairs professionals tend to share four different values: (1) an interest in holistic student development; (2) collaboration over autonomy; (3) teamwork; and (4) a preference for doing over thinking and reflecting (Love et al., 1993). When student affairs professionals and faculty understand both cultures and sets of values, they can work together to create an institutional culture that encourages student learning and development. The two groups can fill the gaps in each other's knowledge, values, and roles (Price, 1999).

In a study of differences among academic disciplines, Braxton and Hargens (1996, cited in Eimers, 1999) suggested that faculty in "soft" sciences (e.g., education, business, humanities) were more likely than faculty in the natural sciences (e.g., math, engineering) to encourage in- and out-of-class contact with students and to create opportunities for students to share their skills and knowledge in the classroom. Thus, student affairs professionals may want to seek out faculty in the soft sciences with whom to collaborate. Again, this will depend on institutional culture and other variables.

In recent years, the number of collaborations between student affairs and academic affairs has increased, resulting in an overall shared commitment to student success (Bourassa & Kruger, 2001). Before such collaboration, though, new professionals should spend significant time learning about their own professional cultures and those of their constituents (Philpott & Strange, 2003). This will increase the effectiveness of the working relationship. As one new professional said,

> *We don't always get much training in how to deal with faculty in our preparation programs. We need to understand that it's all about relationships. Faculty are people, too.* —Ryan; Greek affairs; mid-sized, public institution

Other new professionals offered the following advice:

> *Take initiative and don't be frustrated with a few isolated pockets of cynicism and disinterest among faculty. Find out each faculty member's niche and how it might fit with your program. It may take many contacts on your part, but be patient and persistent, and stay committed.* —Miguel; career center; small, public institution

> *Student affairs and academic affairs folks speak a different language. Fundamentally, we are all in higher education to help and serve students. However, to be effective, we cannot assume knowledge between the "two sides of the house" and must take the time to explain and create a common language.* —Kirsten; hall director; large, private, four-year institution

Conditions for Collaboration

There are several conditions for effective collaboration (Brown, 1990). Student affairs professionals (new and seasoned) must understand and acknowledge that the mission of colleges and universities—academics—comes first. They must also understand the nature of faculty preparation, priorities, and daily activities. On the academic side, certain emerging environmental factors promote collaboration. Faculty professional development has expanded; as a result, faculty's conception of their role and obligation to students and their learning has broadened. Broader definitions of scholarship, with a focus on teaching and assessment of student outcomes, favor collaboration (Banta & Kuh, 1998). Significant numbers of new faculty are joining the academy—they may be more open to collaboration. To build a bridge between silos, each culture must take time to learn about the other.

In *Learning Reconsidered*, Keeling (2004, p. 13) says it is realistic to consider the entire campus as a learning environment. This overall learning includes both in- and out-of-class experiences. Collaborative institutional efforts to assess this overall learning are important and should become part of the campus culture. One of six themes common to effective academic and student affairs collaborations is joint planning of curriculum and assessment (Banta & Kuh, 1998). Student affairs has the opportunity to take the lead in these assessment efforts (in collaboration with faculty) and to capitalize on them to build evidence of learning in and out of the classroom. Sharing the results of these assessment efforts can promote discussion and empower both faculty and staff to continue assessment of student learning. Faculty-staff partnerships can help students who need additional support and can help broaden the learning of all students (Eaker & Sells, 2007). Student surveys, focus groups, observations of student engagement, and other assessment methods may provide useful data for assessing the effectiveness of collaboration and suggesting ways to improve the learning environment.

Student affairs staff offer expertise in student characteristics, development and learning, program development, supervision, administration, policy development, networking with diverse groups, conflict mediation, and student conduct (Dannells, 1997; Engstrom & Tinto, 1997). This knowledge should be promoted to faculty as an incentive to engage in collaborative efforts. Student affairs professionals should emphasize their expertise as educators along with their administrative skills. As Magolda said, to be successful, these partnerships must be "meaningful, reciprocal, and responsive" (2005, p. 17).

Collaboration in the Community College Setting

About 40% of all college students attend community colleges, so it is important to address collaboration in this setting (Martinez, 2004). Students of color and first-generation students are more likely to attend a community college because of open admissions policies, proximity to home, and affordability. Because of the diversity of students enrolled at community colleges and the need to help these students succeed, it is important for faculty and student affairs professionals to collaborate in designing services, programs, and systems to put students at the center of learning (Shenk & de la Teja, 2007).

With learners at the center of the community college culture, Keeling (2006) says it is essential to create learning outcomes that support student success and engage all campus community members in creating experiences that support learning. Student affairs staff can become "dialogue experts" to help bring diverse groups together, stimulate discussion, and promote student learning (Keeling, 2006). The need for intentional collaboration is critical in this environment—to identify and assess learning outcomes of diverse community college students and to address student success in a holistic manner. Student affairs staff can help interpret the data collected and be advocates with faculty for student learning.

In a survey of community college best practices, O'Banion (1997) found that essential elements of collaboration include assessment of learning outcomes, involvement of key staff on joint committees and with shared responsibilities, and a commitment to ongoing professional staff development and to identifying ways academic affairs and student affairs can work together to facilitate student learning.

Along with assessment, another way to partner with faculty is to help community college students with the transition from two-year to four-year institutions. Effective transitions for these students involve collaborative advising and orientation programs that address the challenges community college students face in transferring to a four-year institution. New professionals have an opportunity to connect with faculty in helping students understand how things like classes, registration, advising, internship, job search, and involvement opportunities may differ.

We need to help faculty see that we are educators, too. —Sharisse, advising center, community college

Opportunities for Collaboration

Brown (1990) described several areas that call for collaboration. These major themes have important implications for how student affairs professionals work with their colleagues in academic affairs to improve undergraduate education. With the renewed emphasis on learning, the academic community needs to focus on different methods of teaching and how to help students learn more effectively. Student affairs professionals can design co-curricular experiences to reinforce course content, identify high-risk classes, and work with instructors to improve success rates, as well as organizing discussion groups for students enrolled in common courses.

Engstrom and Tinto (2000) described a three-phase continuum for involvement with faculty: (1) serve as a clearinghouse of information; (2) work cooperatively with faculty while maintaining traditional roles; and (3) work cooperatively with faculty in a relationship in which the roles and expertise of both parties are appreciated and utilized. Residential learning communities are excellent examples of how to accomplish these goals. Models of faculty involvement include faculty-in-residence, faculty fellows who coordinate regular programs with specific halls, first-year programs, classes that meet in the residence hall, students who live in proximity and take the same courses, and theme halls with affiliated faculty. Residence halls are particularly productive settings in which to integrate academic and social life by bringing faculty and students into regular contact with one another. Student affairs staff can provide opportunities for student involvement and meaningful conversations with faculty outside the classroom; this increases the level of comfort students feel when interacting with faculty (Nesheim et al., 2007). These interactions also offer faculty the opportunity to work with student affairs colleagues. Students benefit from these interactions through greater satisfaction with the overall college experience (Astin, 1985). Faculty also benefit—some report improvements in their teaching as a result of getting to know students better (Kuh, Schuh, Whitt, & Associates, 1991). Thus, it is important for student affairs professionals to broker opportunities for connections between students and faculty.

Residential students have a continuous presence on campus, offering an opportunity for faculty and staff to create truly seamless learning environments. However, student affairs staff are not always trained in how to build academic collaborations, and faculty do not always think about addressing student learning from a broader institutional perspective. It is essential to create learning environments not in isolation but in collaboration. To do this, we must look for components of partnerships that already exist on our campus (e.g., pairing service learning with residence hall community service programs). Pilot projects using existing resources provide evidence of feasibility that will change minds and increase the likelihood of ongoing partnerships (Masterson, 2008). Faculty need to have clearly defined roles and responsibilities, and understand the benefits (e.g., increased student-centeredness, a more holistic understanding of students) and drawbacks (e.g., reduced time for research, possible impact on promotion or tenure). Faculty at transition points in their careers (i.e., just completed an administrative appointment, a few years away from retirement, want a different experience, between research projects) are good candidates to approach about involvement in residential partnerships (Stewart, 2008).

Curricular reform with an emphasis on the general education curriculum is another collaboration opportunity. The liberal education curriculum (e.g., psychology, history, philosophy, the natural sciences, and literature) promotes student development and contributes to the development of identity, competency, autonomy, appreciation for diversity, and the clarification of values. Coupled with a focus on active learning, the general education curricular reform movement provides an opportunity for student affairs professionals to serve as advocates, facilitators, and reinforcers; helping students understand the developmental aspects of the core academic disciplines (Brown, 1990). Some methods to achieve these goals are freshman year integration and transition programs (Banta & Kuh, 1998; Garland & Grace, 1993); incorporating faculty's vocational or career interests into residential life programs (Garland & Grace, 1993); cooperative education/internships; new faculty orientation (Finley, 1996); academic support programs (e.g., study skills labs, writing labs, tutoring); academic advising; honors programs (Brown, 1990); early warning systems for students in academic difficulty; and living–learning communities (Schroeder, 1999).

Opportunities for collaborative relationships in an institution emerge from the need to focus on different methods of teaching and find ways for students to learn more effectively. Gaff (1983) said that student affairs professionals and other administrative staff should be included in the debates about general education, because they "can help set high expectations" and advance learning goals for students outside the classroom. Collaborative ways to accomplish these goals include leadership training (Martin & Murphy, n.d.); service learning (Engstrom & Tinto, 1997; Fried, n.d.); advising student organizations; and facilitating career decisions by connecting academic programs with course and career choices (Garland & Grace, 1993). Other issues that call for collaboration are values education, dealing with diversity issues, and teaching social responsibility (Brown, 1990).

A broad range of interactions occur with some frequency between faculty and student affairs professionals (Brown, 1990), including standing committees and councils; university programs and functions (e.g., admissions, orientation, honors programs, academic support programs); residence halls; health and counseling services; career planning and placement; and student activities and cultural programming. Other opportunities for interaction and collaboration are campus diversity initiatives and decentralized student services in colleges within a university.

Over the past 20 years, many institutions have focused on integrating service learning across the curriculum (Engstrom & Tinto, 1997). Through service learning, students are encouraged to create tangible relationships between classroom content and real-life experiences. Engstrom and Tinto (1997) said that service learning provides ideal opportunities for collaborative activities between academic and student affairs, in which both parties can make significant contributions. They cited several institutions that are creatively and effectively forging partnerships in this area. Service learning excels in bringing students, faculty, staff, and community agencies together to develop and define mutual goals to build effective, collaborative, and reflective learning experiences (Stein, 2007).

Banta and Kuh (1998) described outcomes assessment in higher education as "one of the most promising but underused opportunities for collaboration." They said it is one of the few activities on campus in which student affairs professionals and faculty can participate equally. New student programs and experiences, as well as co-curricular transcripts, are examples of collaboration in the assessment process to focus institutional effort on student learning. Especially at larger, research-oriented institutions, it may be beneficial for student affairs professionals to demonstrate their ability to collect and analyze outcome data to faculty immersed in a research culture.

The Council for Higher Education Accreditation and several regional accrediting agencies would like to see evidence to validate the assessment of learning outcomes in and outside the classroom (Newman, Couterier, & Scurry, 2004). The council's emphasis is on creating an organizational structure and culture in which the chief academic and student affairs officers work closely to create a learning-centered environment. The call from external constituents for accountability, increased graduation rates, employable graduates, and evidence of learning outcomes highlights the need for collaborative partnerships between faculty and student affairs staff (Cook & Lewis, 2007). Keeling and colleagues (2008) stressed the importance of collaborative use of all campus resources to promote student success. Both student affairs professionals and faculty members must address internal and public questions about the functioning of postsecondary institutions by reconsidering assessment policies, patterns, and practices in colleges and universities, and responding to expectations for greater institutional accountability. Faculty and staff can address common concerns by engaging in evidence-based, reflective practice and supporting one another in doing their best work.

Table 1 summarizes a number of ways student affairs professionals can collaborate with their academic colleagues to provide seamless learning environments in which students make the most of learning resources both inside and outside the classroom, and in which the curricular and co-curricular are a holistic, continuous experience (ACPA, 1994).

Table 1. Opportunities for collaborative efforts between student affairs and academic affairs.

Enrollment management, retention, admissions efforts (Brown, 1990; Martin & Murphy, n.d.)
Precollege enrichment courses
Undergraduate research and other creative opportunities with faculty (Cook & Lewis, 2007).
Freshman year integration and transition programs (Banta & Kuh, 1998; Fried, n.d.; Garland & Grace, 1993)
Incorporating faculty's avocational or career interests into residential life programs (Garland & Grace, 1993)
Cooperative education, internships, field experiences (Stein, 2007)
Residential life programs: Theme housing, freshman interest groups, living–learning communities, residential communities, faculty-in-residence efforts (Brown, 1990; Fried, n.d.; Martin & Murphy, n.d.; Schroeder, 1999)
Student discipline (Dannells, 1997; Garland & Grace, 1993)
Including faculty on unit advisory boards (Brown, 1990)
Participating in annual week/month events (e.g., Women's History, Alcohol Awareness, Black History)
Co-curricular transcripts or portfolios (Banta & Kuh, 1998)

Table 1. Opportunities for collaborative efforts between student affairs and academic affairs *(continued).*

Advising student organizations (Brown, 1990)
Involvement with student newspaper or radio (Brown, 1990)
Assessment (Banta & Kuh, 1998)
International programs and study/education abroad
Serving on faculty governance committees (Brown, 1990)
University day care centers (Brown, 1990)
New faculty orientation (Finley, 1996)
Academic support programs (e.g., study skills labs, writing labs, tutoring) (Brown, 1990)
Honors college/honors program involvement and involvement with academic honor societies connected to specific majors (Brown, 1990; Cook & Lewis, 2007)
Faculty development workshops (Finley, 1996)
Teach individually or as a team (e.g., freshman experience course, graduate course in college student personnel, or undergraduate course) (Cook & Lewis, 2007; Martin & Murphy, n.d.)
Protection of human subjects committees
Early warning systems for students in academic difficulty
Facilitating career decision by making connections between academic programs and course and career choices (Brown, 1990; Garland & Grace, 1993)
Involvement in adventure learning or outdoor programs (e.g., ropes course, wilderness experiences) (Cook & Lewis, 2007)

Table 1. Opportunities for collaborative efforts between student affairs and academic affairs *(continued).*

Responding to increased violence/decreased civility on campus (Garland & Grace, 1993)
Long-range planning groups (e.g., space, resources)
Joint appointments in student affairs and on the faculty
Leadership training and coursework on leadership efforts (Martin & Murphy, n.d.)
Service learning (Engstrom & Tinto, 1997; Fried, n.d., Stein, 2007)
Serving as consultants for each other
Joint research, joint publications, or joint professional presentations (Cook & Lewis, 2007)

To build effective relationships, we must assess the environment and identify institutional issues that cross the boundaries between academic affairs and student affairs.

Advice for Building Collaborative Relationships

As *The Student Learning Imperative* (ACPA, 1994) implored, we should attempt to bridge the functional silos on campus, make seamless what are often perceived by students to be disconnected experiences, and develop collaborative partnerships with faculty and others to enhance student learning. One new professional said,

We need to reach out more to faculty and make our invitation well known. —Darien; student activities; mid-sized, public institution

To build effective relationships, we must assess the environment and identify institutional issues that cross the boundaries between academic affairs and student affairs (e.g., retention, assessment). We facilitate collaboration, for example, by building relationships with colleagues in learning centers and advising offices that straddle the functional silos, and by developing a shared vision with academic colleagues. By creating cross-functional teams of staff and faculty with diverse skills and experiences, we can understand that faculty are people like ourselves and find ways to connect with them. Making persistent attempts to connect with faculty, recognizing them publicly for their collaborative efforts toward student learning, and continually identifying the major issues that lend themselves to collaboration will increase our opportunities to work effectively together. We must leave the comfort and security of organizational boundaries and take some appropriate risks (Schroeder, 1999). One new professional described it this way:

> *We must educate faculty about what we do and be sensitive to their needs. Listen to them and reach out. However, be "ready to be railed" (challenged) for your efforts. Faculty are paid to think and articulate ideas. Be prepared to help faculty understand our decisions and don't back down, but provide data and information. Don't be defensive, but always do your best to be "even" and a professional, and you will gain their respect.* —Sharona; student leadership program; small, private university

Another new professional said,

> *After working on a number of initiatives that involve faculty, I have found that you may need to work further in advance than you would with others at the university. Faculty typically like to have things scheduled and on their calendars well in advance. Waiting to the last minute usually leads to disappointment.* —Charlie; residence life coordinator; large, public, research university

To create seamless environments through collaboration, we should start with small projects to achieve some success and then build on them. We should demonstrate how student affairs programs promote personal and academic development, and engage faculty in discussions about how to make this an outcome of the academic curriculum as well (Brown, 1999). As student affairs professionals, we need to quit worrying about being second-class citizens and "not getting any respect." One new professional described his experience this way:

> *I sometimes think faculty see student activities as the "gym decorators" of the university and our staff as paraprofessionals. To show them otherwise, it is important to be professional and honest, to stand up for the decisions you make, and be proactive and consistent. It's important to be intentional with our programs and services, and serious about our work.* —Stephen; union programs; mid-sized, public institution

Student affairs professionals should be confident that they make a difference in students' lives and be comfortable living in the breach between being a service provider and a faculty member (Hossler, 2001).

Student affairs as a profession must relinquish the weak self-identity that leads to ineffectiveness, an anti-intellectual culture, concern that territory will be gained or lost, and a need to be seen at the center of the institution. Instead, we should begin recognizing the value we have as educators and include a focus on learning. We should "transcend real and imagined boundaries, strengthen our identity, and lead effectively from the margins" (NASPA's Think Tank, 2001, p. 2). Right or wrong, initial contacts for collaboration may have to come from student affairs professionals, because it is unlikely that faculty will initiate such contact.

Kuh (1996) suggested several ways to create seamless learning environments in collaboration with faculty: invite faculty members to present research findings at student affairs staff meetings; have student life and academic deans, as well as other faculty, attend professional conferences together; and hold occasional joint meetings of senior staff. Finley (1996) recommended finding faculty allies who appreciate what student affairs brings to the educational experience, participating in new faculty orientation and following up with these faculty afterward, writing articles for faculty newsletters about services and programs, using brief e-mail messages to keep faculty informed about what is happening in student affairs, and offering to guest lecture in their classes. Helping faculty access students as research participants and serving on institutional review boards for the protection of human subjects are other ways to develop faculty allies. As one new professional in student activities suggested,

> **To build effective relationships, we must assess the environment and identify institutional issues that cross the boundaries between academic affairs and student affairs.**

> *I started a dialogue with all faculty advisors. The dean of students and I talked with the provost about ways to add some value to faculty merit portfolios through involvement as an advisor. As a result, I have the vice president for student affairs send letters each semester thanking faculty for their service. Faculty want a tangible benefit.* —Danielle; housing; large, public institution

Another new professional in residence life described faculty recognition this way:

I write the president at the end of each year, naming faculty who have been involved and their contributions to retention. We make sure that events involving faculty are well publicized on campus so their peers recognize their involvement. We also try to make sure there is a benefit for them. For example, for nontenured faculty, we talk about possible research and publication opportunities. —Drew; leadership programs; mid-sized, private institution

Cook and Lewis (2007) offered several tips for student affairs practitioners related to building collaborative partnerships with faculty. They suggested that new professionals in particular tend to expect that partnerships will be on a 50-50 basis, and that this is unrealistic. Student affairs staff should identify themselves as educators and not just logistics people. Being a spokesperson for active student involvement in academic life (e.g., service learning, cooperative education, academic honor societies, undergraduate research, and field experiences) is important. Another way to engage with faculty is to ask students about faculty members who have influenced them and use their recommendations to engage those faculty members. The authors of *Learning Reconsidered* suggested trying to determine and map out where learning opportunities occur and looking at the intersections of academic affairs and student affairs as opportunities to discuss partnering on projects and programs (Keeling, 2004).

New professionals can also become engaged by: (1) getting involved with the academic side of the institution (e.g., taking a class, teaching a class, or serving on a committee; or through joint research, writing, or professional presentations); (2) getting involved with faculty by collaborating on projects, playing "noon ball," running, or finding other neutral ground on which to establish relationships; (3) personally inviting faculty to be involved in structured, time-limited tasks in student affairs (e.g., orientation planning, staff screening and selection, judicial boards); (4) making faculty experiences comfortable by having a structured segment so they know what to expect, providing an escort to introduce them and show them what to do, or having more than one faculty member present; (5) viewing every interaction as an opportunity to introduce faculty to the values and goals of your unit and the profession; for example, serving on advisory boards to your unit or program; and (6) following through and having fun (Love et al., 1993). One new professional made the following suggestion:

It can be challenging for a faculty member to step out of the familiar (e.g., the classroom) and enter a new environment (e.g., a residence hall) because it is new and can be intimidating. We need to educate them about what we do and escort them into the new surroundings. —Juan; residence life; mid-sized, public university

Student affairs professionals complain that they are the ones who always have to approach the faculty, and they wish faculty would do the initiating sometimes. We need to realize that this is not likely to happen very often, considering faculty culture and values, the size of the institution, and campus culture. We must approach faculty to build bridges and create effective learning environments for our students. The key to this involvement is persistence. One new professional described it this way:

It is important to reach out to faculty, because the academic mission is central to our mission in student affairs. We must take the initiative and not see ourselves as second-class citizens. Some new professionals get frustrated by being the initiators. It is important to look for common ground (e.g., academic expectations, the university as a learning community) and work with faculty from that point. —Jessie; international student programs; large, research university

Although comprehensive research has not been conducted to assess the outcomes of collaboration on student learning, the potential for improved cognitive, interpersonal, and organizational skills; responsibility for self and community; increased leadership and citizenship; self-understanding; and academic success and retention (Bloland, Stamatakos, & Rogers, 1996) makes it worth the effort. Persistence and optimism with faculty, while maintaining a focus on issues and themes around student learning, will pay big dividends in the end. Historical, organizational, and cultural obstacles may impede easy progress; however, the greatest barrier to collaboration with faculty—and the one most within our control—is attitude.

The principles of good practice for partnership programs state that effective collaborations: (1) reflect and advance the institution's mission; (2) embody and foster a learning-oriented ethos; (3) build on and nurture relationships; (4) rec-

> **Some new professionals get frustrated by being the initiators. It is important to look for common ground (e.g., academic expectations, the university as a learning community) and work with faculty from that point**

ognize, understand, and attend to institutional culture; (5) value and implement assessment; (6) use resources creatively and effectively; and (7) demand and cultivate numerous expressions of leadership (Whitt et al., 2008). New professionals should know the context within which they work, focus on student learning, create partnerships with allies, engage in assessment, and expect partnerships to require sustained effort. With this kind of focus, the new professional can create successful, lasting collaborative relationships.

References

American Association for Higher Education (AAHE), American College Personnel Association (ACPA), & National Association of Student Personnel Administrators (NASPA). (1998). *Powerful partnerships: A shared responsibility for learning.* Washington, DC: Authors.

American College Personnel Association (ACPA). (1994). *The student learning imperative: Implications for student affairs.* Washington, DC: Author.

American College Personnel Association (ACPA). (1999). *Higher education trends for the next century: A research agenda for student success.* C. S. Johnson & H. D. Cheatham (Eds.). Washington, DC: Author. www.acpa.nche.edu/seniorscholars/trends/trends.htm.

American College Personnel Association (ACPA) and National Association of Student Personnel Administrators (NASPA). (1997). *Principles of good practice for student affairs.* Washington, DC: Authors.

Astin, A. (1985). *Achieving education excellence: A critical assessment of priorities and practices in higher education.* San Francisco: Jossey-Bass.

Banta, T. W., & Kuh, G. D. (1998, March/April). A missing link in assessment. *Change, 30,* 40–46.

Bloland, P. A., Stamatakos, L. C., & Rogers, R. R. (1996). Redirecting the role of student affairs to focus on student learning. *Journal of College Student Development, 37,* 217–226.

Bourassa, D. M., & Kruger, K. (2001). *The national dialogue on academic and student affairs collaboration.* New Directions for Higher Education, no. 116 (pp. 9–38). San Francisco: Jossey-Bass.

Brown, R. D. (1999, February). Shaping the future. *ACPA Developments, 25,* pp. 1, 16.

Brown, S. S. (1990). Strengthening ties to academic affairs. In M. J. Barr, M. L. Upcraft, & Associates, *New futures for student affairs* (pp. 239–269). San Francisco: Jossey-Bass.

Cook, J. H., & Lewis, C. A. (Eds.). (2007). *Student and academic affairs collaboration: The divine comity.* Washington, DC: NASPA.

Cook, J. H., Ghering, A. M., & Lewis, C. A. (2007). Divine comity: The basics. In J. H. Cook & C. A. Lewis (Eds.), *Student and academic affairs collaboration: The divine comity* (pp. 1–15). Washington, DC: NASPA.

Dannells, M. (1997). *From discipline to development: Rethinking student conduct in higher education.* ASHE-ERIC Higher Education Report 25(2). San Francisco: Jossey-Bass.

Eaker, R. E., & Sells, D. K. (2007). Circle five: Mutual understanding through frequent communication. In J. Cook, & C. Lewis (Eds.), *Student and academic affairs collaboration: The divine comity* (pp. 105–116). Washington, DC: NASPA.

Eimers, M. T. (1999, March/April). Working with faculty from diverse disciplines. *About Campus, 4,* 18–24.

Engstrom, C. M., & Tinto, V. (2000). Developing partnerships with academic affairs to enhance student learning. In M. Barr, M. Desler, & Associates (Eds.), *The handbook of student affairs administration* (4th ed.) (pp. 425–452). San Francisco: Jossey-Bass.

Engstrom, C. M., & Tinto, V. (1997, July/August). Working together for service learning. *About Campus, 2,* 10–15.

Finley, D. (1996, March). Faculty and student services: Friends or foes. Paper presented at the annual convention of the American College Personnel Association, Baltimore, MD.

Fried, J. (n.d.). Steps to creative campus collaboration. NASPA invited paper. Washington, DC: NASPA.

Gaff, J. G. (1983). *General education today: A critical analysis of controversies, practices, and reforms.* San Francisco: Jossey-Bass.

Garland, P. H., & Grace, T. W. (1993). *New perspectives for student affairs professionals: Evolving realities, responsibilities, and roles.* ASHE-ERIC Higher Education Report 7. San Francisco: Jossey-Bass.

Hirt, J. B. (2006). *Where you work matters: Student affairs administration in different types of institutions.* Washington, DC: American College Personnel Association.

Hossler, D. (2001). Reflections on the scholarship of application in student affairs. *Journal of College Student Development, 42,* 356–358.

Keeling, R. P. (Ed.). (2004) *Learning reconsidered: A campus-wide focus on the student experience.* Washington, DC: National Association of Student Personnel Administrators and American College Personnel Association.

Keeling, R. P. (Ed.). (2006) *Learning reconsidered 2: A practical guide to implementing a campus-wide focus on the student experience.* Washington, DC: American College Personnel Association, Association of College and University Housing Officers-International, Association of College Unions International, National Academic Advising Association, National Association of Campus Activities, National Association of Student Personnel Administrators, & National Intramural-Recreational Sports Association.

Keeling, R. P., Wall, A. F., Underhile, R., & Dungy, G. J. (Eds.). (2008). *Assessment reconsidered: Institutional effectiveness for student success.* Washington, DC: International Center for Student Success and Institutional Accountability.

Kuh, G. D., Schuh, J. H., Whitt, E. J., & Associates. (1991). *Involving colleges: Successful approaches to fostering student learning and development outside the classroom.* San Francisco: Jossey-Bass.

Kuh, G. D. (1996). Guiding principles for creating seamless learning environments for undergraduates. *Journal of College Student Development, 37,* 135–148.

Love, P., Kuh, G. D., MacKay, K. A., & Hardy, C. M. (1993). Side by side: Faculty and student affairs cultures. In G. D. Kuh (Ed.), *Cultural perspectives in student affairs work* (pp. 37–58). Washington, DC: ACPA.

Magolda, P. M. (2005, January/February). Proceed with caution: Uncommon wisdom about academic and student affairs partnerships. *About Campus, 6,* pp. 16–21.

Martin, J., & Murphy, S. (n.d.). Building better bridges: Creating effective partnerships between academic affairs and student affairs. Invited paper. Washington, DC: NASPA.

Martinez, M. (2004). High and rising: How much higher will college enrollment go? In K. Boswell & C. D. Wilson (Eds.), *Keeping America's promise: A report on the future of the community college* (pp. 21–23). Denver: Education Commission of the States.

Masterson, J. (2008). Academic/student affairs partnerships in residential settings: Principles and practices. In G. Luna & J. Gahagan (Eds.), *Learning initiatives in residential settings* (Monograph No. 48, pp. 19–28). Columbia, SC: University of South Carolina, National Resource Center for the First-Year Experience and Student in Transition.

Merriam Webster's collegiate dictionary (11th ed.). (2008). Springfield, MA: Merriam-Webster.

NASPA's Think Tank. (2001, June). A challenge to change: A statement on the future of the student affairs profession. Salmon Lake, MT: NASPA.

Nesheim, B., Guentzel, M., Kellogg, A., McDonald, W., Wells, C., & Whitt, E. (2007). Outcomes for students of student affairs–academic affairs partnership programs. *Journal of College Student Development, 48,* 435–454.

Newman, F., Couturier, L., & Scurry, J. (2004). *The Future of higher education: Rhetoric, reality, and the risks of the market.* San Francisco: Jossey-Bass.

O'Banion, T. (1997). *A learning college for the 21ˢᵗ century.* Phoenix: Oryx Press.

Philpott, J., & Strange, C. (2003, January/February). On the road to Cambridge: A case study of faculty and student affairs in collaboration. *Journal of Higher Education, 74,* 77–95.

Price, J. (1999, Fall). *Merging with academic affairs: A promotion or demotion for student affairs?* New Directions for Student Affairs, no. 87 (pp. 75–83). San Francisco: Jossey-Bass.

Schroeder, C. C. (1999). Forging educational partnerships that advance student learning. In G. S. Blimling & E. J. Whitt (Eds.), *Good practice in student affairs: Principles to foster student learning* (pp. 133–156). San Francisco: Jossey-Bass.

Shenk, E. J., & de la Teja, M. H. (2007). Collaboration in the community college. In J. Cook, & C. Lewis (Eds.), *Student and academic affairs collaboration: The divine comity* (pp. 201–238). Washington, DC: NASPA.

Stein, J. (2007). Circle six: Service-learning as crossroads. In J. Cook, & C. Lewis (Eds.), *Student and academic affairs collaboration: The divine comity* (pp. 117–154). Washington, DC: NASPA.

Stewart, D. (2008). The role of the faculty in the residential setting. In G. Luna & J. Gahagan (Eds.), *Learning initiatives in residential settings* (Monograph No. 48, pp. 55–62). Columbia, SC: University of South Carolina, National Resource Center for the First-Year Experience and Student in Transition.

Whitt, E. J., Nesheim, B., Guentzel, M., Kellogg, A., McDonald, W., & Wells, C. (2008, May/June). "Principles of good practice" for academic and student affairs partnership programs. *Journal of College Student Development, 49,* 235–249.

MAKING PROFESSIONAL CONNECTIONS

CHAPTER SIX

Lori M. Reesor, Grace Bagunu, and Melissa Hazley

The key to personal and professional success is having a strong support base of people who believe in you, challenge you, and help you grow. Many leadership books in popular literature support this concept. In addition, it is a common belief that having positive and motivated people around you will have a positive impact on your destiny. Student affairs professionals understand these concepts and try to create these kinds of opportunities for our students. Sometimes we can be the positive change agents who make a difference in students' lives. New professionals should work to establish a support system of connections, mentors, and professional involvement to enhance their professional growth and development. This chapter offers suggestions for networking with other student affairs professionals and developing relationships with mentors, as well as recommendations for getting involved in professional organizations.

The Art of Networking

When I first became a professional, networking scared me to death. Going up to a stranger and striking up a conversation while pretending to be confident and smart seemed so tough. My taste of how easy it could be happened during a trip to NASPA IV-West. I decided to join the optional walk on one of the mornings to put myself out there. I enjoy walking, so I figured it was perfect. I ended up walking with another woman who was a professional in the field, and we talked about everything under the sun—personal, professional, etc. I found out after our walk that she was a very well-known and respected professional in the field. I laughed at myself, because I think if I had known who she was in the beginning, I probably would have shied away, but without the introductions and in the casual environment, I made a connection. Later on that morning, I realized I had networked and I didn't even know it! It wasn't as scary as I thought it was going to be. —Sarah; housing professional; large, research institution

New professionals in student affairs need professional involvement and connections with colleagues to begin establishing their professional identity. In the scenario above, Sarah had an "ah-hah" moment. In the student affairs profession, we encounter many opportunities to engage in casual conversations with colleagues, whether we realize it or not. This can occur at your university's basketball game while you're in line to get some popcorn—we all know how long concession lines can be, so take advantage of these few minutes to meet those around you. Maybe you exercise on campus, as many administrators and faculty members do; group exercise classes or trading repetitions on a workout machine is a great way to meet people from across campus. Networking can be scary, but it can also be very basic and easy.

> **Building a professional network is an important aspect of one's career.**

There are many benefits to building a network. As colleges and universities change, the response of student affairs professionals must change. Having a network can be a stress reliever—it's comforting to realize that colleagues face similar issues. Having someone to bounce ideas off of can be a huge asset. Networks can help you stay knowledgeable about current events and opportunities in the field, recruitment processes, information technology trends, campus security issues, and opportunities for advancement.

There are four steps to successful networking: (1) network at all levels in the organization; (2) make it a top priority to seek out colleagues; (3) be sincere and genuine in your relationships; and (4) follow up. Building a professional network is an important aspect of one's career. Although these steps seem to be clearly laid out, networking can still be a puzzling experience. In this chapter, we will attempt to demystify the art of networking.

A network is an important part of professional development. For some people, the word "networking" has a negative connotation. They may envision the old boys network—meeting others to gain favors, loyalties, or personal influence (Pancrazio & Gray, 1982). Networking may sound artificial and manipulative, but it is simply a means of meeting new colleagues and can be a collaborative, collegial process. Networking can be beneficial for the individual as well as the group. This is particularly true for white women and people of color, who can find support with others outside the dominant group of white males. Networks enhance a profession by encouraging competence, communication, and support. One description of a network says,

> It increases the probability of success for its individual members in numerous ways. It acts as an employment service....It gives members useful professional, social, and political contacts, thus expanding their bases of influence....A network also provides members [with] mutually beneficial psychological and economic support...[A network can also provide] genuineness, empathy, respect or warmth...(Pancrazio & Gray, 1982, pp. 16–17)

Networking is a valuable tool that can be used throughout a career. According to Helfgott (1995), networking skills can help you "increase your level of confidence; acquire mentors; tap into the 'hidden' job market; exchange valuable information, knowledge, resources, and contacts; give and receive advice and moral support; [and] form long-term personal and professional relationships" (p. 60). A new professional describes it this way:

[I think] networking is a process of meeting people, getting to know what they know, and letting them know what you know; exchanging information when it may be beneficial. Networking is important in job searches, research, and in learning about new things.

Here are some basic suggestions to help the new practitioner develop a professional network:

1. *Network at all levels in the organization.* Networking is not just an up or down issue. While there may be value to networking with people at higher levels, there are benefits to developing collegial relationships with peers and coun-

terparts in other areas of the college. For example, if you work in admissions, having contacts in the housing department can help you be more successful in your position. Two new professionals share their thoughts about networking:

> *I find this [networking] easiest when I attend professional functions with another person who already knows many people and is able to introduce me. I find this less intimidating and easier to do.* —Admissions recruiter

> *I think an aspect of networking that is often overlooked is peer networking. Most of us think of it as getting to know higher-ups who can help us out. The relationships with colleagues and classmates can be some of the most beneficial networks.* —Scholarship coordinator

    2. Make it a top priority to seek out colleagues. If there is an administrator on your campus whom you especially respect and would like to get to know, take the initiative. Ask him or her to join you for a cup of coffee or lunch. Set up a meeting. It is usually helpful to have a purpose for your meeting beyond building your network. Maybe the person is creating a new program you would like to learn more about, or maybe you are thinking about a doctorate one day and want to get his or her opinion. Most administrators have very busy schedules, and while they should welcome the opportunity to get to know new professionals, the meeting should be purposeful. Most administrators and faculty members (even the very busy ones) will be flattered by your interest and will take the time to meet with you. Examples of networking are shared by two new professionals:

> *I have realized that in order to network, you must get involved professionally whenever you are offered an opportunity, and you must make yourself known. Attendance is simply not enough—you must actively work at meeting more people, finding similarities between yourself and others, and keeping in touch.* —Admissions staff member

> *I network by learning a little about people I come in contact with, whether it is at a conference, professional activity, or social event.* —Financial aid counselor

    3. Be sincere and genuine in your relationships. If you are making artificial contacts with people you might be able to use, you are not networking. You can tell when someone is a fake and just "schmoozing"; others can tell, too. "People are quick to recognize and avoid those who are only interested in 'what's in it for me'" (Helfgott, 1995, p. 63). If you are sincerely interested in someone's background, values, thoughts, and opinions, this is a different type of relationship. Be yourself. Most of us are connected in some way in student affairs, or we share mutual friends. Impressions can be long-lasting, so make sure they are positive.

4. *Follow up.* Sincere follow-up efforts are the key to turning your network contacts into opportunities (Helfgott, 1995). Send a thank you note to anyone who has given you a referral or provided support. Be prepared to develop other contacts to keep the relationship going. A one-time encounter is not networking. With some people, it takes a number of interactions before they start to get to know you and consider you part of their network. Don't be discouraged if you meet someone a dozen times and they still do not remember who you are. This happens to all of us; don't take it personally. It just means that you may not develop a significant relationship with that person.

Another way to follow up with network contacts is through online networks. Just as students participate in social interaction through online networks such as Facebook and MySpace, advances in technology provide a new medium of networking for student affairs professionals. NASPA offers its members networking opportunities through the members-only section of its website (NASPA, 2008). Through the site, members can share tips, gather information for research, counsel prospective graduate students, and engage in discussions with thought leaders. Another medium of networking is iStudentAffairs.com (2008), which connects friends and colleagues in the profession. These online social networking sites enable student affairs professionals to share program ideas and discuss views on policy matters, and to stay connected and up-to-date with colleagues around the country and even the world. One thing to keep in mind about online networking: always be professional, especially with postings and pictures—you never know when a potential employer might see what you've posted. Online social networking is great for follow-up and maintaining networks, but don't let the cyber world be your first interaction with other professionals; face-to-face is always the best place to make a good first impression.

Intentionally put yourself in very normal situations. Attend a brown bag lunch training session, which is an excellent way to meet other members of the campus community. Exchange business cards with a colleague and plan to have coffee together one day. Planning collaborative programs is also a great way to build a network. You can showcase your strengths and learn from others as you build a useful network. Networks can also grow by the "spider web effect": someone you know introduces you to someone else, and so on. A simple inquiry to someone can help grow your network. Although networking can seem difficult and intimidating, it can be fun and very rewarding. The best way to begin is with the basics.

Networking is an important skill in developing relationships within your institution, with colleagues at other colleges and universities, and in professional organizations. A residence hall director observes, "I've found that networking is the key to finding a job, and the resources you develop can prove invaluable later in life."

Mentoring

"The evidence is overwhelming in the literature that significant sources of social support, as well as 'learning,' are professional networks and mentoring" (VanDerLinden, 2005, p. 740). VanDerLinden (2005) says that although finding funding for professional development may be challenging, especially at smaller institutions such as community colleges, taking advantage of human capital can be very cost-effective and often easily implemented.

Finding a Mentor

Various definitions exist for the word "mentor." The following definition was adapted from Moore and Salimbene (1981): A mentor is a more experienced professional who guides, advises, and assists in numerous ways the career of a less experienced, often younger, upwardly mobile protégé in the context of a close professionally centered relationship, usually lasting a year or more. Many research studies (Bell, 1996; Caruso, 1992; Kelly, 1984; Kogler Hill et al., 1989; Tull, 2003) show that a mentor can have a positive effect on a person's career. In fact, some studies show that those who experience supportive relationships such as mentoring have more opportunities for success, advancement, and achievement in their careers (Kogler Hill et al., 1989; Wunsch, 1994). The profession of student affairs is no different. Many of us learn early on as new professionals that mentoring is an important part of our career development (Roberts, 2007). The question is how to develop mentoring relationships.

Networking can be an important factor in meeting a mentor (Helfgott, 1995; Kelly, 1984). In one research study, student affairs professionals suggested that new professionals take a proactive approach in initiating relationships with a mentor (Kelly, 1984). Many new professionals believe that the senior student affairs administrator taps his or her magic wand and picks one new professional to be the protégé. Rarely does it happen this way; often, it is the new professional who initiates the relationship.

Kelly (1984) recommends that, to begin the mentoring process, you first assess your needs. What do you want from a mentor, what kind of help do you need, and who can provide it? Typically, you can expect a mentor to provide emotional support and direct assistance with professional and career development, and to act as a role model (Tentoni, 1995). It is also appropriate to want different things from different mentors. Once you define your needs, ask colleagues to identify potential mentors. Create and take advantage of opportunities to interact. Put yourself in situations that allow you to be highly visible, and always do a good job at whatever you are doing (Kelly, 1984). This is how a few new professionals met their mentors:

> *When I first started my new position at the college, I knew the vice president was involved in our professional association. I made an appointment to talk with him about ways I could get involved. Little did I know that he would ask me to assist him with a national task force. This was the start of our mentoring relationship.* —Residence hall director

> *I find someone whose management or professional work style I agree with, and I try to build a relationship with this person in order to learn more about how he or she became successful.* —Admissions recruiter

> *I found a mentor by attending a conference and hearing a speaker. I really understood and liked her ideas, and thought I could learn from her. So I approached her and introduced myself a couple times and then asked to work for her for free [as an intern]—anything to work for someone who could teach me something new.* —Admissions supervisor

Kelly (1984) provides an excellent list of characteristics to look for in a potential mentor: a similar or shared value system, time availability, professional competence in the area in which you desire expertise, active contributions to the field, a genuine interest in your professional development (a nurturing personality). The mentor should be someone you like and trust, and an open communicator. Fortunately, many people have these characteristics, so you will have plenty of opportunities to select different mentors. "Effective mentors are like friends in that their goal is to create a safe context for growth. They are also like family in that their focus is to offer an unconditional, faithful acceptance of the protégé" (Bell, 1996, p. 7).

It is important to realize that selecting a mentor takes time, effort, and commitment, so be patient if a relationship takes a while to develop. Ideally, you will have a number of mentors with different expectations to challenge and support you. As Batchelor says, "Mentoring relationships often develop into rich and helpful lifelong friendships" (1993, p. 381). You will receive many rewards, as these two professionals attest:

> *The benefit [of having a mentor] is having advice and concern from an individual who has already traveled down the career road you are traveling.* —Financial aid counselor

> *I see many benefits to mentor relationships—it is a great way to learn about new jobs; you can learn from others' experiences; you have a person with whom you can discuss important work issues with the assumption that they may have greater insight into the problem; and overall it produces a more positive work environment, because mentors enjoy their status (I am assuming) and they enjoy the chance to help develop a new professional.* —Admissions recruiter

Challenges with Mentors

Successful mentorships are beneficial not only for the persons involved but also for the organization (Rosenbach, 1993; Sandler, 1993). As with any relationship, it takes two people to make it work—both persons have to cultivate the relationship. Here are a few recommendations to make the most of the relationship with your mentor. They are adapted from Trimble's (1994) suggestions for protégés.

☞ *Clarify needs and expectations.* It is important to acknowledge that your mentor has certain strengths and will not be able to meet every one of your needs. By matching your needs with the mentor's strengths, you should both feel more successful in the relationship.

☞ *Be time-conscious.* Most mentors are busy people, and while they may value the relationship, it is up to you to respect their schedules. Make an appointment in advance and have a specific purpose when you meet. Do not become a burden to your mentor.

☞ *Create a dialogue.* In any relationship, it is important to know when to stop talking and when to be a good listener. Ask for clarification if necessary. Try to understand the values at work and the reasons for decisions. Ask your mentor to share experiences that might help you understand your own situation. Creating give-and-take communication challenges both of you and helps you gain new insights and make new discoveries.

☞ *Foster respect and appreciation for a valued professional.* As a protégé, you are seeking someone to support and care for you and your career. Show the same interest and care for your mentor. A caring attitude is important in the mentor relationship. Provide the mentor with positive feedback. This can occur in many forms, whether it is a personal note, nominating him or her for an award, or just saying thank you. One residence hall director showed appreciation for her mentor in this way:

> *One of my mentors had started a new job at a different campus. I sent her a card during her first week to let her know that even though we were not in the same location anymore, I still thought of her.*

Cross-Race and Cross-Gender Mentors

It is ideal to develop various mentor relationships that meet different needs. The most common relationships tend to be between members of the same gender and race (Kelly, 1984). At the same time, much has been written about the importance and challenges of mentoring for women and people of color (Batchelor, 1993; Evans, 2000; Frankel, 2004; Hawks & Muha, 1991; Kelly, 1984; Luebkemann & Clemens, 1994; Murrell, Crosby, & Ely, 1999; Smith & Davidson, 1992). Since many high-level administrators are white males, mentoring can help with the professional development of underrepresented groups. Some challenges can also arise when the mentor is culturally different from the protégé.

Much literature exists on the potential problems of cross-gender mentoring relationships. At times, men and women may assume stereotypical roles in relating to each other (Rosenbach, 1993). One new professional said, "I greatly respect my mentor, but at times he acts like my father as opposed to my professional advisor." In issues related to gender or sexual orientation, as significant relationships develop, increasing intimacy and sexual tensions can result. "A more frequent disadvantage for women being mentored by men are the innuendoes about the relationship from people who find it hard to believe that any relationship between a man and woman is not sexual" (Sandler, 1993, p. B3). Develop appropriate boundaries so the intentions of the relationship are clear. As with any potential sexual harassment situation, "the dangers in the traditional mentoring model are not necessarily gender-related, but rather are a function of the imbalance of power within the relationship" (Johnsrud, 1991, p. 9).

New professionals of color working in predominantly white institutions may want to connect with people from similar backgrounds or cultures. Ideally, it is helpful to find this support within student affairs, but this can be difficult—some institutions still do not have many professionals of color. Support groups or networks may be available in the larger institution. Many campuses have a Hispanic network or an African American faculty and staff council. These organizations can help you meet other staff members on campus who may share common experiences. If the group you are looking for does not exist, this may be your opportunity to create it. You might also need to look outside your institution to community or civic organizations, or even colleagues at other institutions. There may be some statewide networks or groups that you can join. Regardless of the avenue you choose, it is important to develop relationships.

When I first came to campus, I made contact with the Office of Multicultural Affairs. Through that office, I learned of the African American Network. This group of faculty, professional staff, and support staff met monthly at a local restaurant. We also had a listserv so we could communicate through e-mail. It was a way for me to feel connected with others and learn about special cultural opportunities.
—Multicultural advisor

The literature relating to cross-racial mentoring is limited. The benefits of same-race mentoring include the ability to discover similarities rather than emphasizing differences and the exhibition of cultural sensitivity (Luna & Cullen, 1995). Some research shows that cross-racial mentoring relationships have not been as successful because of organizational and personal barriers (Luna & Cullen, 1995; Rosenbach, 1993). Because socializing and informal activities are often involved in mentoring, there may be pressure to participate only with individuals from a similar background. Cultural differences may lead to misunderstandings, but Rosenbach (1993) says that "racism and sexism in the workplace will disappear as leaders learn to work in diverse teams and begin to view all members as friends and colleagues" (p. 148). Therefore, it is recommended that mentor relationships cross gender and ethnic lines to enhance learning opportunities and improve overall organizational climate (Luna & Cullen, 1995; Rosenbach, 1993; Sandler, 1993).

Cross-racial mentoring relationships can be extremely beneficial. For example, a new professional of color can learn much about the culture of a predominantly white institution through the mentorship of a white professional. This mentor can help usher the new person into his or her role and make the transition smoother. The cultural adjustment can be challenging for new professionals of color, just as it can be for students of color. Having a respectful mentoring relationship with a white professional already on staff can be a great asset. However, some authors believe that sharing an "affinity"—whether it is race, gender, or position level—can have a negative impact on mentoring relationships (Murrel et al., 1999). Stanley and Lincoln (2005, p. 46) assert that "it is especially important that faculty of color be mentored effectively; majority administrators and senior faculty are likely to be perplexed by the task, because they may have no previous experience with minority colleagues to draw upon." Open and honest conversations can avoid the pitfall of miscommunication and the eventual dissolution of the mentoring relationship.

> **New professionals of color working in predominantly white institutions may want to connect with people from similar backgrounds or cultures.**

I have had a wonderful experience being mentored by a former professor. The fact that we are not the same race, I think, has made the experience more enjoyable and rewarding. It is fun to chat about our respective careers, and I know that I can call on her to receive good advice about my next career move. Plus, she gets the whole diversity thing and the challenges that I face. Talking with her about those struggles is pretty easy, and I definitely feel supported. The cultural differences we have also benefit me, being that I am a new professional of color working on a predominantly white campus. I feel that our relationship provides me insight into her culture, thus helping me navigate my own institution. I think the insight I provide benefits her in a similar manner. Although I do have a mentor who shares my ethnicity, I wouldn't give the relationship up with my white mentor for anything! —Lacy; small, private institution*

When I started my first position out of graduate school, I soon realized that being the "only" person of color in my department would be quite an adjustment. I called my mentor to vent a little and ask for guidance. Even though she is not a person of color, she coached me on how to talk about my adjustment issues. We also discussed possible projects or appointments I could gain in multicultural affairs or other diverse areas. I found this a great relief! To see that she understood where I was coming from and that she even offered to coach me on how to talk about it with my supervisors was awesome. —Madison; mid-sized, public institution

Stages of Mentoring

Johnsrud (1991) describes a developmental process common to the relationship between mentors and protégés. In the early stages, the relationship tends to be more dependent. The protégé may rely more on guidance from the mentor and have a strong desire to please the mentor. Protégés may need more confirmation. As protégés move on to the independent stage, they are more likely to establish their purpose as distinct from the mentor. They may ask questions such as "Am I competent and independent if I am still being helped?" "Will I always be a protégé?" At the interdependent stage, "persons have the ability to fulfill for one another the yearning for connectedness and the yearning for identity" (Johnsrud, 1991, p. 15).

> **Networking and seeking out mentors are two ways of developing connections, but professional organizations provide different learning experiences than those obtained on one's own campus.**

Working through developmental stages with a mentor is a normal process. Just as our parents will always see us as children, mentors may always see us as their protégés. It is not uncommon to outgrow mentors or to disagree or have ethical conflicts with them. Mentors are not perfect; they are human beings and make mistakes. They may disappoint you. They may give you bad advice. At these times, reassess your needs and their strengths, and try to have realistic expectations for the relationship.

While the mentoring relationship may include challenges, it is usually mutually beneficial and caring. If you have numerous mentors, you will be able to hear many perspectives on complex issues. One residence hall coordinator says,

Every time I am contemplating a major issue related to my career, I touch base with all my mentors. Each one provides a different angle

and perspective that I may not have thought of. I value all of their thoughts.

Mentoring relationships take time and effort. The result can be long-lasting, meaningful relationships that allow you to grow and develop as a person and a professional. "With a supportive environment and the right attitude, mentoring can be a powerful force to empower followers to be leaders" (Rosenbach, 1993, p. 149).

Getting Involved in Professional Associations

A common question asked by new professionals is "Should I get involved in professional organizations?" The answer is a resounding "Yes!" and the reasons are many (Nuss, 1993). Networking and seeking out mentors are two ways of developing connections, but professional organizations provide different learning experiences than those obtained on one's own campus. They allow new professionals to observe leadership styles in a different venue. They are outlets for socializing and identifying colleagues who share the same values and interests or hold positions you may aspire to in the future (Gardner & Barnes, 2007). For many, being involved in professional organizations involves a "sense of obligation to help advance the status of the profession and fund programs that assist it" (Nuss, 1993, p. 368). Professional organizations can also be a way to develop new friendships, networks, and mentors. Two new professionals described their involvement this way:

I have become involved in professional organizations by meeting others within my field, developing friendships, and then volunteering to serve on committees with these other professionals. This has been a great way to learn more about my field and other organizations and to grow professionally. —Admissions supervisor

My involvement in NASPA as a new professional in student affairs has definitely eased my transition from graduate student to full-time professional. As a graduate student, the student affairs world seemed so big, full of seasoned professionals, opportunities, and lots to learn. The resources and networking opportunities that NASPA provides have made things a lot less scary! I am now able to navigate the student affairs world with ease, and I know that it is really a tight-knit community of individuals who are passionate about student development, just like I am. My involvement in NASPA has also introduced me to members

of the "NASPA family," new professionals like myself and experienced professionals across the nation whom I can turn to as a resource.
—Coordinator of student activities; large, research institution

Preparing on the Home Front

In this section, we suggest various ways of getting involved in professional organizations. We don't tell you which ones to join or which ones are the best. For a list of the best known student affairs associations, see Appendix A. Read through the list and check out the organizations' websites, then talk to your colleagues, faculty, mentors, and other network members about the history, organizational structure, culture, and purpose of the organizations in which you are interested. Again, discuss with your supervisor his or her expectations or support for certain organizations.

Before you rush out and join a number of professional organizations and get involved with them, make sure that things are in place in your job and on your campus. This means consulting with your supervisor about his or her thoughts on and support for professional involvement. Support might include financial support to attend conferences or meetings; time off work (rather than using vacation time); and the use of office supplies (postage, phone calls, etc.) to assist in your professional development.

For example, a hall director might be interested in getting involved in the American College Personnel Association (ACPA). The housing director might think ACPA involvement is inappropriate for the hall director and suggest that the person get involved in the Association of College and University Housing Officers-International (ACUHO-I) instead. It is common for new professionals to receive some funding for a regional conference, but you might have to pay to go to a national conference yourself. Sometimes this policy differs if you are presenting a program. Clarify all these things in advance so your supervisor supports your involvement and you are aware of the parameters. The bottom line is that you were hired to perform the duties and responsibilities of your job. When you are performing those to your fullest ability and meeting the expectations of your supervisor, you are ready to get involved in professional associations. This new professional gives another example of consulting your supervisor:

Many professional connections I made were a result of my supervisor pushing me to get involved in the National Association for Campus Activities (NACA), an organization that's very supportive and welcoming of new professionals. My experience with NACA paved the way to new volunteer opportunities in the National Association for Student Personnel Administrators (NASPA). —Joy, major research institution

Having a meaningful conversation with your supervisor about involvement in professional organizations is an essential step as you begin your journey into your professional development.

Making the Most of Professional Conferences

Attending conferences is one way of getting involved in professional organizations. It is an effective way to learn more about what the organization has to offer, its members, and future opportunities. For new professionals, it might be advantageous to start by attending a state or regional conference. These events are usually smaller, allowing for more personal connections and easier navigation. No matter what your position (whether you are a new professional or a mid-level manager), being a newcomer to a conference can be intimidating.

You may feel as though everyone already knows one another and you are the outsider. Be careful before you make hasty judgments about the friendliness or openness of an organization on the basis of your initial observations. Student affairs professionals are rarely exclusionary. What may seem like a clique is really a group of friends and colleagues who have known one another for years and are getting together for their annual event. One new professional described his first conference this way:

I had just arrived at the hotel, tired because the plane was late and it took longer than I thought to arrange for transportation. I immediately felt like a new freshman on campus trying to find the registration area. After asking for directions several times, I found the area, only to notice several small groups of people talking. I wondered if anyone would ever talk to me. Then someone shouted my name—it was a good friend from grad school. I realized that I, too, knew people here, and it would be okay. —Residence hall director

Here are some important tips for making the most of your first (or second or third) professional conference (Swanson, 1996):

☞ *Attend the session for newcomers or first-time attendees.* This session will provide helpful information regarding the conference and the organization. Often, you will have an opportunity to meet some of the leaders of the organization. You will also meet other newcomers, so you can start building your own network at the conference.

☞ *Attend as many keynote speeches and interest sessions as possible.* Review the conference program guide carefully and mark the sessions you would like to attend. Select two or three options for each time block, as some sessions may be full by the time you get there. If you are with other staff members from your institution, split up and get to as many different sessions as you can. Arrive early at sessions, because some fill up quickly. Go to the opening session and the reception. This will help you get a sense of the conference, the association, and the leadership.

☞ *Meet new people.* Introduce yourself to people around you. Contacts are one of the greatest benefits of the conference. You will be amazed at the small size of the world of student affairs. If you meet someone with whom you would like to stay connected, exchange business cards. Visit as many college- or university-sponsored receptions as you can. You will meet a lot of people and can learn how to get more involved. You could even end up with a full meal, which is important given the low budgets of new professionals. Attend task force or commission meetings.

☞ *Attend business meetings.* This is an opportunity to learn more about network, commission, or regional activities. Business meetings may sound formal and only for those who have invitations, but most business meetings are open to all members. Again, these activities are a great time to volunteer and get involved. Also, by attending your state or regional business meetings, you will learn more about professional development activities closer to home.

☞ *Enjoy the time away.* Treat yourself to some fun and excitement. Use your free time and meals to get to know others and share ideas. If special tours or events are offered, try to take advantage of them. You may have budget limitations, but often some low-cost activities are provided. If you are in a new area, try to visit some of the local highlights. Seeing new places is a perk of attending conferences—take advantage of the opportunity. Not all learning occurs in the interest sessions.

☞ *Reflect on the experience.* When the conference is over and you return to campus, it is natural to feel exhausted and exhilarated. Focus on what you learned. Share the information and handouts with your colleagues. Follow up on the contacts you made at the conference by sending a short note. Thank your supervisor for the opportunity to attend.

Levels of Organizational Involvement

Over the course of your career, your interest in certain organizations may vary. Some new professionals maintain constant membership in a more general association like NASPA or ACPA and, depending on their job responsibilities, also join a more specialized interest organization (Nuss, 1993). Once you determine which organization is most interesting to you, it is possible to become involved at various levels (Nuss, 1993).

☞ *Passive member or consumer.* At this stage, you are an official member who receives the mailings and documents to stay current in the profession. You may want to take advantage of some of the technological services provided by the organization; for example, joining a listserv. At some point you may start attending the state, regional, or national conferences, but you still feel more like an observer or spectator. You may want to consider joining one of the committees or special interest groups. For example, NASPA has a New Professionals Knowledge Community; other organizations may have a Black Caucus. Some professional organizations also have electronic learning communities, which allow you to develop connections and gain new knowledge online. These organizations are effective ways to connect with other professionals with similar interests.

Once you are ready to increase your involvement in the association, there are a number of steps you can take. The first is to volunteer at the conference. This is an excellent way to meet people and start learning about the workings of the operation. Find an area you are interested in and look for others who share that interest. Knowledge and interest groups form on almost every topic in student affairs for professionals to share information. When you attend the conferences, be sure to go to the business meetings and socials. These events enable you to meet the leaders of the organization and hear about current activities and events. At almost every business meeting, officers will ask for volunteers to help with future programs. This is your chance to get involved.

☞ *Contributor.* Another way to be involved in the professional association is as a contributor (Nuss, 1993). You might write a proposal to present a program, write an article for the newsletter, or submit research results for publication. If you are interested in presenting a program, talk with people who have done it. Ask to see a copy of their proposal so you get an idea of how to complete one. Ask a mentor or active member in the organization to review your proposal and give you feedback. Ask one of your mentors or a colleague at another institution to help you present. This is a great way to continue a networking relationship and become more involved at the same time.

☞ *Coordinator.* This means you are responsible for planning, coordinating, or directing the efforts of other volunteers (Nuss, 1993). Typically, this responsibility is on a state, regional, or national level; it may require a time commitment of six months to two years. You will likely be working with volunteers all over the country, which could involve interaction by phone, e-mail, or regular mail. You will need good skills in coordinating, budgeting, and supervising, as well as strong interpersonal and communication skills (Nuss, 1993). The expectations for volunteers in professional associations are no different than those for employees. Be thorough, dependable, responsible, and effective. Although you are working for a volunteer association, the accountability and expectations of high quality are no less than those for your paid position.

☞ *Officer.* The highest level of involvement is governance (Nuss, 1993). This means being elected or appointed to a regional or national board. At this level, individuals affect policy and long-term planning for the organization. The time commitment can be significant. While this is not typically the level at which new professionals participate, it is appropriate to set goals and plans to reach this stage at some point in your career.

Getting involved is not limited to professional organizations at the regional or national level, but can include committees and associations within your campus community. There are a variety of opportunities to network and develop as a professional at your current institution. Involvement in search committees, steering committees, staff associations, and campus meetings are just a few ways to engage and network in your local community. This is illustrated by one new professional:

When I first started working at the university, I felt like an outsider, I walked the campus and didn't know any faces. I would have lunch with office coworkers who had worked at the university for multiple years, and they would know a number of other colleagues from other departments eating lunch around us. Working on a campus that was so large, I thought I would never be able to connect with colleagues. Then I was asked to sit on a campuswide committee and a steering committee, and through both experiences I have networked with more colleagues around the campus. Now, when I eat lunch on campus, I run into colleagues I have networked with while serving on committees, and I feel like a connected member of the university. —Activities coordinator

So where do you start in this area of professional involvement? As always, it starts with self-assessment. What do you hope to accomplish? What talents do you have? How can you contribute? What are some areas you wish to develop? Once you have decided on your goals, let your mentors know of your plans. Have them introduce you to the leaders of the association. When you meet the leaders, instead of simply saying, "I want to get involved," tell them some of the specific things you would like to do. If it seems appropriate, follow up in writing and include a resume so the leader or decision maker can know how best to use your talents and skills. Following up with an e-mail is also useful. Finally, if it does not happen the first time, try again. Many leaders receive a lot of communication from their professional associations (and about their own work), so be patient and contact them again if you do not hear from them right away.

Professional associations play an important role in your career. The benefits include meeting valued colleagues and making friendships, learning about campus issues from new perspectives, and having access to cutting-edge research and vital federal, state, and local updates related to students and higher education. Research shows that involvement in professional associations influences the ability to network for future career opportunities and expands networks to foster future collaborations among colleagues (Gardner & Barnes, 2007). Once you become involved, you have an opportunity to establish a professional reputation beyond your campus, and you can influence the future of the profession. The expectation is that you should be professionally involved, and the rewards are great.

Conclusion

One out of three new professionals leaves student affairs every year (Woodard & Komives, 1990). This is a disadvantage to the professionals as well as to specific campuses. One factor that helps new professionals remain in the profession is to develop connections. These connections can occur through networking, mentor relationships, and involvement in professional associations. The suggestions and stories contributed by new professionals around the county illustrate the importance of developing and maintaining professional connections. Over time, with patience and perseverance, a new professional can network at any level, find a diverse group of mentors, and join professional organizations that will build a network of challenges and supports. These relationships will foster growth and development throughout your professional and personal life. All it takes is a little courage, a bit of hope, and some know-how. It is up to you to begin this process. While it takes time and effort, the personal and professional benefits make it worthwhile.

References

Batchelor, S. W. (1993). Mentoring and self-directed learning. In M. Barr (Ed.), *The handbook of student affairs administration* (pp. 378–389). San Francisco: Jossey-Bass.

Bell, C. R. (1996). *Managers as mentors: Building partners for learning.* San Francisco: Berrett-Koehler.

Caruso, R. E. (1992). *Mentoring and the business environment: Asset or liability?* Brookfield, VT: Dartmouth.

Evans, G. (2000). *Play like a man, win like a woman.* New York: Broadway Books.

Frankel, L. (2004). *Nice girls don't get the corner office.* New York: Warner Business Books.

Gardner, S. K., & Barnes, B. J. (2007). Graduate student involvement: Socialization for the professional role. *Journal of College Student Development, 48,* 369–387.

Hawks, B. K., & Muha, D. (1991). Facilitating the career development of minorities: Doing it differently this time. *Career Development Quarterly, 39,* 251–260.

Helfgott, D. (1995). Take 6 steps to networking success. *Planning Job Choices: 1995.* Bethlehem, PA: College Placement Council.

iStudentAffairs.com. (2008). More about iStudentAffairs.com. Retrieved August 4, 2008, from www.istudentaffairs.com/forum/topic/show?id=1348277%3ATopic%3A230.

Johnsrud, L. K. (1991). Mentoring between academic women: The capacity for interdependence. *Initiatives, 54*(3), 7–17.

Kelly, K. E. (1984). Initiating a relationship with a mentor in student affairs: A research study. *NASPA Journal, 21,* 49–54.

Kogler Hill, S. E., Bahniuk, M. H., Dobos, J., & Rouner, D. (1989). Mentoring and other communication support in the academic setting. *Group & Organization Studies, 14,* 355–368.

Luebkemann, H., & Clemens, J. (February, 1994). Mentors for women entering administration: A program that works. *National Association of Secondary School Principals Bulletin, 78,* 42–45.

Luna, G., & Cullen, D. L. (1995). *Empowering the faculty: Mentoring redirected and renewed* (ASHE-ERIC Higher Education Report, No. 3). Washington, DC: Association for the Study of Higher Education.

Moore, K. M., & Salimbene, A. M. (1981). The dynamics of the mentor-protégé relationship in developing women as academic leaders. *Journal for Educational Equity and Leadership, 2*(1), 51–64.

Murrell, A., Crosby, F. & Ely, R. (1999). *Mentoring dilemmas: Developmental relationships within multicultural organizations.* Mahwah, NJ: Lawrence Erlbaum Associates.

NASPA. (2008). NASPA members only. Retrieved October 1, 2008, from http://naspa.myu360.com/home.

Nuss, E. M. (1993). The role of professional associations. In M. Barr (Ed.), *The handbook of student affairs administration* (pp. 364–377). San Francisco: Jossey-Bass.

Pancrazio, S. B., & Gray, R. G. (1982). Networking for professional women: A collegial model. *Journal of NAWDAC, 45,* 16–19.

Roberts, D. M. (2007). Preferred methods of professional development in student affairs. *NASPA Journal, 44*(3), 561–577.

Rosenbach, W. E. (1993). Mentoring: Empowering followers to be leaders. In W. E. Rosenbach & R. L. Taylor (Eds.), *Contemporary issues in leadership* (pp. 141–151). Boulder, CO: Westview.

Sandler, B. R. (March 10, 1993). Women as mentors: Myths and commandments. *Chronicle of Higher Education,* p. B3.

Smith, E. P., & Davidson, W. S., (1992). Mentoring and the development of African American graduate students. *Journal of College Student Development, 33,* 531–539.

Stanley, C., & Lincoln, Y. (2005, March/April). Cross-race faculty mentoring. *Change Magazine,* 44–50.

Swanson, R. M. (1996). *How to do a conference* [brochure]. Washington, DC: American Association of Collegiate Registrars and Admissions Officers.

Tentoni, S. C. (1995). The mentoring of counseling students: A concept in search of a paradigm. *Counselor Education and Supervision, 35*, 32–42.

Trimble, S. (February, 1994). A protégé's guide to mentoring. *National Association of Secondary School Principals Bulletin, 78*, 46–48.

Tull, A. (2003, July 22). Mentoring of new professionals in student affairs: Part one – introduction. *NetResults*. Retrieved September 29, 2008, http://www.naspa.org/membership/mem/pubs/nr/default.cfm?id=1103.

VanDerLinden, K. (2005). Learning to play the game: Professional development and mentoring. *Community College Journal of Research and Practice, 29*, 729–743.

Woodward, D. B., & Komives, S. R. (1990). Ensuring staff competence. In M. Barr and M. L. Upcraft (Eds.), *New futures for student affairs* (pp. 217–238). San Francisco: Jossey-Bass.

Wunsch, M. A. (1994). Giving structure to experience: Mentoring strategies for women faculty. *Initiatives, 56*(1), 1–10.

RECONCILING LIFE AND WORK FOR THE NEW STUDENT AFFAIRS PROFESSIONAL

CHAPTER SEVEN

Joy Blanchard

"Be aware of wonder. Live a balanced life—learn some and think some and draw and paint and sing and dance and play and work every day some."
—Robert Fulghum, *All I Really Need to Know I Learned in Kindergarten*

Though a career in student affairs is not as simple as navigating the challenges of kindergarten, Fulghum does offer cogent advice: Do what you enjoy and revel in the small pleasures of life. Student affairs professionals choose the work they do for altruistic reasons (Rhoades et al., 2008; Tull & Medrano, 2008). However, the work is not all "fun and games." In addition to long hours, modest pay, and the daily stress of life as an employee, student affairs professionals must challenge themselves to find balance among the many constituencies they serve: students; supervisors and university administrators; spouses/partners and children. No one's life operates in a vacuum, and the more one can achieve happiness and balance, the less likely one is to experience burnout.

For the new student affairs professional, finding balance can be difficult, but it is essential. Balance is more complicated than applying simple time management tips (Roberts, 2008). It requires us to step back and truly examine our lives. The self-help literature asserts that balance is within our reach if we become more efficient, make choices, and establish boundaries. However, the issue of work–life balance involves not only the individual but also the broader societal climate of the American workplace. Just as consumers want products that are more efficient and make their lives easier, organizations have begun to expect the same of their employees (Reich, 2002).

Student affairs professionals too frequently subscribe to the norm that success is measured, in large part, by productivity at work. Still, their personal life is also important to them. New professionals want to succeed at both, but how can they do it all?

> Unfortunately, the external markers of success—which reflect the satisfaction of others regarding our performance—may not translate into feelings of personal satisfaction. Searching for more and better ways to work efficiently is, I think, a strategy built on the implicit assumption that accomplishing more will lead to more recognition from others and, therefore, more personal satisfaction....This logic is flawed....There are, after all, human limits to how much one can accomplish—incremental gains in efficiency and its associated rewards (internal as well as external ones) become harder to achieve as one becomes more efficient and productive. (Jackson, 1996, 354)

In an effort to find more time for personal commitments, some professionals may attempt to become hyperefficient. Anyone who works with college students knows that the job is not one in which you report at 8:00 a.m., take an hour for lunch, and leave at 5:00 p.m. In fact, the job often is most demanding, most interesting, and least flexible during those hours when other professionals have typically gone home for the evening. In a time-intensive field like student affairs, with its ambiguous boundaries, practitioners often find that work crowds out the time that can be spent at home. However, to find balance, personal time is key, as this professional attests:

> *There is life outside of housing! It is critical that you put effort into making friends outside of your job. You will end up talking about work when you're not at work if you only have support inside the department. I can't emphasize this enough...get outside your comfort zone, make the extra effort...and don't forget—the world is bigger than hous-*

ing. You will enjoy your life and position infinitely more if you do this!
—Marite; medium-sized, public, land-grant institution

Though the goal of balance often is described dualistically (work versus life, or career versus family), the two often are interdependent. The right job improves self-esteem, satisfaction with personal growth, and health (Reich, 2002). But the psychological spillover of work thoughts and worries can cause problems when you are engaged in outside activities. When psychological involvement in work detracts from involvement outside of work, the professional will probably be less satisfied with his or her personal life (Friedman & Greenhaus, 2000).

> **For the new student affairs professional, finding balance can be difficult, but it is essential.**

Advice abounds on how to achieve work–life balance. The problem is a common one among professionals, and adjusting to a new job—as well, perhaps, as a new location and peer group—can complicate the issue for student affairs practitioners. The need for balance is even more compelling because the profession is built on an ethic of service, so major responsibilities involve responding to students at unpredictable times.

As soon as you step foot off campus, leave all your work behind. For two years I did work at home or worked late. That led to burnout really quickly. I see a lot of my peers let work rule their life because they are new in town and without a significant other or family. However, I strongly encourage them to find a social network, to volunteer, find something to do outside work. If you are connected 24/7, you won't last long in this profession. I used to have anxiety-ridden dreams about work; then I realized that I needed a break. I just said to myself, "Once I leave, it's done for the day." Obviously, there are situations that require attention after hours; but for the most part, once you leave work, turn your attention to something else. —Grace; assistant director; large, public university

When work consumes too much attention, it leaves little energy for developing satisfying personal relationships, which then leaves a void that encourages the investment of still more energy in work (Friedman & Greenhaus, 2000). Managing family issues is an important factor in predicting job satisfaction (Appel & Kim-Appel, 2008; Innstrand et al., 2008). Studying workaholics, Bonebright, Clay, and Ankenmann (2000) found that even for those who were highly driven at work and enjoyed it greatly, high work involvement did not lead to increased life satisfaction or sense of purpose. They hypothesized that lack of life balance was a factor.

Ironically, student affairs administrators spend much of their professional lives encouraging students to discover balance in their lives. However, that same advice often is not so easy to follow, as this professional noted:

> *I have noticed that we always teach students to live balanced lives, yet we set the worst examples. I can remember several days when I would be in the office for 12 hours, then attend a program, lead a meeting, and spend some time with students in the evening. If I was lucky, I would be in bed by 1:00 in the morning and get six hours of sleep before it was time to get up and do it all over again.* —Residence life professional

Working toward some sort of work–life balance is a process of integration, not one of defining separate areas. A new professional's enthusiasm, combined with the fast pace of the job, can further confound the boundaries of home and work.

> *Sometimes work and home really blur. When I am at work, I am on the telephone home about something with my son; and when I am at home, I am on the phone dealing with something from work.* —Student affairs professional

Some professionals prefer to separate the professional from the personal. However, given the growing number of hours work demands, and the pervasive technology that links us to the office—such as the Internet, e-mail, cell phones, and text messages—this solution may become increasingly difficult to implement. Another blurry area is relationships. New professionals often are close in age to the students they supervise and advise. They must draw a work–life boundary to avoid confusion in the advisor–advisee relationship, given the often close relationships student affairs professionals form with their students (Dial, 2005).

> *As a new professional in higher education, finding balance can be one of the most challenging goals. In addition to the unorthodox hours required of most entry-level positions, often new professionals are nearly the same age as the students they supervise, making it easy for relationship lines to blur. One strategy I employed to create a separation between work and home was to communicate to my students (and supervisors) that when I was at home, I was not at work. It was a challenge not to answer that 2 a.m. text message from a student or the 6 a.m.*

e-mail from a supervisor, but it did help me keep my personal boundaries intact. —Katrina; programming advisor; large, public university

From research and their own sensibilities, new professionals know that they need to take the time to step back from their full work schedules, not only to avoid stress and burnout but to become better professionals. Making more time for one's personal relationships should not be viewed as a negative; professional and personal life can work in tandem to increase satisfaction and decrease burnout. "The downside of these trade-offs can be mitigated, at least in part, by seeing them as opportunities to make conscious choices among life priorities; to become clearer about our values" (Friedman & Greenhaus, 2000, p. 38). However, placing aspects of your life in a hierarchy of importance is difficult.

It is hard for me to think about my life as "life" and work as "work." Most of the time, the two seem to blend together. I'm not sure this is always a good thing, but it is something I am aware of. —Residence life professional

Another problem many new professionals face is the transition from student to student affairs practitioner. Student affairs graduate programs tend to emphasize the importance of student development in preparing future practitioners. However, professional life in student affairs can be marked by a bureaucracy and formality more commonly associated with the business world. New professionals in student affairs often feel tension between the desire to help students—usually the primary reason they selected this career path—and the need to fulfill their administrative duties. Many attempt to do both perfectly, which can lead to ever-longer hours.

> **Making more time for one's personal relationships should not be viewed as a negative; professional and personal life can work in tandem to increase satisfaction and decrease burnout.**

Entry-level positions usually are accompanied by high levels of student contact, which can make managing professional responsibilities difficult. Entry-level admissions counselors travel the most; resident directors supervise the highest number of staff members; and entry-level student activities professionals advise the most groups. Not only do these positions include planned time that new professionals will devote to students, but the high contact also makes them the likely first responder for the inevitable but unpredictable crises that require additional time to resolve. The typical responsibilities in an entry-level position are time-consuming; it is especially important at this juncture to find appropriate strategies and networks to work toward a healthy balance.

> *As a new professional in student affairs, it was difficult to create time for personal activities because of the expectations to work late and be on campus for evening programs. It was also very difficult to find healthy social outlets away from work. Some coworkers chose to spend a lot of time outside of work together, but I did not find that to be a healthy option, as the conversation always turned toward frustrations about work. I also needed separation between work and personal time, and spending time with coworkers at night and on the weekends tended to blur the lines of professionalism. Thus, I was left with the very difficult task of meeting new people in a new city. I guess this would be a typical problem for new professionals in any field; however, it was a large hurdle for me.* —Daniel; judicial affairs officer; mid-sized, public university

Lessons to Take Away

Balance occurs when work and life augment each other. When resources derived from one role are applied to other roles in fruitful ways, the positive emotions initially experienced in one part of life can spill over to enrich other domains as well (Friedman & Greenhaus, 2000). Pursuing balance is a constant and dynamic effort that involves many facets. Based on the current literature and advice from working professionals, the next section offers practical recommendations for achieving balance. Though each journey is different, some areas are common to all. New professionals must make important choices as they carve out a career path and fit that into the dreams they have for a satisfying personal life. Everyone should make time for themselves and learn how to draw appropriate work–life boundaries.

In today's workplace, one can be more successful by learning how to effectively navigate institutional cultures and mores while also challenging any status quos that hinder a bias-free, inclusive work environment. Networking is important for all new professionals, and employers and employees should develop an open dialogue to establish expectations for both sides. And, finally, everyone must remember that life is a journey. Decide where you are in your career and establish attainable goals. Learn from mentors and see your own mistakes as an opportunity to grow and hone your skills and goals. Outside of work, happiness can be attained by reveling in one's hobbies, interests, family, and friends. An enriched personal life can serve one in good stead to enjoy the rigors and rewards of a career in student affairs.

Making Choices

When you are barraged with opportunities, making choices at work is difficult. Job descriptions and supervisors can help guide and prioritize. Making decisions about career and personal life is impossible without personal reflection. For some, the choices may include whether to work full time or part time because of familial obligations or raising children. For others, the decision may be whether to switch jobs and location in the interest of career mobility (Rhoades et al., 2008). For yet others, both partners in a relationship may be involved in higher education, and they may have to modify their career plans so that both can find employment in the same area or at the same university. However, some institutions today have special programs to accommodate dual-career couples (Wolf-Wendel, Twombly, & Rice, 2003).

Learning how to tap into various support systems can be very helpful, even just for knowing what options are available. Because people lead such different lives, there is no universal formula, despite what some self-help gurus might profess. Each new professional must find an approach that works. And any formula for balance will change in response to modifications at work or in life. Updating is an essential component of reflecting and planning.

Taking Time for Yourself

Time spent relaxing is a significant contributor to life balance. Without personal time, one is trading work busy-ness for personal busy-ness. Carving out the time can be difficult. New professionals can work with their supervisors and colleagues to anticipate some of the high-demand times inherent in the job and create buffers for personal renewal, such as allowing for flexible work hours when late-night work or overtime is anticipated.

Paying attention to one's physical health, as well as one's spiritual and emotional health, is important to reduce burnout and maintain productivity. Casey and Grzywacz (2008) found that employers who allow flexibility in the workplace or working from home increased their employees' job performance and persistence. Indiana Wesleyan University offers a concierge service to help employees accomplish daily tasks, such as picking up dry cleaning (June, 2008).

Other universities, such as Southern Methodist University, provide incentives like additional personal leave days, campus dining vouchers, and free parking for staff and faculty who participate in campus wellness programs (Wellpower SMU, 2008).

Establishing and Maintaining Boundaries

With the pervasiveness of e-mail, cell phones, and text messages, the physical boundaries of old—when professionals worked at an office and then went home to pursue personal interests—barely exist anymore. Boundaries need not be spatial; they can be based on issues or priorities. New professionals can educate their staff and students, and perhaps even their supervisor, about priorities to prevent inappropriate interruptions at home (Roberts, 2008). For example, as it would be inappropriate for a student to interrupt a presentation to the board of trustees for assistance with a noise violation, new professionals can discuss with co-workers and students their personal priorities so that after-hours interruptions can be kept to a minimum.

Understanding Organizational Culture

Tull and Medrano (2008) found that employee-institution fit increased when the values of the institution aligned with the values and attitudes of the employee; this sort of fit resulted in higher employee job satisfaction. Organizations, including universities, transmit their values and culture via policies, practices, rituals, and traditions (Martin, 2002; Scott, 2001). Early in your career, you should identify the values (e.g., philosophical, theological, or educational) most important to you and discuss them with your supervisor—or even look for a job at an institution whose mission most mirrors your value system. One new professional realized the consequences of working in a department with values that conflicted with hers when she was told that increasing revenue was the number one goal of her unit:

> *...this led to several instances of "keeping the customer happy" at the expense of student development and a lot of decisions that I had trouble accepting and supporting; for example, our director cut the number of resident assistants in a freshman hall so that instead of one RA for every 35–40 residents, there is now one for every 60–70.* —Anna, coordinator of new student orientation, former residence hall director, regional university

Learning the culture of an organization is not an overnight process. The new professional is well advised to observe and dissect information before making assumptions about the organizational culture and the norms that guide the institutional philosophy and policy. The idea is not to attempt to change organizational culture all alone or all at once, but to think about organizational dissonance and dysfunction in terms of culture, and to act accordingly. Job applicants should ask employers about the organization's values regarding personal issues. For example, does the institution offer child care? What is the workplace like for lesbian, gay, bisexual, and transgender, and queer (LGBTQ) employees? Are they generally "out"? Are same-sex partners welcome at department socials (Albin & Dungy, 2005)? Is the workplace safe and inclusive for LGBTQ employees? Does the institution offer domestic partner benefits? Does it support people with disabilities? What is the university's family leave policy? Does it offer paternity leave? Are multiple faiths accepted on the campus? Is there a strong multicultural community?

Working with Your Employer

Balancing the personal and the professional begins with exploring organization-level assumptions and values that involve cultures and climates, behaviors and habits, policies and practices. Some assumptions that run counter to work–life balance are stereotyped gender roles, performance evaluations that stress face time rather than outcomes, and a mindset that the pursuit of a satisfying personal life means a compromised career. Employers should provide opportunities based on an employee's abilities and interests rather than making assumptions about values on the basis of stereotypes (Friedman & Greenhaus, 2000), be they racial, gender, socioeconomic, or ethnic. Student affairs professionals generally are attuned to issues of equality and discrimination, and are committed to their elimination; they are better positioned than professionals in many other fields to address bias.

Changing a destructive organizational culture is easier said than done, particularly for new professionals who have limited power in the organization. As workplace mores and employees' expectations of work–life balance change, it is essential to open the lines of communication and discuss job expectations. New professionals can help their supervisors by initiating such discussions (Kernel, Kerenge, & Jauneaud, 2008). Employees are more likely to make good decisions when employers are clear about business priorities; likewise, employees need to clearly inform the employer of their own personal and career priorities (Roberts, 2008). (See chapters 2 and 4 for more discussion of employee–employer expectations.)

Networking

New professionals can benefit from finding people in similar professional or personal situations and creating social and career support through networking. Discussing strategies with mentors and colleagues can help clarify values and generate feedback for growth. Supervisors can help employees find work–life balance by encouraging them to network and build communities. Other methods of networking include memberships in professional associations, campus-community associations, and special interest communities within and outside the field of student affairs. (See chapter 6 for more discussion of networking.)

Enjoying the Journey

New professionals generally aspire to move into positions with greater autonomy and broader reach; however, the path to mid-level and upper administration can be long and circuitous. New professionals should relish the rich experiences inherent in entry-level positions and view each position as a means to gain greater professional and personal wisdom. They should challenge the conventional wisdom that professionals must first establish their careers and then work on their personal lives. One new professional spoke of the need for a change in perspective:

> *It took me a while before I decided that my mental and physical health were worth more to me than being the super student affairs professional. I learned to say no and to set limits with my time. New professionals want to be superhuman, but we need to know that it is okay to be human every once in a while.* —Assistant registrar

When the focus is on the journey, not the destination, spontaneity and unforeseen opportunities can provide priceless teachable moments. Many practitioners try different specialty areas (e.g., housing, judicial affairs, orientation) during their career. This should not be viewed as failure or indecision but as a way to explore the student affairs profession and garner invaluable skills that can be transferred throughout the university community. Many administrators identify themselves as generalists rather than specialists. The skills needed in student affairs administration are quite varied; new professionals should savor the freedom early in their career to explore many options. Just as student affairs practitioners help students find meaning in their college experiences, new professionals should capitalize on these early years to find meaning and satisfaction in their own careers.

Conclusion

The search for balance often involves compromise, frustration, and disappointment. This may be distressing for student affairs professionals, because they are generally motivated not by extrinsic rewards but by a true enthusiasm for what they do, and their work is typically deeply intertwined with their personal values. They are rarely "on the clock" in a way that allows them to easily separate work and home. But it is possible to be passionate about work and still maintain a balance. The trick is to feed the passion in such a way that it fuels other aspects of one's life. Trying to achieve harmony between the professional and the personal is an inherently messy task. Balance is a dynamic goal that requires constant reflection and adjustment.

> **New professionals should relish the rich experiences inherent in entry-level positions and view each position as a means to gain greater professional and personal wisdom.**

Focusing solely on work will only make it harder to achieve balance now or in the future. New professionals would do well to take time for themselves and invest in their personal life in ways that will create positive overflows into their work, and vice versa. Although the quest for balance is a deeply personal one, it should not be undertaken in isolation. It is up to everyone to address work–life balance publicly and privately to create positive changes for people, families, organizations, and society.

References

Albin, J. A. & Dungy, G. J. (2005). Professional associates: Journeys of colleagues in student affairs. In R. L. Sanlo (Ed.), *Gender identity and sexual orientation: Research, policy, and personal perspectives.* New Directions for Student Services, no. 111. San Francisco: Jossey-Bass.

Appel, J., & Kim-Appel, D. (2008, July). Family systems at work: The relationship between family coping and employee burnout. *Family Journal,* *16*(3), 231–239.

Bonebright, C. A., Clay, D. L., & Ankenmann, R. D. (2000) The relationship of workaholism with work–life conflict, life satisfaction, and purpose in life. *Journal of Counseling Psychology, 47*(4), 469–477.

Casey, P., & Grzywacz, J. (2008, March). Employee health and well-being: The role of flexibility and work-family balance. *Psychologist-Manager Journal, 11*(1), 31–47.

Dial, D. (2005). GAs within offices of student judicial affairs: A best practices discussion. *Student Affairs Law and Policy Weekly, 3, 13.*

Friedman, S. D., & Greenhaus, J. H. (2000). *Work and family: Allies or enemies? What happens when business professionals confront life choices.* New York: Oxford University Press.

Innstrand, S., Langballe, E., Espnes, G., Falkum, E., & Aasland, O. (2008, January). Positive and negative work-family interaction and burnout: A longitudinal study of reciprocal relations. *Work and Stress, 22*(1), 1–15.

Jackson, S. E. (1996). Dealing with the overenriched life. In P. J. Frost & M. S. Taylor (Eds.), *Rhythms of academic life: Personal accounts of careers in academia* (pp. 351–355). San Francisco: Jossey-Bass.

June, A. (2008, July 18). Indiana Wesleyan helps employees stay fit and well fed. *Chronicle of Higher Education, 54*(45), B6+.

Kernel, V., Kerenge, K., & Jauneaud, S. (2008, January). What are your tips for an effective work–life balance? *Communication World, 25*(1), 13–13.

Martin, J. (2002). *Organizational culture: Mapping the terrain.* Thousand Oaks, CA: Sage Publications.

Reich, R. B. (2002). *The future of success.* New York: Vintage Books.

Rhoades, G., Kiyama, J. M., McCormick, R. & Quiroz, M. (2008). Local cosmopolitans and cosmopolitan locals: New models of professionals in the academy. *Review of Higher Education, 31,* 209–235.

Roberts, E. (2008, September). Time and work–life balance: The roles of 'temporal customization' and 'life temporality.' *Gender, Work and Organization, 15*(5), 430–453.

Scott, W. R. (2001). *Institutions and Organizations* (2nd edition). Thousand Oaks, CA: Sage Publications.

Tull, A., & Medrano, C. I. (2008). Character values congruence and person-organization fit in student affairs: Compatability between administrators and the institutions that employ them. *Journal of College and Character, IX*(3), available at www.collegevalues.org.

Wellpower SMU. (2008). Wellpower. Retrieved September 27, 2008, from http://smu.edu/hr/healthy/Wellpower.asp#Overview.

Wolf-Wendel, L., Twombly, S. B., & Rice, S. (2003). *The two-body problem: Dual-career-couple hiring policies in higher education.* Baltimore: The Johns Hopkins University Press.

PATHWAYS TO SUCCESS
IN STUDENT AFFAIRS

CHAPTER EIGHT

Florence A. Hamrick and Brian O. Hemphill

Congratulations! The strains of "Pomp and Circumstance" and the alma mater are fading. Final assistantship and practicum duties, as well as papers and exams, are in the past. Fond hugs, goodbyes, and updated contact information have been exchanged with classmates at spring picnics. Your job search has yielded, or will soon yield, a full-time professional position in student affairs. And perhaps you already have some years of full-time student affairs experience behind you. Your diploma is in hand but, if you are lucky, learning will not cease.

In many ways, a first full-time position in student affairs is an embarkation, the beginning of one's professional career. Early career experiences provide the basis for starting or continuing the processes of determining what career advancement will mean, working toward these goals, and evaluating previous choices and goals in light of new information and emerging trends. Career advancement considerations include mulling over options for future professional

147

positions, thinking about various types of institutional work settings, and deciding whether (or when) to pursue graduate work—most often a doctoral degree. While these are separate decisions, they also represent learning processes described by John Dewey almost 100 years ago (Dewey, 1926). They entail collecting information and, more important, continuing to reflect on individual experiences. The process of reflection brings personal meaning to the experiences and the new information, and helps with identifying options. This chapter provides information to help new professionals envision their own student affairs professional careers. We discuss career path development, professional maturation, and strategic considerations in career advancement.

Determining Career Paths

Some career fields and large organizations specify career paths or ladders for new staff members to maximize their readiness for senior management positions. Higher education career paths are much less well-defined, as various paths can lead to the top of the opportunity pyramid (Moore, 1984; Task Force, 1990; Twombly, 1990). While the idea of a career path is a viable guiding notion for new professionals because of the planning and focus it encourages, your career path will most likely be an individual creation influenced by mentors, supervisors, colleagues, and others. Indeed, although supervisors or mentors can assist by incorporating professional development into expectations for job performance (e.g., Winston & Creamer, 1997), new professionals are also well-advised to take direct, proactive responsibility for identifying and pursuing opportunities relevant to advancing their career and life goals. Looking ahead, looking around, and looking over your shoulder may provide the best analytic perspective from which to identify personally-viable paths, including previously unseen spurs or switchbacks.

Organizational and financial constraints on institutions of higher education and student affairs units—such as the elusive "right-sizing"—challenge the wisdom of relying on a prefabricated career path to direct your choices, since institutional needs and goals can change at any time. But professionals can make the best possible career decisions by using the best available information about themselves and about social, economic, and educational developments. The following sections on personal, environmental, and institutional factors offer perspectives for new professionals who are building careers in student affairs and higher education.

Personal Factors

Understanding your motivations for engaging in a particular type of work will help you define the work settings that offer the rewards you seek. Derr (1986) proposed a typology of five career orientations—such as "getting ahead" and "getting balanced" (pp. x–xi)—to help individuals and organizations match motivations with desired rewards. Persons who are most concerned with getting ahead are predominantly motivated and rewarded by promotions and money; those concerned with balance are more motivated and rewarded by flexible work environments and measures of deference to family responsibilities and personal pursuits. Motivations and preferred rewards may also shift in different life stages. For example, a college president who was formerly a student affairs administrator put a premium on balance during his early career: "[Working as a senior administrator] would have distracted so much from family life when our youngsters were in their formative years. We would have paid a price for absenteeism that I don't think I would have recovered from as a dad and as a husband." The process of lifelong development begins in childhood; as it moves forward, our evolving commitments and priorities are reflected in our work and career choices. Career goals and work preferences have recently been linked to generational characteristics; for example, millennials are said to prefer clear supervisory expectations and working in cooperative, technologically savvy groups (DeBard, 2004), while generation X members tend to consider themselves free agents (Coomes & DeBard, 2004) who are building "portable" careers (DeBard, 2004, p. 40).

> Looking ahead, looking around, and looking over your shoulder may provide the best analytic perspective from which to identify personally-viable paths, including previously unseen spurs or switchbacks.

Dual-career relationships, divorce or termination of intimate relationships, successful cultivation of support networks, birth and growth of children, concerns of blended families, and needs of aging parents are familiar examples of personal considerations that affect career-related choices, especially (but not only) with regard to geographic mobility. Despite the widespread perception that women professionals are less mobile because of personal and family considerations, the gender gaps in geographic mobility and rates of position change are not significant (Sagaria & Johnsrud, 1988). Nobbe and Manning (1997) concluded that student affairs administrators who were mothers positioned motherhood as a counterbalance to work-related stress.

Many environmental factors have implications for student affairs professionals who seek a job change and/or advancement to a senior administrative position. For example, years of stable or declining state and federal support for higher education have resulted in a less seasonal and more tentative student affairs job market, in which anticipated and funding-contingent positions are advertised along with actual vacancies (Janasiewicz & Wright, 1993). Additionally, student affairs as a career field offers a kind of opportunity pyramid, with many entry-level positions and comparatively few senior-level positions. Consequently, only a small proportion of today's new professionals will attain senior administrative positions. Additionally, Evans (1988) explained that supervisory configurations in higher education have relatively few hierarchical levels, resulting in career ladders with fewer vertical rungs and wider career "steps" and suggesting that dramatic vertical movement occurs less frequently than horizontal movement. Institutionally, this organizational configuration is particularly characteristic of small colleges and universities (Heida, 2006; Hirt, Amelink, & Schneiter, 2004). Finally, because senior administrators also move horizontally among deanships or vice presidencies across multiple campuses, not all senior administrative positions are filled from the ranks of mid-level student affairs administrators, which can become highly stable on campuses (Heida, 2006). Increasingly, mid-level management positions are regarded as more than simply preparation for senior administration, prompting a reexamination of traditional assumptions of career success and achievement (Belch & Strange, 1995; Fey & Carpenter, 1996; Gordon, Strode, & Mann, 1993). At least one additional factor plays a role in the high level of competition for senior student affairs positions: Successful candidates for these positions also come from the ranks of faculty members and others who do not always have direct experience or educational preparation in student affairs administration or higher education (Task Force, 1990).

Institutional factors also influence career path development, since individuals work on specific campuses as well as within the broader student affairs profession. Specific decisions regarding positions and responsibilities, restructuring, and professional development are made at institutional, division, or program levels. Institutions or divisions may offer formalized internship and cross-training opportunities (e.g., Robinson & Delbridge-Parker, 1991) to facilitate career development, but attendance costs or lack of information may complicate new professionals' access to these opportunities (Young, 1994). Division and program support for professional advancement of staff vary widely; candidates should not hesitate to inquire about levels and types of professional development support for staff members.

New professionals may begin a first job only to be surprised by an unfore-seen mismatch between themselves and their positions or an uneasy person-en-vironment fit (e.g., Shriberg & Wester, 1994). Not all first professional positions "click," and entry-level turnover is frequently high (e.g., Bass, 2006; Oblander, 2006). One new professional remarked: "There's been a high turnover lately among the six program coordinator positions, so even in my second year I am the second most senior program coordinator." Regular turnover at entry-level positions also plays a facilitative role, as new professionals change jobs one or two times in search of appropriate challenges and environmental supports. Al-though prolonged job-hopping can raise suspicion, new professionals need not worry that a first negative job experience will be fatal to their careers. The first author of this chapter spent a long and unsettling year in her first professional position before she found a position that was a much closer match for her skills and work style.

Some student affairs positions may not be located within a division or department of student affairs; these jobs can offer different perspectives and potentially attractive work settings. According to a professional currently serv-ing as admissions and financial aid officer in an MBA program office,

The School of Business here is very much like a small college, but with the additional benefits of being in a university community. Personally, my primary efforts are spent on recruitment and admissions, but I sit in meetings to discuss the curriculum, students' preparation and prog-ress through the program, placement issues, and evaluation of our pro-gram's fit with employers' needs. I know what's going on throughout the school. In other admissions positions, I would bring in students and then never see them again, but here I work with them throughout their two years here and afterwards. I have a much greater understanding of the student experience from beginning to end.

For personal reasons (e.g., priorities, aspirations) and environmental and institutional reasons (e.g., job market dynamics, professional development re-sources), a career path is more likely to result from a series of best judgments rather than from unquestioning adherence to a pre-specified route. Some of the environmental and institutional factors mentioned, however, are also cited as sources of frustration and reasons for leaving the student affairs field.

An early study placed the attrition rate from student affairs jobs at 39% among master's and doctoral recipients, 1 to 10 years after degree completion (Burns, 1982). A subsequent study of a 10-year span of master's graduates from one graduate program found a lower overall attrition rate of 33% (Holmes, Verrier, & Chisholm, 1983). Although 80.9% of respondents were employed in student affairs jobs one year after graduation, only 39.0% held student affairs positions five years later. The combined rate for graduates employed in student affairs or other higher education positions was 89.3% after one year and 58.5% after six years (Holmes et al., 1983). The reasons for attrition are not easily determined, although one study links departure with poor supervision and diminished job satisfaction early on (Tull, 2006). Student affairs professionals may also discover that their skills and knowledge are transferable to other career fields (Carpenter, Guido-DiBrito, & Kelly, 1987) that they find more attractive in terms of career development potential or more feasible in terms of current or anticipated life circumstances.

Student affairs careers can be less financially competitive than other career options available to master's degree recipients (Task Force, 1990). Factors related to attrition in student affairs include limited opportunities to grow, pursue scholarship, or use knowledge (Bender, 1980); limited mobility due to relocation difficulties, hiring practices, or limited or unclear career paths (Evans, 1988); age (attrition increases with age); years past the master's degree (Burns, 1982), and reevaluation of student affairs as a career choice (Lorden, 1998). On the other hand, advantageous factors related to student affairs work include quality of life within an academic community; professional association involvement; research and development opportunities; and intrinsically rewarding work (Task Force, 1990). New professionals should carefully weigh their own sense of the advantages and disadvantages as they plan their careers.

Career advancement can be construed as a series of positions that serve as stepping stones to a desired culminating position; it can also be regarded as a process directed toward greater actualization of one's potential as a student affairs educator (Manning, 1994). To prompt personal deliberations on values, self, and actualization, Rhatigan (1996) offers the following:

> What directs your life? What are the sources of the answers you have achieved? How does this bear on your work? Often the word "journey" is used, an appropriate metaphor, reminding us that the answers to these questions are not always the same, even in an individual life. Most importantly, the word journey recognizes movement toward a destination. The pursuit occurs across time in our relationships with people and in our journey into the self. (p. 73)

Although the career path for many is designed to lead to upper administrative positions, not all aspirants will realize that goal and not all professionals will aspire to it. Career ambitions are often vertically directed or vertically realized, but not always. Most concepts of career advancement include the ideal of maturity that can be achieved in part through professional experiences.

Maturing As a Professional

A college president who was formerly a student affairs administrator remarked, "Were I to have been offered a senior-level administrative position before I had reached a certain experiential level and maturity in my own career, I would not have been able to do this job. Impossible. Absolutely impossible." To call someone a "seasoned" professional is to recognize his or her professional maturity, capabilities, and readiness for more complex challenges. As a result of work experience, new professionals develop maturity in their own professional practice. Although mere accumulation of years does not necessarily yield maturity, years of experience provide opportunities to test and refine one's skills, capabilities, and instincts.

As a new professional, it is easy to forget Scher and Barr's (1979) admonition that "individuals must carefully attend to their survival as people who have professional jobs rather than as professionals who also have a personal life" (p. 530). For new professionals in one study, finding balance "took a back seat to concerns about fitting in and appearing competent" (Renn & Hodges, 2007, p. 386). Entry-level student affairs positions often entail long days that can extend into evenings and weekends; it is not surprising that being new to the student affairs profession was a significant factor in predicting job-related stress (Berwick, 1992). New professionals must simultaneously learn the culture and mores of a new campus while searching for niches and connections on campus and within the local community. This acclimation may be particularly critical for people of color and gay, lesbian, bisexual, and transgendered professionals as they seek communities or networks that offer support and acceptance. In the case of new professionals who work at the same institution from which they earned their degrees, they must make transitions in practice and perspective from student or paraprofessional to full-time

> New professionals must simultaneously learn the culture and mores of a new campus while searching for niches and connections on campus and within the local community.

professional staff member, and this effort can be complicated by perceptions of colleagues, support staff, and others who may still view them as students. Skilled supervisors often anticipate such concerns and work directly with new professionals (and staff members) to ease the transition.

When asked about their transitions from being the new person at their campuses to being a contributor and leader, new professionals often spoke in terms of finding their feet and finding their voice. Consider these excerpts:

> *I had the opportunity to work for two directors in two different career services offices as a coordinator prior to this position. As a coordinator, I tended to rely on advice from the directors and learn from them. Much of what I learned was constructive and useful to my understanding of how I would organize and administer my own career services program, and some of what I learned helped me decide what I would not want to do and how I would not want to be. Now that I am a director, I feel very confident about my career services knowledge and my professional abilities. In addition, I do not hesitate to make major decisions on my own, and I am responsible for my department's budget. I have also challenged myself by assuming leadership roles in two state professional associations. Through this involvement I have been able to provide advice and mentoring to current graduate students and new professionals.* —Career services director

> *In my experience, I felt less like a newcomer when problems arose and my staff and supervisors began to look to me for solutions and suggestions instead of thinking, "Well, he's new here." Then I started to be heard and acknowledged as a resource and as someone with expertise who can help us get from point A to point B. It has been important for me to listen and learn about the campus's history and culture, and then show that I have a true understanding of the issue or problem at hand. For me, colleagues' feedback was the signal that I was less "new" and on target with my understandings of the campus and important issues here. I brought my own personal philosophies of working with students and groups, and my own sets of theoretical approaches, but I try to match these with what I continue to learn about the campus. It will be important for me to complete an academic year, too, so that I experience a full cycle on campus.* —Student activities director

> *I remember coming [here] and being almost overwhelmed with all there was to learn about the field, my job, the college, and my new home, and I*

wondered when, if ever, I would feel that sense of not being new anymore. I had this conversation with friends from grad school who were going through similar things. It was a gradual process for me of getting to know people and feeling comfortable in a new place. I began feeling that sense of not being the "new professional" sometime during the spring and summer of my first year. I think it takes a solid year to begin to understand the cycle and rhythms of an institution. I knew I was emerging as a not so new professional when I began taking on tasks because they made sense and needed to be done. And when people began calling me to serve on committees and work on projects because they knew my skills and interest areas, not because the project fit my job description. So I guess the realization was gradual for me, but it was triggered when I noticed more and more requests for my participation or new projects coming into my area. What helped me most in making this transition was confidence in my skills and preparation and immersing myself in the job and the institutional culture. —Study abroad coordinator*

Much of finding your feet entails getting used to a new campus and new ways of doing things; finding your voice is realizing that you, as a new staff member, have valuable insights and perspectives to share. Both are necessary. According to Van Maanen (1983), professional socialization is a reciprocal and ongoing process. As the excerpts above make clear, new professionals' contributions are often judged by their grasp of institutional nuances. By considering their own perspectives in light of their growing knowledge of the campus, new professionals can reach mature judgments about the extent to which their contributions will be welcomed or resisted.

This learning process can deepen your knowledge about yourself and your own strengths and weaknesses, presenting opportunities for reflection-in-action (Schön, 1983) and reflective practice. The practices are not so much a product of formal coursework and formal learning, but they are enhanced through internships and practica, watching, participating in mentoring relationships, and personal trial and error (Brown et al., 1992; Richmond & Sherman, 1991), underlining the critical importance of fit with an environment that supports and encourages risk taking as a form of learning and professional development.

New professionals may not have decided on specific job targets or strategies for attaining them, but entry-level professional positions provide opportunities to observe, learn from, and work with established practitioners who may be models if not mentors. There can be rich opportunities for reflective learning, cultivating professional instincts, and "catching" an assortment of skills that are not often the subject of formal educational settings (Task Force, 1990). These competencies include developing a feel for optimal decision timing, dealing with consequences of decisions, and delegating expediently and appropriately (Appleton, Briggs, & Rhatigan, 1978). Even in first professional positions, new staff members form or continue to form their professional identities and personal lives in ways that will influence their career advancement decisions and options.

Seasoning and maturity are critical for student affairs practitioners who are called on to deal with some of the most puzzling and distressing issues on campuses. New student affairs professionals bring their own levels of maturity and knowledge to help their campuses capitalize on potential opportunities represented by, for example, electronic communications and social networking, social justice efforts, and broadened considerations of multiculturalism and campus diversity. Although we should attempt to anticipate future challenges, we do not have a crystal ball. Preparation for meeting professional challenges and opportunities includes using reflection and continued learning to maintain a positive, open disposition. Change and associated challenges can wrack campuses and student affairs professionals, yet change also provides opportunities for positive transformation of campuses, practices, and attitudes (Rhoads & Black, 1995).

Strategic Issues in Career Advancement

Identifying and addressing strategic career advancement issues are major challenges and concerns for most new professionals. Mentoring and professional association involvement are also integral factors in career advancement, and these issues are addressed in detail in chapter 4 of this book. The following sections address the critical yet often puzzling issues of doctoral degree attainment, conventional and non-conventional career paths, institutional crossovers, and "accrual mobility" in student affairs.

Practical Experience and the Doctorate

According to one student affairs professional, "Young professionals in student affairs should be striving to achieve educational excellence." While a doctoral degree might not be the be-all and end-all for every aspiring new professional, it should be strongly considered. For student affairs professionals in the field to gain credibility from colleagues (and the all-influential faculty), they must contribute to the academic experience of students, document those contributions and their effects, and relay them to the entire campus community, including students, faculty, and administrative colleagues. Simply put, pursuing a doctoral degree is a commitment beyond practice. It signifies the pursuit of knowledge that contributes to a field that promotes personal growth and development. New professionals who understand the complexities of higher education should see the doctorate as an opportunity to continue discovering themselves as learners, while promoting both professional and intellectual skill building.

Does advancement in student affairs require a doctoral degree? This question is frequently asked by new professionals, yet is difficult to answer because of the many related contingencies, such as position aspirations and types of institutions. Those who aspire to professional positions as directors (e.g., of student activities or, of multicultural affairs) may be able to attain their goal with a master's degree, but this depends on the traditions, expectations, size, and organizational structure of the college or university. According to Rickard (1985):

> Position listings in *The Chronicle of Higher Education* capsulize, both implicitly and explicitly, institutional values and expectations. Position requirements typically include degree minimums, years of experience, and experience in similar kinds of institutions. In a study of 103 vacancy listings for senior and mid-level student affairs officers, four-year public institutions expressed a clear preference for a doctorate, while private institutions required a master's degree. The top-ranked requirement for both public and private was experience in similar kinds of institutions. (p. 5)

Increasing numbers of job listings in *The Chronicle of Higher Education* contain the phrase "master's required; doctorate preferred." There are no absolute patterns of expectation among colleges and universities because of institutional differences in philosophy, size, type, and other factors. However, the doctoral degree increasingly functions as a gatekeeper to higher level positions and advancement in student affairs. In discussing the importance of the doctorate as a professional credential, one vice president and dean of students remarked,

> *You do not have to have a doctorate to be a dean of students or a vice president for student affairs, as a select few institutions do not require one. However, by having an earned doctorate, your opportunities to be selected as a finalist from a candidate pool will increase significantly.*

The doctorate broadens the range of institutions at which a candidate may successfully compete for director, assistant or associate dean, dean, or vice president positions—particularly at large universities—and even influences future salaries (Engstrom et al., 2006; Reason, Walker, & Robinson, 2002).

Career advancement in student affairs frequently involves combinations of education and work experience. Both help prepare professionals to undertake increasingly complex responsibilities, although the relative emphasis placed on each has evolved. Various perspectives have emerged regarding the doctoral degree (and field of study), work experience, and career advancement. Twenty-five years ago, senior student affairs administrators in one study identified work experience as the primary qualifier for advancement and ranked experience ahead of one's terminal degree field of study (Lunsford, 1984). A later study by the National Association of Student Personnel Administrators (NASPA) reported that the majority (56%) of senior student affairs administrators had an earned doctorate (as cited in Komives & Taub, 2000). Komives and Taub noted that the experience gained through earning a doctorate helps senior student affairs administrators be competitive in job searches. Finally, according to a 1992 study by Townsend and Wiese, although senior student affairs administrators who hold doctorates in higher education regarded the degree as useful preparation, presidents and senior academic affairs officers (with the exception of those at community colleges) regarded the higher education doctorate as useful but not essential for a senior student affairs officer. Combinations of work experience and graduate education, rather than only one or the other, now constitute superior preparation for career advancement.

Years of work experience can also be factored into decisions regarding perceived readiness for Ph.D. study. Many higher education and student affairs doctoral programs require that applicants have several years of full-time work experience—often between two and five years—as a criterion for admission. Although opinions range widely about the need for full-time experience, obtaining a doctorate without previous full-time experience can be detrimental to the student. Work experience provides a valuable basis for practical reflection as part of doctoral study. Further, new doctoral recipients may find themselves regarded as overqualified for some positions by virtue of education yet under-qualified for others by virtue of experience, negatively affecting their marketability. A professional who has earned a master's degree and worked with program development, supervision, policies, procedures, and budgets is more attractive than is an applicant with a doctorate and little or no prior experience in these areas.

A student affairs professional who served as dean of students and vice president for student services echoed this view:

The professional standards and guidelines for student services programs support the popular belief that student services leaders must have substantial work experiences in one of the functional areas of student services and an advanced degree to command respect for their leadership on campus. Part of commanding respect comes from a working knowledge and experience in student personnel.

Many options are available to the professional interested in pursuing a doctorate, whether the choice is to attend as a full- or part-time student at a local university or from home. Online degrees have emerged as an additional option. To accommodate busy schedules, institutions of higher education have begun offering accredited distance education courses as well as online degrees.

The increasing selectivity of the job market and the adherence to more formalized hiring practices also suggest that competitive candidates will demonstrate a balance of professional study and experience (Kuk, Cobb, & Forrest, 2007). As Komives and Taub (2000) wrote, "Few would argue...that there is a growing expectation of doctoral study for both advancement and credibility in student affairs" (p. 509). Again, no one road map guides new professionals to success, but new professionals who gain theoretical knowledge and practical experience in program development, supervision, policy development, and budgeting will open doors to advancement in student affairs.

Conventional versus Nonconventional Career Paths

New professionals in student affairs are confronted immediately with career decisions that may appear confusing—a situation that is complicated by the fact that different people give different advice on career strategies. This section provides an overview of traditional and nontraditional career paths in student affairs.

Historically, those who aspired to be senior student affairs administrators started their careers in residence life (Birch, 1984). Frederiksen (1993) said, "The housing and residence life career field has become a primary provider of basic student affairs professional work experiences and, in so doing, offers an excellent experience foundation for other career fields within student affairs" (p. 176).

In Richmond and Benton's 1988 study of placement results, the largest category of new professionals in student affairs (regardless of career aspiration) found their first professional position in residence life, despite initially lower anticipation of a residence life job. This career beginning was also common during the 1960s and 1970s, when residence life was viewed as a key starting point because of the variety of experiences a new professional acquired in the residence hall setting. In residence life, new professionals observe and influence student development by managing responsibilities from student counseling to judicial affairs, experiences commonly seen as the cornerstone of a successful student affairs career. The experiences of one new master's degree recipient suggest that a residence life position also provides a departure point for closer involvement with, and understanding of, other programs in student affairs:

> *Student affairs as a profession is similar to other professions...there are those who believe only one path should be traveled in an effort to be successful. However, I come from the school of thought that there are many directions one can take to be successful in our field. Although I have taken what historically has been thought of as a traditional path through residence life, I think it imperative to be familiar and involved with other areas of student affairs as well as other facets of the university...I think the contemplation should not be if one will be limited because of the choice to pursue residence life, admissions, multicultural affairs, or student activities. The contemplation should be more about you as a new professional limiting yourself. Any facet of student affairs will most likely provide an avenue to pursue your ultimate goals. One must be careful not to build walls and close oneself in nor allow others to apply such limitations.*

Today, new professionals take multiple routes to senior-level administration. In the 1980s and 1990s, an increasing number of practitioners began their careers in student activities, academic advising, financial aid, volunteer services, career services, multicultural affairs, and admissions, leading to increased diversity in background experiences (J. Claar, personal communication, January 2002; M. B. Snyder, personal communication, January 2002). One advantage of this variety of entry points to student affairs is that new professionals with primary interests in areas other than residence life can be accommodated earlier in their careers. It is unclear to what extent beliefs persist about residence life as a preferred basis for a student affairs career. Time will tell whether increasing numbers of professionals with nontraditional career beginnings are able to realize their career advancement goals. As the above individual suggested, new professionals gain a tremendous advantage in the job search by acquiring early experience in various areas of student affairs (e.g., residence life, student activities, career services, multicultural affairs) through full-time work and also through internships and practica.

In some cases, new professionals may fear that several successive years in one functional area will typecast them as an expert in one area and limit their marketability for generalist administrative positions. Sustained expertise in one area provides a valuable track record of success and an additional set of opportunities for advancement within that specialty; professionals who are concerned about being locked into one area can seek out committee assignments and collaborative projects in other student affairs areas or in professional associations to demonstrate a breadth of commitments and expertise. For new professionals, positions that entail responsibilities in more than one student affairs area may be particularly attractive. One example of such a position, often referred to as a "split" or "joint" appointment, is a job that specifies 60% time in a residence life appointment and 40% time in career services. Although this arrangement can offer valuable skill-building opportunities, new professionals and their supervisors must take care to ensure that the "split" does not become two full-time jobs that one person is expected to perform.

Building transferable skills improves competitiveness but does not guarantee that a move to the desired specialty area will follow. Such transfers can be more or less readily accomplished depending on, for example, the existing number of professionals with the requisite knowledge base and experience. Participating in cross-training experiences, pursuing continuing education, and holding split positions can help professionals demonstrate a new set of goals and skills to a prospective employer.

Determining a career path is not an easy task, but new professionals can take advantage of a valuable source of information by participating in professional conferences. As student affairs professionals, we advise students that a critical aspect of success in college is involvement; the same advice applies to our own careers. The networking that occurs at conferences enhances skills and provides insight into various career opportunities. By participating in conferences and other professional development programs, newcomers can learn, sharpen abilities, and evaluate career decisions while they increase their marketability. As Harned and Murphy (1998) said, "New professionals must understand that there is hard work ahead. There is potential for many rewards, so an investment in their own growth and development will pay many dividends in the future" (p. 52).

Institutional Crossovers: Public, Private, and Community College

Working in three private and two public institutions, my career choice was one of professional development. Except for my residential life experiences, I had become a generalist. Although I realized that many employers (especially those in small private liberal arts institutions) seek generalists, it was important for me to find a job that would help

me develop my skills in one particular area of student development.
—Admissions professional

New professionals obtain employment in various types of institutions—doctoral-degree-granting universities, comprehensive institutions, liberal arts colleges, community colleges, and vocational-technical colleges. Community colleges are growing at a faster rate than four-year institutions (AACC, 2006); currently, among the more than 4,000 higher education institutions in the United States, approximately 1,195 are community colleges (AACC, 2008). As the proportion of student affairs career opportunities in community colleges continues to increase, so will the knowledge base about strategic career issues characteristics of student affairs professionals in community colleges. With this said, the services and programs present in community colleges are familiar and recognizable to those present at four-year institutions (Culp, 2005; Helfgot, 2005).

Professionals in the field of student affairs may wonder whether they can or should "cross over" to different types of institutions in the course of their careers, and question how competitively crossover candidates are regarded. The admissions professional quoted above observed that one of the major differences between public and private institutions involves being a generalist or a specialist. New professionals in public colleges and universities are traditionally hired to perform one or two major duties and are not expected (and perhaps not encouraged) to venture into other areas of responsibility. Most public institutions have a large student affairs staff; therefore, professionals tend to specialize in specific programmatic areas—and may need to do so for advancement. Mid- and upper-level managers in large public institutions have more opportunities to venture into other areas of student services as they supervise diverse program offices or plan cooperative ventures.

Student affairs positions at small private colleges and universities are more fluid in nature, and professionals (including new professionals) are expected to move beyond expertise in any one narrow specialty. Many private colleges expect their multicultural affairs and student activities staffs to play active roles in residence life, health services, volunteer services, and freshman orientation. In short, private colleges tend to expect new professionals to be generalists. A new professional must possess the skills and confidence, as well as the desire, to work outside his or her area of expertise.

Some employers are impressed by professionals who have worked in a variety of settings early in their careers; those who work in one setting for 7–10 years may find themselves defined by that choice of institutional type. Kauffman (1983) found that faculty members on selection committees were wary of candidates who attempted crossovers; for example, an administrator in a small private institution might have difficulty moving to a large public college or university, or from a two-year to a four-year institution. Although there are no set rules in this area, institutional crossovers can be used early in one's career to determine whether a public or private environment best matches one's professional needs and goals, personality, or preferred work style. Once professionals are established and identified in a given area, they may find it difficult to change the perceptions of others who associate them with a particular type of institution. Direct experience is one of the best determinants of fit with respect to institutional type. As is true for students, we grow and develop best when we are in a comfortable yet stimulating environment that includes but transcends working relationships.

The opportunity to work with and for professionals and institutions whose values match our own contributes to the "goodness-of-fit" principle (Birch, 1984) and the "person-organization" fit (Tull & Medrano, 2008). But there is more to these principles than good working relationships. One needs to feel equally good about the quality of the new environment and the institutional values (Birch, 1984; Tull & Medrano, 2008).

One faculty member and student affairs administrator recommends that new professionals try to experience multiple settings during the course of their academic preparation:

> *New professionals in graduate school must be sensitive to the issue of marketability during the process of completing an academic program. Practicums and internships are excellent ways to take a close look at the market availability for new professionals. It is critical that they develop courses of study which provide the opportunity to experience both public and private institutions.*

A dean of students advises new professionals to evaluate and reevaluate their decisions:

> *New professionals must realize that the decision to work in a public or private institution does not have to be permanent. Select the best setting for yourself, but realize that the career decision-making process does not end with your first job. Research and evaluate the different settings, and make a professional decision about your future.*

New professionals should ask themselves questions about an institution's traditions, environment, and values, and consider how the answers correlate with their own personality, values, and beliefs. Wise decisions will contribute to a rewarding student affairs career.

Promotions and Accrual Mobility in Student Affairs

In student affairs administration, the prevailing attitude seems to be that the way to move up is to move out—to move on to another institution or position (Rosser, 2000). According to Burkhalter (1984), an administrator in student affairs will generally work for five different institutions during his or her career. However, accrual mobility and internal promotions may account for an increasing number of promotional opportunities. Accrual mobility "occurs through evolved jobs in which the employee accrues responsibility and/or knowledge well beyond normal growth in the job" (Miner & Estler, 1985, p. 121); it results in the creation of a new position or unit in recognition of the employee's growth that matches an institutional need. Consider the following assistant dean of students' career thus far:

> *While initially content to do the proverbial "two-year tenure" of most new professionals, I found that the opportunity for accumulated knowledge and experience was increasing exponentially each year I remained with the university. After year three, I was regularly engaged in institutional activity far beyond any that could have been experienced in that time period by taking a position at another college or university. In addition, I found myself with a promotion and an opportunity to attend graduate school at minimal cost. Despite the rural isolation, the scarcity of African American professionals, and the newness of my functional area, extending my stay was one of the most professionally profitable decisions I ever made.*

Financial constraints often cause institutional administrators to reevaluate potential job openings. During times of severe financial stress, colleges and universities may reduce the number of job opportunities for both new and seasoned professionals (e.g., Burkhalter, 1984). Additionally, new organizational structures have emerged with student affairs offices reporting to academic affairs administrators or residence life programs reporting to business officers. And finally, because of financial constraints, the duties of a departing staff member are often distributed temporarily or permanently among the remaining staff.

Decreases in institutional financial resources have prompted many changes that will affect careers in student affairs and may result in longer "insider" affiliations with one institution (Sagaria & Dickens, 1990) and a subsequent intra-institutional career path. A career at one institution may also proceed through the process of accrual mobility. The professional quoted above had a successful career start as an insider, since he began as the university's coordinator of multicultural services and was promoted to assistant dean of students two years later. In student affairs, advancement through accrual mobility or by an inside path provides an alternative to a more typical assumption that position advancements always occur inter-institutionally. Increasingly competitive job markets may well establish an atmosphere in which professionals can view their careers, or significant portions of them, as long-term commitments to a particular higher education institution.

Conclusions and Recommendations

Career advancement is an ongoing process that unfolds as individuals, institutions, and social and economic trends evolve; new professionals should monitor these personal and environmental developments and their career-related implications. We suggest that new professionals set long-range as well as mid-range (5–10 years) and short-term (1–5 years) career goals, and audit themselves on a regular basis. Such an audit evaluates not only *progress* toward specific goals but also the continued *appropriateness* of those goals. Realigning goals or revisiting time frames may both be in order if progress has not met earlier expectations. Mentors and supervisors can be helpful resources in these reflection and reevaluation processes, and career counseling may also benefit professionals who desire more focused attention to their career concerns.

Systematic attention to career advancement can be crucial. Financial advisors recommend calculating a net worth statement as part of annual income tax preparation, and manufacturers of smoke detectors recommend replacing old batteries twice a year when clocks are adjusted for daylight savings time. A reasonable time for career auditing may coincide with annual performance appraisals and/or meetings regarding merit salary adjustments. In addition to reflecting about specific job accomplishments, professionals should ask themselves questions such as these: What am I good at? What do I enjoy? What are my contributions to students, staff, and the campus? Am I satisfied and successful with what I am doing? Am I able to do the work I want to here? Am I accepted and validated as a professional and as a person? What are my opportunities for further growth? What do I want to do next? What has changed in my life during the past year, and how do I respond to that? How do I want my life to change in the next year or two?

You can supplement your own answers to these questions with performance appraisal feedback. Answering the questions can help you identify your accomplishments, your promise, your desires, and your commitments. Of course, the answers may change as staff, colleagues, and supervisors arrive or depart campus, and as work settings are reconfigured. If these changes are rapid, your answers may be different even from one year to the next. Setting goals and addressing these questions will help you regularly evaluate the fit with your current position, measure your progress on your career path, and identify possible changes or accommodations to your path.

In general, we suggest the following activities as beneficial for professionals in student affairs at all levels when considering career issues and goals. Identify your strengths and acknowledge your weak areas. Seek or create opportunities to demonstrate your strengths and address your weaknesses through professional development activities. Seek opportunities to learn from others and to teach and help others. Consider personal, institutional, and environmental developments, and determine how these changes might affect your plans and goals. Identify sets of constraints and opportunities, and accept professional opportunities for risk-taking and skill development. Finally, work hard. Student affairs careers are challenging but also rewarding and, at times, exhilarating. As one student affairs professional wryly remarked, "I don't get a high salary, but that's not why I'm in this line of work. I'm in it for the [holiday] cards." Our work as educators, advocates, counselors, and life-long learners provides its own set of rewards to those who value the satisfactions of contributing to students' lives and to the colleges and universities in which they work.

References

American Association of Community Colleges (AACC). (2006). *Community college growth by decade*. Retrieved July 29, 2008, from www.aacc.nche.edu/Content/NavigationMenu/AboutCommunityColleges/HistoricalInformation/CCGrowth/CC_Growth_1991-2000.htm.

American Association of Community Colleges (AACC). (2008). *CC stats.* Retrieved July 30, 2008, from www2.aacc.nche.edu/research/index.htm.

Appleton, J. R., Briggs, C. M., & Rhatigan, J. J. (1978). *Pieces of eight: The rites, roles, and styles of the dean by eight who have been there.* Portland, OR: NASPA Institute for Research and Development.

Bass, J. H. (2006). Vice president for student affairs and dean of students: Is it possible to do it all? In S. B. Westfall (Ed.), *The small college dean.* New Directions for Student Services, no. 116 (pp. 45–52). San Francisco: Jossey-Bass.

Belch, H. A., & Strange, C. C. (1995). Views from the bottleneck: Middle managers in student affairs. *NASPA Journal, 32,* 208–222.

Bender, B. E. (1980). Job satisfaction in student affairs. *NASPA Journal, 18,* 2–9.

Berwick, K. R. (1992). Stress among student affairs administrators: The relationship of personal characteristics and organizational variables of work-related stress. *Journal of College Student Development, 33,* 11–19.

Birch, E. (1984). Thoughts on career advancement. In A. F. Kirby & D. Woodard (Eds.), *Career perspectives in student affairs* (NASPA Monograph Series, Vol. 1., pp. 43–52). Washington, DC: National Association of Student Personnel Administrators.

Brown, R. D., Podolske, D. L., Kohles, R. D., & Sonnenberg, R. L. (1992). Becoming a reflective student affairs administrator. *NASPA Journal, 29,* 307–314.

Burkhalter, J. P. (1984). *Career patterns of chief student personnel administrators.* Unpublished doctoral dissertation, University of Georgia, Athens.

Burns, M. (1982). Who leaves the student development field? *NASPA Journal, 20,* 9–12.

Carpenter, D. S., Guido-DiBrito, F., & Kelly, J. P. (1987). Transferability of student affairs skills and competencies: Light at the end of the bottleneck. *NASPA Journal, 24,* 7–14.

Coomes, M. D., & DeBard, R. (2004). A generational approach to understanding students. In M. D. Coomes & R. DeBard (Eds.), *Serving the millennial generation.* New Directions for Student Services, no. 106 (pp. 5–16). San Francisco: Jossey-Bass.

Culp, M. M. (2005). *Increasing the value of traditional support services.* New Directions for Community Colleges, no. 131, 33–49. San Francisco: Jossey-Bass.

DeBard, R. (2004). Millennials coming to college. In M. D. Coomes & R. DeBard (Eds.), *Serving the millennial generation.* New Directions for Student Services, no. 106 (pp. 33–45). San Francisco: Jossey-Bass.

Derr, C. B. (1986). *Managing the new careerists.* San Francisco: Jossey-Bass.

Dewey, J. (1926). *Democracy and education.* New York: Macmillan.

Engstrom, C. M., McIntosh, J. G., Ridzi, F. M., & Kruger, K. (2006). Salary determinants for senior student affairs officers: Revisiting gender and ethnicity in light of institutional characteristics. *NASPA Journal, 43*(2), 243–263.

Evans, N. J. (1988). Attrition of student affairs professionals: A review of the literature. *Journal of College Student Development, 29*(1), 19–24.

Fey, C. J., & Carpenter, D. S. (1996). Mid-level student affairs administrators: Management skills and professional development needs. *NASPA Journal, 33*, 218–231.

Frederiksen, C. F. (1993). A brief history of collegiate housing. In R. B. Winston, Jr., S. Anchors & Associates, *Student housing and residential life* (pp. 167–183). San Francisco: Jossey-Bass.

Gordon, S. E., Strode, C. B., & Mann, B. A. (1993). The mid-manager in student affairs: What are CSAOs looking for? *NASPA Journal, 30*, 290–297.

Harned, P. J., & Murphy, M. C. (1998). *Creating a culture of development for the new professional.* New Directions for Student Services, no. 84 (pp. 43–53). San Francisco: Jossey-Bass.

Heida, D. E. (2006). The student affairs portfolio in small colleges. In S. B. Westfall (Ed.), *The small college dean.* New Directions for Student Services, no. 116 (pp. 15–29). San Francisco: Jossey-Bass.

Helfgot, S. R. (2005). *Core values and major issues in student affairs practice: What really matters?* New Directions for Community Colleges, no. 131 (pp. 5–18). San Francisco: Jossey-Bass.

Hirt, J. B., Amelink, C. T., & Schneiter, S. (2004). The nature of student affairs work in the liberal arts college. *NASPA Journal, 42*, 94–110.

Holmes, D., Verrier, D., & Chisholm, P. (1983). Persistence in student affairs work: Attitudes and job shifts among master's program graduates. *Journal of College Student Personnel, 24*, 438–443.

Janasiewicz, B. A., & Wright, D. L. (1993). Job market trends in student affairs: Ten years later. *NASPA Journal, 30*, 145–152.

Kauffman, J. F. (1983). Commentary on examining the myths of administrative careers. *ASHE Bulletin, 35*, 7–8.

Komives, S. R., & Taub, D. J. (2000). Advancing professionally through doctoral education. In M. J. Barr, M. K. Desler & Associates (Eds.). *The handbook of student affairs administration* (pp. 508–534). San Francisco: Jossey-Bass.

Kuk, L., Cobb, B., & Forrest, C. (2007). Perceptions of competencies of entry-level practitioners in student affairs. *NASPA Journal, 44*(4), 664–691.

Lorden, L. P. (1998). Attrition in the student affairs profession. *NASPA Journal, 35*, 207–216.

Lunsford, L. W. (1984). Chief student affairs officer: The ladder to the top. *NASPA Journal, 22*, 48–56.

Manning, K. (1994). Liberation theology and student affairs. *Journal of College Student Development, 35*, 94–97.

Miner, A. S., & Estler, S. E. (1985). Accrual mobility: Job mobility in higher education through responsibility accrual. *Journal of Higher Education, 56*, 121–143.

Moore, K. M. (1984). The structure of administrative careers: A prose poem in four parts. *Review of Higher Education, 8*(1), 1–13.

Nobbe, J., & Manning, S. (1997). Issues for women in student affairs with children. *NASPA Journal, 34*, 101–111.

Oblander, D. A. (2006). Student affairs staffing in the small college. In S. B. Westfall (Ed.), *The small college dean*. New Directions for Student Services, no. 116 (pp. 31–44). San Francisco: Jossey-Bass.

Reason, R. D., Walker, D. A., & Robinson, D. C. (2002). Gender, ethnicity, and highest degree earned as salary determinants for senior student affairs officers at public institutions. *NASPA Journal, 39*(3), 251–265.

Renn, K. A., & Hodges, J. P. (2007). The first year on the job: Experiences of new professionals in student affairs. *NASPA Journal, 42*(2), 367–391.

Rhatigan, J. J. (1996). Simple gifts: Reflections on the profession. *NASPA Journal, 34*, 67–77.

Rhoads, R. A., & Black, M. A. (1995). Student affairs practitioners as transformative educators: Advancing a critical cultural perspective. *Journal of College Student Development, 36*, 413–421.

Richmond, J., & Sherman, K. J. (1991). Student-development preparation and placement: A longitudinal study of graduate students' and new professionals' experiences. *Journal of College Student Development, 32*, 8–16.

Richmond, J., & Benton, S. (1988). Student affairs graduates' anticipated and actual placement plans. *Journal of College Student Development, 29*, 119–124.

Rickard, S. T. (1985). The chief student affairs officer: Progress toward equity. *Journal of College Student Personnel, 26*, 5–10.

Robinson, D. C., & Delbridge-Parker, L. (1991). A model job rotation plan: A 10-year follow-up. *NASPA Journal, 28*, 172–178.

Rosser, V. J. (2000). Midlevel administrators: What we know. In L. K. Johnsrud & V. J. Rosser (Eds.), *Understanding the work and career paths of midlevel administrators*. New Directions for Higher Education, no. 111 (pp. 5–13). San Francisco: Jossey-Bass.

Sagaria, M. A. D., & Dickens, C. S. (1990). Thriving at home: Developing a career as an insider. In K. M. Moore & S. B. Twombly (Eds.), *Administrative careers and the marketplace*. New Directions for Higher Education, no. 72 (pp. 19–28). San Francisco: Jossey-Bass.

Sagaria, M.A.D., & Johnsrud, L. K. (1988). Mobility within the student affairs profession: Career advancement through position change. *Journal of College Student Development, 29*, 30–40.

Scher, M., & Barr, M. J. (1979). Beyond graduate school: Strategies for survival. *Journal of College Student Personnel, 20,* 529–533.

Schön, D. A. (1983). *The reflective practitioner: How professionals think in action.* New York: Harper Collins.

Shriberg, A., & Wester, S. R. (1994). Employment satisfaction among non-Catholic student affairs professionals at Catholic colleges and universities. *Journal of College Student Development, 35,* 109–112.

Task Force on Professional Preparation and Practice. (1990). *The recruitment, preparation, and nurturing of the student affairs professional.* Washington, DC: National Association of Student Personnel Administrators.

Townsend, B. K., & Wiese, M. (1992). The value of a doctorate in higher education for student affairs administrators. *NASPA Journal, 30,* 51–58.

Twombly, S. B. (1990). Career maps and institutional highways. In K. M. Moore & S. B. Twombly (Eds.), *Administrative careers and the marketplace.* New Directions for Higher Education, no. 72 (pp. 5–18). San Francisco: Jossey-Bass.

Tull, A. (2006). Synergistic supervision, job satisfaction, and intention to turnover of new professionals in student affairs. *Journal of College Student Development, 47*(4), 465–480.

Tull, A., & Medrano, C. (2008). Character values congruence and person-organization fit in student affairs: Compatibility between administrators and the institutions that employ them. *Journal of College and Character, IX*(3), 1–16.

Van Maanen, J. (1983). Doing new things in old ways: The chains of socialization. In J. L. Bess (Ed.), *College and university organization: Insights from the behavioral sciences.* New York: New York University Press.

Winston, R. B., Jr., & Creamer, D. G. (1997). *Improving staffing practices in student affairs.* San Francisco: Jossey-Bass.

Young, R. B. (1994). Student affairs professionals' perceptions of barriers to participation in development activities. *NASPA Journal, 31,* 243–251.

CRISIS MANAGEMENT
FOR NEW PROFESSIONALS

CHAPTER NINE

Eugene L. Zdziarski and Dawn Watkins

M any people in a college or university community feel at least some-what responsible for managing campus crises, but in a true crisis, they typically look to student affairs professionals for leadership. A recent survey of provosts in higher education found that the person most frequently identified as integral to the management of a crisis is the senior student affairs officer (Mitroff, Diamond & Alpaslan, 2006). With this in mind, having a framework in place for understanding crisis management is key for all student affairs professionals and, in particular, new professionals.

The skill set for handling crises is required throughout the careers of student affairs professionals. Although the crises most often discussed are the major or catastrophic events, in reality it is the smaller events—those that most people in the college or university community never even hear about—that student affairs professionals deal with on a regular basis. These day-to-day crises make up the majority of the work of student affairs professionals and, in particular, new professionals who are on the front line. Understanding how to manage small incidents prepares a student affairs professional to manage day-to-day crises and the large-scale incidents that, sadly, often make national news. In this chapter, we will introduce some theoretical crisis management concepts, apply them to higher education, and then relate them to specific events that new professionals in student affairs might face in their work.

Crisis Management As a Process

> *No matter what, you can't stop crazy; you just have to be prepared for the worst, but I worry that I'm not prepared.* —New student affairs professional

Crisis management planning is not something that is done once, involving a pretty notebook that sits on a shelf, to be used in the event of an incident. Crisis management is a continuous process that evolves as higher education administrators move through both small- and large-scale events. Many authors (Abent, 1999; Coombs, 1999; Federal Emergency Management Agency [FEMA], 1996; Koovor-Misra, 1995; Mitroff, Pearson & Harrington, 1996; Ogrizek & Guillery, 1999; Pauchant & Mitroff, 1992) describe the process as a series of stages or phases. We think it is best described as a cycle. On a fundamental level, it is often viewed as a three-phase process: pre-crisis, crisis, and post-crisis (Birch, 1994; Coombs, 1999; Guth, 1995; Koovor-Misra, 1995; Meyers, 1986; Mitchell, 1986; Ogrizek & Guillery, 1999). In this model, certain actions and steps are taken before, during, and after the crisis event to effectively manage the incident. FEMA (1996) proposes a four-phase model: mitigation, preparedness, response, and recovery. This model adds mitigation—planning to avoid a crisis altogether or to reduce the impact of a crisis should it occur.

The skill set for handling crises is required throughout the careers of student affairs professionals.

To ensure crisis management is a continuous process of learning from our work with small and large scale crises, we offer the following five-phase model to student affairs professionals: planning, prevention, response, recovery, learning (Zdziarski, 2006) (see Figure 1). A planning process is when deliberate and intentional steps are taken to prepare organizations to deal with potential crises that may be faced. The *planning* phase of our model might include a crisis audit to identify potential crisis events and stakeholders who would be part of the response.

Figure 1. Crisis management cycle.

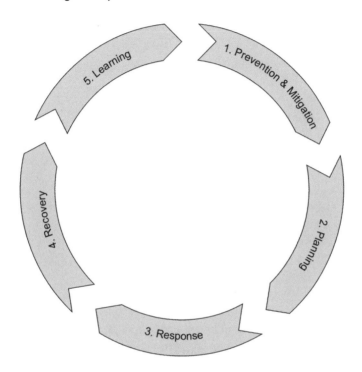

Note. From Crisis Management: Responding from the Heart (p. 7), by K. S. Harper, B. G. Paterson, and E. L. Zdziarski II. Washington, DC: NASPA. Copyright © 2006 NASPA. Reprinted with permission.

In the *prevention* phase, one examines existing prevention efforts. Student affairs professionals frequently manage prevention programs, although they are often not recognized as part of the overall crisis management process; for example, conducting and implementing alcohol education programs, providing instruction for the use of college or university vehicles for sport clubs, and conducting fire drills in residence halls. Crisis *response* is putting the plans and protocols we developed in earlier phases into action to respond to a crisis event. This is the phase people focus on when they discuss or analyze crisis management.

Crisis managers must understand that the *recovery* phase may last days, weeks, months, or—as with the aftermath of Hurricane Katrina on the Gulf Coast of the United States—even years. This phase is often both overlooked and underestimated for its importance in responding to individual needs as well as restoring the affected community. Sometimes people are so anxious to get back to business as usual that they overlook the needs of individuals and of the affected community as a whole. Student affairs professionals are frequently the people who attend to the human needs—they are adept at recognizing and responding to persons in crisis.

Throughout the recovery phase and afterwards, *learning* must occur so crisis mangers can understand what worked well and what could have been done better. The learning phase closes the loop and makes crisis management a continuous improvement process, so the organization and its people are increasingly better equipped to manage crises on campus.

The Crisis Matrix

The reality is that my coursework and field experience throughout graduate school prepared me for the profession to a certain extent. When it comes to handling crises, all of that was learned on the job.
—New professional in Greek Life

A matrix provides a conceptual framework for examining crisis management. It allows the student affairs professional to capture an understanding of a crisis and how to respond following predetermined steps for each phase. The Crisis Matrix (Zdziarski, Dunkel, & Rollo, 2007) involves three dimensions: type of crisis, level of crisis, and intentionality of crisis (see Figure 2).

Crisis events in higher education can generally be grouped into three *types*: environmental, facility, and human. *Environmental* crises include weather-related events such as hurricanes, tornados, earthquakes, and floods. *Facility* crises include such events as fires, power outages, structural collapses, and computer failures. *Human* crises include death, serious injury, and mental health issues. Understanding the differences between types of crises brings about distinct ways of responding to the varying crises.

Figure 2. Crisis matrix.

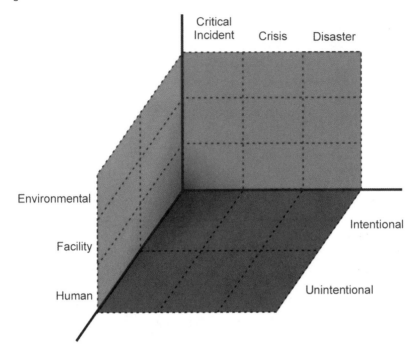

The second dimension in the Crisis Matrix is the *level* of the crisis. Generally, a *campus crisis* is defined as an event, often sudden or unexpected, that disrupts the normal operations of the institution or its educational mission and threatens the well-being of the personnel, property, financial resources, or reputation of the institution (Zdziarski, 2006). In this context, crises affect the entire institution, disrupting normal operations.

Some crises affect not only the institution but the surrounding community as well—these events are usually considered *disasters* and typically place significant demands on community resources. For example, in the case of a hurricane, everyone in the area is affected by high winds and flooding, and support must go to the entire community. Colleges and universities must be aware of the availability of support should a disaster strike.

Another level of crisis may affect only a segment of the campus community. These crises, called *critical incidents*, may affect a residence hall, a student group, or a specialized sub-set of a student population. Institutional plans typically operate at the level of campus-wide crises and major disasters, while student affairs professionals typically deal with critical incidents on a daily basis. New professionals should focus their own learning in this area and hone their crisis management skills. This experience will serve them well in the future as they move into senior roles within student affairs, where they are likely to lead the response to major crises.

The third dimension of the Crisis Matrix is the **intentionality** of the crisis; this refers to the continuum from an act of God to an intentional act by or toward someone. When someone dies from natural causes or in an accident, people can understand and accept the death. However, when a person dies as the result of an act of violence—such as terrorism or a shooting—the psychological impact on people is much more significant, as are the level and nature of the immediate response, the investigation, and the follow-up.

The Crisis Matrix allows student affairs professionals to develop and enhance their understanding of existing crisis management plans. Then they can take the events listed in a crisis audit and fully explore and understand the resources and response modalities that can be set in motion for a critical incident, a campus-wide crisis, or a disaster. The student affairs professional can see how the management of the crisis changes depending on whether the event is intentional or not.

The student affairs professional must understand the difference between crisis management *plans* and crisis management *protocols*. In putting together a plan, one creates a basic outline for managing a crisis. The outline defines: (a) the purpose of the plan, (b) who has the authority to initiate the plan, and (c) which aspects of the plan remain the same regardless of the type or nature of the crisis event. The plan includes individual protocols for different types of crisis events. Each protocol provides a series of action steps to address a specific kind of crisis event. Ultimately, the crisis portfolio would include a protocol for every potential type and level of crisis.

Crisis Management and Institutional Type

What IS the crisis management plan at my new institution?
—New professional at a small, liberal arts college

Crisis management is more than just responding to a set of circumstances, and a one size plan does not fit all. Everyone who might be involved in crisis response should be included in the institution's crisis management planning. Whether at a large university, a small college, or a community college, students and their families expect that a crisis response will include personal attention. Larger institutions have more resources. For example, most large colleges and universities have their own commissioned police officers, while smaller institutions are more likely to rely on local law enforcement. On the other hand, student affairs professionals at smaller colleges and universities may know most students on an individual basis, which can make it easier to respond to individual needs in a crisis.

There are no hard and fast rules associated with managing a crisis at a smaller or larger institution. Student affairs professionals must understand the strengths of their institution and maximize them in times of crisis, and understand the limitations of their institution and minimize them in a crisis. For example, a small college that relies on local law enforcement should have detailed discussions as part of the planning process about the type and level of support. Will institutional managers have access to campus buildings if local law enforcement is handling a crisis? If so, how will this work? Should college personnel have badges to alert local law enforcement of their role in assisting with an institutional crisis? Will local law enforcement provide information to college or university personnel in the midst of a crisis? In a large university, "while there may be a desire for personal attention, there is also likely a realization that students will be more anonymous on campus" (Rollo & Zdziarski, 2007, p. 5); thus, student affairs professionals should plan how to respond to students individually with the available staff resources. These kinds of discussions must occur during the planning process.

The challenge to the new professional is how to put all this information together. Managing a crisis might sound overwhelming but, to a certain extent, student affairs professionals do it every day. Applying sound management principles is the key to resolve both daily incidents and large-scale events.

Crisis Events

My campus is as safe as it can be, but how do I teach students not to take that for granted but not live in fear? —New professional in student activities

The case studies that follow illustrate the kinds of critical incidents that new student affairs professionals encounter in their work, and how they can apply crisis management principles to resolve them.

Case #1

You are an area coordinator at a mid-size university. One of your hall directors reports that a custodian has noticed vomit in the community bathroom area on a regular basis. You have the resident assistant ask a few questions in that particular hall, and she reports to the area coordinator that (1) food has been disappearing out of people's individual refrigerators in that hall; (2) one woman in the hall has experienced significant weight loss since the beginning of the academic year; and (3) the same woman said she has been experiencing flu-like symptoms throughout the fall semester and has occasionally vomited in the community bathroom.

Case #2

You are the assistant director of student activities at a small college. Because you and the director take turns attending events, you are the sole student activities staff person overseeing an outdoor evening concert. Two hours before the start of the event, the concert chair of the activities board comes to you in a panic because she just heard that a tornado watch has been called for your county. She asks you whether the concert should be canceled. The stage is already set and the technical crew is currently setting up microphones and speakers. To attract students to the event, dinner is currently being served on the lawn area adjacent to where the concert will occur.

Case #3

You are a coordinator for campus recreation at a large university and have worked closely with the lacrosse sport club to arrange their game at a university about 100 miles away. A team member calls to say that one of the vans in their caravan of four has had an accident. Local police are on the scene. The student reports that there are no injuries but the police may be arresting the student driver. As you question the student further about why the student driver is being arrested for a minor accident, you learn that there may have been open containers of alcohol in the van at the time of the accident.

Applying the Principles

Applying some of the theoretical concepts discussed above, how does a new professional plan, prevent, respond, and recover from these kinds of crises? Case #1 involves what appears to be a hall resident with an eating disorder. The area coordinator identifies the situation as a human crisis and reports it to the university's at-risk committee, which then helps the coordinator determine the next steps to involve the student in some sort of intervention. The at-risk committee (which has different names at different institutions) is usually a committee of college or university staff who review situations in which students are considered at risk, which can be anything from academic jeopardy to mental health concerns.

> New professionals must know and understand existing institutional plans to address human crises and make sure their actions are consistent with institutional expectations.

New professionals must know and understand existing institutional plans to address human crises and make sure their actions are consistent with institutional expectations. This case also illustrates the need for prevention planning. Has this area coordinator trained residential life and custodial staff about eating disorders and the need to communicate with other student affairs professionals even for what may seem like insignificant or unrelated events? To answer such questions, a new professional should conduct a crisis audit for his or her scope of responsibility.

In Case #2 involving the assistant director of student activities with a tornado watch announced shortly before the start of an outdoor concert, the planning aspect of crisis management is key. Is there a system or mechanism in place to receive such information on a regular basis, or is the department truly dependent on a student listening to the radio? Weather cannot be prevented, but action can be taken to reduce the impact of a weather emergency. The assistant director must be familiar with the authority structure in place to make a decision about continuing or canceling the event. In the time available, can this new professional research the likelihood that a tornado will occur and weigh the risks? Does the department have a "rain plan"? Is a shelter specified and available if the decision is made to continue the concert outdoors and the storm hits? The new professional must consider such questions in planning events, and when making decisions about how to prevent further escalation of crisis events and how to manage overall college risk.

In Case #3, the new professional who is advising a student over the phone about a lacrosse sport club van accident can rely on the recovery and learning aspects of the theoretical framework. The first step is to confirm the well-being of those involved; in this case, there is no loss of life or injury requiring medical treatment, and damage to the vehicle appears minimal. Should the trip continue? How would you accommodate the students who were traveling in the wrecked van? Maybe a colleague at a neighboring institution, who is closer to the accident, can provide immediate support and assessment of the situation. Who else in the institution needs to be notified? Moving into recovery, you may have to attend to individual needs of students who are traumatized by the accident. What should you do about the student who has been arrested? Should campus disciplinary action be considered for all the students in the van? From a learning perspective—to close the loop—what educational programs exist to stress no-alcohol policies and practices on sport club trips and during other student activities? Do the existing educational programs need to be modified?

Those three cases illustrate the kinds of events a new professional might encounter and how he or she might apply the crisis management cycle to develop protocols for responding to them. If you get used to applying the crisis management model to crises at every level of student affairs work, you will be better prepared to apply it to a critical incident, campus emergency, or disaster. While crisis events may differ in terms of scope and magnitude, the theoretical elements of crisis management remain the same. New professionals should feel empowered in their work as day-to-day crisis managers and recognize that this work is preparing them to manage serious crises in their future professional careers.

References

Abent, R. (1999). Managing in time of crisis. *NASPA NetResults*. [Online serial.] Accessed: November 30, 1999, at www.naspa.org/Results/pubrelat/managing.html.

Birch, J. (1994). New factors in crisis planning and response. *Public Relations Quarterly, 39*, 31–34.

Coombs, W. T. (1999). *Ongoing crisis communication: Planning, managing, and responding* (Vol. 2). Thousand Oaks, CA: Sage.

Federal Emergency Management Agency (FEMA). (1996). *State and local guide (SLG 101): Guide for all-hazard emergency operations planning.* Available at www.fema.gov/pte/gaheop.htm.

Guth, D. W. (1995). Organizational crisis experience and public relations roles. *Public Relations Review, 21*(2), 123–136.

Koovor-Misra, S. (1995). A multidimensional approach to crisis preparation for technical organizations: Some critical factors. *Technological Forecasting and Social Change, 48*, 143–160.

Meyers, G. C. (1986). *When it hits the fan: Managing the nine crises of business.* New York: Mentor.

Mitroff, I. I., Diamond, M. A., & Alpaslan, C. M. (2006, January/February). How prepared are America's colleges and universities for major crisis? *Change*, 61–67.

Mitroff, I. I., Pearson, C. M., & Harrington, L. K. (1996). *The essential guide to managing corporate crisis: A step-by-step handbook for surviving major catastrophes.* New York: Oxford University Press.

Mitchell, T. H. (1986). Coping with a corporate crisis. *Canadian Business Review, 13*(3), 17–20.

Ogrizek, M., & Guillery, J.-M. (1999). *Communicating in crisis: A theoretical and practical guide to crisis management.* H. Kimball-Brooke & R. Z. Brooke (Trans.). New York: Aldine De Gruyter.

Pauchant, T. C., & Mitroff, I. I. (1992). *Transforming the crisis-prone organization: Preventing individual, organizational, and environmental tragedies.* San Francisco: Jossey-Bass.

Rollo, J. M., & Zdziarski, E. L. (2007). The impact of crisis. In E. L. Zdziarski, N. W. Dunkel, & J. M. Rollo (Eds.), *Campus crisis management: A comprehensive guide to planning prevention, response and recovery* (pp. 1–33). San Francisco: Jossey-Bass.

Zdziarski, E. L. (2006). Crisis in the context of higher education. In K. S. Harper, B. G. Paterson, & E. L. Zdziarski (Eds.), *Crisis management: Responding from the heart* (pp. 3–24). Washington, DC: NASPA.

Zdziarski, E. L., Dunkel, N.W., & Rollo, J. M. (2007). The crisis matrix. In E. L. Zdziarski, N. W. Dunkel, & J. M. Rollo (Eds.), *Campus crisis management: A comprehensive guide to planning prevention, response and recovery* (pp. 35–51). San Francisco: Jossey-Bass.

MANAGING THE FIRST JOB SEARCH PROCESS

CHAPTER TEN

Brent G. Paterson and Christa Coffey

The first major job search can be exhilarating, a climax to the successful completion of a graduate program and recognition that you have made it. It can also be scary, exhausting, and harmful to the checking account. In writing this chapter, we offer our joint experiences with job searches: as candidates, as employers, as members and chairs of NASPA Career Services and The Placement Exchange, and as faculty in master's degree programs in student affairs.

We have focused our thoughts on those who are conducting their first major job search. Many paths into the field do not require a degree in student affairs. We have found, however, that most people experience similar issues in conducting a job search, regardless of the path they take.

Competencies

The first stage of the job search involves knowing yourself—identifying your strengths, weaknesses, and values. Investing time and effort in this process will help you find a position that suits you.

As a starting point, we suggest that you review *Skills Analysis Survey for Graduate Students in Higher Education and Student Affairs Graduate Preparation Programs* (Cooper et al., 2002). The survey will help you determine your current and desired ability level for a variety of important competencies. Before the beginning of the second year of your graduate program, identify—perhaps with the help of a supervisor—your strengths and weaknesses in terms of skills and abilities. Understanding the areas in which you need improvement will enable you to focus on these areas; analyzing your strengths will allow you to search for positions that will maximize those abilities and help you sell yourself to potential employers. Matching the competencies you possess with the requirements of a position is one aspect of finding "fit," which leads to decreased job stress and increased job satisfaction.

> Many soon-to-be new professionals do not realize how different the environment can be from one institution to the next, and how important it is to think about professional values.

Most of the competencies essential for entry-level student affairs work should come as no surprise. As a helping profession, we need "people skills." These include skills in creating interpersonal relationships, communication (both verbal and written), and advising and counseling, along with the ability to work with people of diverse backgrounds. Organizational and administrative skills, including program development and budgeting, are also helpful for entry-level practitioners.

In addition, each functional area requires certain competencies or levels of competence. Many skills are transferable not only among functional areas in student affairs but also between positions inside and outside the field. To determine what competencies are essential for the areas you are interested in, refer to the professional associations that specialize in those areas (e.g., Association of Fraternity Advisors) and speak with colleagues who work in those areas.

We also suggest that you review the document *Professional Competencies*, published by the American College Personnel Association (ACPA, 2007). This document lists competencies for student affairs professionals in the areas of advising and helping; assessment, evaluation, and research; ethics; leadership administration and management; legal foundations; pluralism and inclusion; student learning and development; and teaching. Within each area, the competencies are grouped by proficiency level: basic, intermediate, and advanced.

Once you understand the competencies essential for entry-level work, you must be creative in connecting the competencies you possess to those the hiring entity seeks. For example, if you have experience advising student organizations, you should be able to connect that experience to a position that will include providing financial aid counseling to students. If you need help making these connections, ask a supervisor or mentor to assist you.

Values

If you are in your final quarter or semester of graduate school, or looking for your first position, it can be nerve-wracking to have no idea where you will be living or what you will be doing in six months. But even if you find yourself in a "desperate" situation, do not accept just any position just because it was offered. You will have a better experience, one in which you can grow professionally, if you accept a job in which your values match those of the institution, department, and supervisor. This is the other part of fit—the part that goes beyond ensuring a match between your competencies and the job responsibilities. This part of fit matches your personality and preferences with those of the organization, institution, and supervisor.

> *Don't waste time on institutions that will be a bad fit or in areas that you don't like. If you do the work right and have the patience to support it, you can find the place you really want to work.* —Marite; medium-sized, public, land-grant institution

Many soon-to-be new professionals do not realize how different the environment can be from one institution to the next, and how important it is to think about professional values. Institutions and departments differ in what they value, perhaps because of who funds them or the influence of their leaders. For example, some institutions are organized to provide staff-driven programming for students, while others provide student-driven programming. Imagine your ideal institution and department. What values would it have (e.g., regarding student development and staff)? What is your advising style in working with students? What is the advising style of the department or institution in which you have an interest? What values and management style would your ideal supervisor have, and how do these line up with those of your potential supervisor?

Make sure you pay very close attention to the climate of the department/division you're interviewing with, and ask a lot of questions to try to figure out if the mission, vision, and goals of the department/division match your own. —Anna, coordinator of new student orientation, former residence hall director, regional university

While your values and the values of the institution, department, and supervisor may not match perfectly, it is important that you do not feel as though you are compromising your personal student affairs values in the execution of your responsibilities.

Types of Positions

The field of student affairs offers a variety of ways to work with and for college students. They are typically grouped by functional areas, which can be found via the search categories of the two major placement conferences and websites (see the section below on "Finding Available Positions"). While the wording may differ slightly from one placement entity to another, candidates can generally search for the following types of positions: adult learner and commuter student services; career services; counseling; Greek affairs; housing and residential life; judicial affairs; gay, lesbian, bisexual, and transgender (GLBT) services; leadership development; multicultural affairs; orientation and new student programs; service learning and volunteerism; student activities and student union; and wellness and alcohol/drug education. For additional information on the history, purpose, role, function, and even entry-level qualifications for most of these functional areas, review *Rentz's Student Affairs Practice in Higher Education* (MacKinnon, 2004).

While these are the most common functional areas in student affairs, the distribution of positions is uneven. At least for the two major placement conferences (see below), housing and residential life positions typically outnumber the combined total of all other positions, comprising 50% to 60% of positions. The next largest category has traditionally been student activities and student union, comprising approximately 15% of total positions.

Types of Institutions

A common question from jobseekers is "Does it matter at what type of institution I work?" The simple answer is that it does not matter as long as you are comfortable at that institution. But be aware that institutions of the same type may not be similar places.

Your graduate program should expose you to student affairs work at different types of institutions. Student affairs faculty members often encourage students to complete a practicum at a different kind of college or university from their undergraduate or graduate school. For example, if you are attending a public university, you might be surprised to find that you like the student affairs work environment at a community college or a religiously affiliated liberal arts college.

In *Where You Work Matters* (Hirt, 2006), Joan Hirt describes student affairs work at different types of institutions: liberal arts colleges, religiously affiliated institutions, comprehensive institutions, research universities, historically black colleges and universities (HBCUs), community colleges, and Hispanic-serving institutions (HSIs). Hirt's characterization of student affairs workers at different types of institutions provides helpful insights for anyone who is considering a position at one of these kinds of institutions. For each type of institution, Hirt describes the professional life of a student affairs staff member in terms of the nature of the work environment, the nature of relationships, and the nature of rewards.

Hirt calls student affairs staff at liberal arts colleges "standard bearers." She says they "believe in working closely with students to encourage development across a broad array of realms" (2006, p.19). They have a holistic approach to their work that closely follows the philosophy of student affairs. She calls staff members at religiously affiliated institutions "interpreters," because they spend their time and energy "interpreting their personal faith in light of their professional responsibilities and interpreting their professional responsibilities in light of their personal faith" (p. 40). Hirt views student affairs staff at comprehensive colleges as "generalists" and those at research universities as "specialists." At the latter type institution, expertise in one functional area is common and relationships tend to be intradepartmental (p.197). Hirt says student affairs staff at HBCUs view themselves as surrogate family for their students (p. 109). At HSIs, change is a way of life, and staff deal with changes in their institutions (academic, programmatic, cultural, and administrative); the changes engaged students' experiences; and the change in how they view themselves as a result of working at an HSI (pp. 159–160). Hirt refers to these staff members as "guardians." Finally, Hirt views student affairs staff members at community colleges as "producers," who provide high-quality services for a diverse population of students with fewer staff than other institutions typically have (p. 136).

We encourage you to explore other institutional types and student affairs work environments in Hirt's book.

Size of Institution

Does institution size really matter? The size of the institution does make a difference in the work environment, job duties, and how you will interact with students. Size often correlates with type of institution. For example, small institutions (fewer than 2,500 students) tend to be private, religiously affiliated liberal arts colleges; whereas institutions with enrollments greater than 20,000 are often public research universities.

Student affairs professionals at small institutions are frequently generalists with responsibilities in more than one area. For example, a staff member may be a hall director and director of student activities. Because there are fewer layers in the student affairs organization at a small institution, a new professional may hold the title of director or associate dean. In addition to titles, small colleges may offer other perks not found at larger universities including the possibility to build closer relationships with faculty and senior administrators because of the flattened hierarchy or to teach an undergraduate course from time to time.

By contrast, student affairs professionals at large universities are specialists. They have very specific duties and usually have limited interactions with students. The staff member who is responsible for student conduct may never encounter a particular student in another setting. The size and decentralized nature of the student affairs division at a large university also means that student affairs staff members may have limited interactions with each other and with other units on campus. At times, student affairs professionals at large universities may feel as though they deal with numbers rather than students.

Location of Institution

Geographic location may be an important factor to some job seekers. Location is more than just climate; it may include the culture of an area. It is easier to adapt to a new culture in some communities than in others. Community values and beliefs about issues such as religion, race, politics, and the environment may affect whether or not you would be comfortable living and working in that community.

Some job seekers are geographically bound by reasons such as the spouse's/ partner's employment or schooling, or family responsibilities. Or they may simply want to stay in a certain area. If you are in this category, you might be limiting your job opportunities and career advancement. Many people happily and successfully spend their entire career at the institution from which they graduate; however, there is a hiring bias toward student affairs professionals who have experience at more than one institution. Innovation and creativity are valued traits in student affairs professionals; if you have worked at only one institution, the assumption will be that you know only one approach to student affairs work.

The size of the community also has implications for the job search. An urban community may offer endless social and entertainment opportunities, but the cost of living (e.g., housing, transportation, food, and utilities) may be high. It may be cheaper to live in a rural setting, but shopping and social and entertainment opportunities may be limited. Living in an urban setting allows a greater measure of anonymity for the student affairs professional; in a rural community, the interplay between the institution and the community may appear seamless, and it may be hard to get away from students. Suburban institutions sometimes have the best of both worlds.

Career Goals

Although high aspirations can be motivating, we suggest that you establish realistic career goals for the near future (the next 5 to 10 years) and reevaluate them periodically. The general rule of thumb is that a person should stay in his or her first professional position for approximately three years. After three years in an entry-level position, you should consider moving into a more responsible position or transitioning into another functional area of student affairs.

New professionals are often concerned about being pigeonholed in one area of student affairs. If you seek opportunities to gain knowledge and skills in areas outside your primary responsibilities, you will have little difficulty selling your transferable skills when you apply for a position in another area of student affairs. If you work in housing but want to move into programming, find opportunities to do programming for your hall or the campus residence hall community. Co-program with the campus programming board. Volunteer to help with a campus program. The number of ways to build your skills and gain experience is limited only by your imagination.

Finding Available Positions

You can search for positions in various ways. Through technology advancements, most search methods are online, which allows you to search at any time and from anywhere.

Professional Associations

NASPA and ACPA each offer two methods candidates can use to look for jobs. The first is the online job board, which allows candidates to search for positions and post résumés free of charge. The second method is used by many aspiring entry-level professionals: the placement conference connected to the annual national convention. Both associations typically hold their conferences in March or April, so this avenue is very popular for candidates who wish to start working in the summer or early fall. Especially if you are not limiting yourself to a specific geographic or functional area (e.g., admissions and enrollment), you will probably benefit from attending a placement conference.

> During my four days at Placement I had 19 first round interviews, 6 second round interviews, got invited to 5 socials and went to 3 of them, interviewed with 43 different professionals, wrote countless thank you notes, and came back with around 40 pounds of folders stuffed with every possible variety of schools. (Pick Me-Choose Me-Hire Me, 2007)

Professional associations that specialize in a functional area of student affairs—such as academic advising, admissions and enrollment, or career services—may have their own online job boards or conference placement services. These services can be especially helpful if you know you want to work in a certain area. We encourage you to review the positions listed with the specialized professional associations, even if the functional area you prefer (e.g., Greek affairs) is one of the major search categories of the NASPA and ACPA processes.

Other Sources of Job Information

In addition to those sponsored by NASPA, ACPA, and other professional associations, online services exist for student affairs and higher education job searches (including faculty positions). These services generally offer more specific functional area search capabilities than the professional association services do, and several include search functions for city, state, institution, and institution type (including community colleges). You can find online job boards by searching for "student affairs" and "jobs" in your favorite Internet search engine.

Some hardcopy publications, including *The Chronicle of Higher Education*, include job listings; however, most companies and organizations have moved to online listings, either exclusively or to supplement hardcopy publications. Online listings are typically updated immediately, so we suggest that you use them.

Institutional Websites

If you are looking to work in a certain city or at a specific institution, the most effective approach is probably the institutional website, as most institutions require that positions be posted through their human resources (HR) department. For a list of higher education institutions and links to their HR websites, go to www.academic360.com.

The challenge in searching for positions on some HR websites is that the descriptions are limited and you may not be able to distinguish among them, especially if the department or office is not listed. For example, you might see five "coordinator" positions listed on the HR website, but if the department or office is not listed, you'll have to figure out if it is a student affairs coordinator or a library coordinator. We suggest that you also check the websites of the student affairs division and the department or office related to your functional areas of interest. If these sites have job listings, they will generally be more descriptive than the ones posted by HR.

Networking

In the business world, many job searchers find positions through networking; student affairs is no different. The profession is a small one—not in the numeric sense but in "degrees of separation"—so networking is a powerful means of searching. Networking is especially helpful if you are in graduate school. Your faculty members, assistantship and practicum supervisors, and undergraduate and graduate school mentors have professional colleagues at institutions around the world. Let them know when you begin your job search, and tell them what you are interested in, including geographic and functional areas. As you apply and interview for jobs, keep them informed of your progress. If you have developed strong relationships with these people during graduate school, they will be more than willing to tell you about potential opportunities, introduce you to colleagues at other institutions, and put in a good word to potential employers.

Application

The great challenge in applying for a position at an institution of higher education is that there are almost as many processes as there are institutions. While almost all institutions require that an application be submitted to the HR department at some point, the timing differs from institution to institution. For example, some institutional HR policies require that a potential candidate submit an application before the hiring unit can make any kind of contact with the candidate. Some policies allow the hiring unit to have a few informal conversations before the candidate submits an application. Still others allow the hiring unit to conduct a few interviews (such as at a placement conference) before requiring an application.

Many institutions use an online application process through the HR website. Even if you gave the interviewer at a placement conference a letter of interest, a résumé, and references, the institution may require you to complete the online application process. This may also be true if you sent information directly to the student affairs department.

Résumé

Student affairs allows for some creativity in how you present yourself through cover letters and résumés. There is nothing wrong with creating your own style, as long as it is professional, organized, easy to read, and consistent.

The purpose of a résumé is to help you obtain an interview, not to describe every experience or skill you have. Employers who are conducting a search—whether at a placement conference or through the institution's HR process—typically receive a large number of applications. In the early part of the process, when they weed out applicants, they typically do not read each résumé in depth. Therefore, especially for entry-level positions, it is best to limit your résumé to two or three pages plus a reference page (discussed below).

Employers are always busy. Use formatting (e.g., bold, different font sizes, and underlining) to draw their attention to specific words, sections, or phrases to ensure that they extract the most important information from your résumé as easily as possible. People read left to right and top to bottom, so place the most important information in the upper left quadrant of the page and in the upper left portion of each section of the résumé (e.g., education, student affairs experience, certification).

You will always need to have a generic résumé, but you should tailor your résumé to each position—or, at the very least, to each functional area—of interest. Many student affairs competencies are transferable, but, for example, some of the skills needed by a Greek advisor are different from those needed by a residence hall director or judicial officer. Organize your résumé to highlight the skills, knowledge, and experience needed in the specific position as explained in its job description. Quantify and use specifics whenever you can—numbers look great. For example, instead of saying that you have budgeting experience, say that you managed a $20,000 budget.

We cannot stress enough the importance of a grammatically correct and error-free résumé. Some employers see a mistake as a lack of attention to detail or even a lack of interest in the position, and will not consider your résumé, despite your qualifications. Ask several people, including at least one professional who coordinates hiring in your functional area of interest, to review your résumé (including content and formatting) and provide you with feedback.

Finally, print your résumé on paper that copies well. Whether you are at a placement conference or an on-campus interview, the employer may make copies of your résumé for an interview team. You want to make sure the copy will be clear. Experiment on a copy machine before you decide what kind of paper to use.

Cover Letter

A typical cover letter is three to five paragraphs and not more than one page. It should be consistent (in font, formatting, header, and paper) with your résumé. It may include the following information: the position for which you are applying, how you learned of the position, why you are interested, why you think you are qualified, what you think you can bring to the position, experiences that are relevant to the position, your current position and significant job responsibilities, contact information, and a request to discuss the position and your qualifications. As you did with your résumé, tailor each letter, highlighting the competencies and experiences that will help you obtain an interview for the specific position. The cover letter is your first chance to explain things in your résumé in more detail, including, for example, time gaps between positions held and information related to the position requirements and your qualifications.

Try to avoid addressing a letter "To whom it may concern" or "Dear Sir or Madam." If you don't know the name of the person to whom you should address the letter, call the department or office in which the position resides and get the name. If you are not able to secure a name that way, address your letter to a specific person in an upper-level position.

References

An infrequently discussed facet of the job search is the selection of references. Your references could be the tipping point in your ability to secure an interview, which is why we suggest that you include a list of references as the last page of your résumé, rather than stating that references are "available upon request."

You will need three to five references. If you are about to complete or have completed a student affairs graduate program, your list should include one or two student affairs supervisors (graduate assistant or practicum/internship); ideally, one of these will be your current supervisor. You will also want to include one or two faculty members. Finally, consider using a student with whom you have worked in an advising/mentoring role. This combination of references allows you to showcase a variety of perspectives on your experience and talents.

How do you decide which individuals to select? Create a list of professional staff, faculty, students, and non-student-affairs contacts with whom you have worked. Then select three to five people who have had the opportunity to observe your strengths and abilities over a period of time (at least one quarter or semester) and who can speak about them in depth. Including a "big name" professional on your reference list can help you secure an interview, but if the person does not have a close relationship with you, he or she may not be able to sell you over another candidate. In the long run, using someone who knows your skills and talents is a lot more helpful in securing a position.

If you are entering the field from outside the graduate school track or you do not have student affairs graduate connections, we suggest selecting references who can talk about the skills and experiences you have that would be transferable to the position. Depending on the amount of time that has passed since your undergraduate career, you might also consider using a reference related to collegiate involvement (e.g., resident assistant or orientation leader).

After you have selected the people you want as references, ask each person if he or she is willing to serve in that role. If they agree, provide them with information about yourself and your search, including a copy of your résumé, and keep them informed of your progress—including the positions for which you have applied, where you are in the process, and your level of interest in each.

Keep in mind that people who are not your "official" references can serve in an unofficial capacity, especially at professional conferences. Make sure your mentors, colleagues, program faculty, and peers know about your interests. These people can connect you to potential job opportunities.

Interview Types

Placement Conference

Interviewing at a placement conference is a unique experience; one that requires great patience, energy, and stress management skills. Placement conference interviewing can be overwhelming, but it is popular because of the potential to meet with a number of institutions in one location.

Placement conferences may differ in minor procedural matters, but most schedule interviews in a similar way. The scheduling process begins when you receive written verification (if you requested the interview) or a written request to schedule an interview from an employer who identifies you from the placement registry you have completed. Upon receipt of that note, you contact the placement conference staff to set a time to meet with the employer.

Interviews are typically scheduled in 30-minute blocks; some employers may invite you back for a second, hour-long interview, which may occur on the same day or later in the placement conference. We strongly encourage you not to schedule back-to-back interviews, in case the first one runs long. Always leave at least a 30-minute block between interviews. This will ensure that you are never late to an interview and will give you time to collect your thoughts after one interview and relax before the next one.

While the setup varies somewhat from one location to another and from one association to another, the concept is similar: Several hundred tables are placed in the convention facility, very close to each other on all sides. During your interview for a position, other interviews will be going on simultaneously at tables all around you—the facility can get very noisy. Because of this setup, and because candidates and employers are constantly walking up and down the narrow aisles between the rows of tables, you have to work hard to maintain your concentration and eye contact during the interview.

You may have several interviews in one day. No matter how tired you are of talking and interviewing, you must stay enthusiastic. Even if you are asked the same question over and over again, you must act as if it is the first time. The employer will perceive a lack of enthusiasm as a lack of interest in the position.

Telephone Interview

The telephone interview is common in student affairs. Typically, hiring entities use it to narrow the field of candidates and determine who will continue to the next step in the process, which may be a campus interview. These calls are also a great follow-up to interviews held at placement conferences, because they allow the hiring entity to involve a number of interviewers, perhaps the entire hiring committee.

If you are invited to participate in a phone interview, find a quiet area where you will not be disturbed. Do not use a mobile phone, as reception is not generally as clear as on a landline, and you do not want any distractions or obstacles to the interviewers hearing your responses clearly. During the introductions, it may be helpful to write down the name and position of each interviewer, so you can make personal connections with people during the conversation. You might also have notes and other references in front of you, as if you were taking an open-book test.

Campus Interview

Typically, when the hiring entity has narrowed the search to three to five candidates, it offers them on-campus interviews. This interview gives you the opportunity to experience the campus and department or office environment personally. Entry-level interviews are typically five to eight hours long over the course of a day; you meet and interview potential coworkers, student affairs division colleagues, students, and the supervisor. It is very strenuous to be interviewed all day, especially if you traveled far to get to campus, so do whatever you can to keep your energy level up (e.g., eat little snacks, drink water, walk around on breaks). Remember, no matter how many times you are asked the same question, act as though it is the first time you have heard it.

Preparation

Regardless of the type of interview, it is important to be prepared. Lack of preparation is obvious to the interviewer, who may think you are not really interested in the position and may, therefore, not want to continue the process with you.

Preparation for interviewing begins with knowing who you are (i.e., your strengths, weaknesses, values, and student affairs philosophy) as discussed earlier in this chapter. Think about your experiences, the skills required for the position, and specific situations you have encountered. Think about why you are interested in working at that type of institution and within that functional area. If you have not thought about these things, you will not be able to answer the inevitable questions. Ask your professors and supervisors for a list of typical questions, and look for them on professional association placement websites. Practice your responses.

Not only do you need to prepare answers for questions you might be asked, you also need to make a list of questions to ask the potential employer. Employers expect and appreciate these questions. What do you want to know about the position, department or office, and institution that will help you decide if it is the best fit for you? This part of the process is very important; after all, you are interviewing them as much as they are interviewing you. Typically, the interviewer will ask if you have any questions. In 30-minute placement conference interviews, you will probably receive 5 to 10 minutes for questions. You will not be able to ask all your questions in this short amount of time, so group them into several sets, starting with the most important ones. If you progress to additional interviews with the same employer, you can proceed down your list of questions, each of which delves deeper into employment issues.

Be patient. The search process takes time.

We are often asked when it is appropriate to talk about salary. Everyone has an opinion on this topic; generally, you should not ask about salary in your first interview with a prospective employer. The HR or department/office website may specify the salary in the job posting or description. If it does not, try to hold out as long as you can before asking, as employers usually bring up salary issues on their own, typically after a few meetings with the candidate. If it still hasn't come up, ask before you accept an invitation for a campus interview.

In addition to general preparation, you should prepare specifically for the position by reviewing the institutional, divisional, and departmental or office websites. This task is difficult at placement conferences because of the quick turnaround and the number of interviews in a short time. If you are attending a placement conference, set up some interviews before you get there. That way, you can do this research in advance, thus freeing up some onsite research time and building in some flexibility to add new interviews onsite.

Preparation is not complete without practice. Mock interviews will give you the experience of the interviewing environment, the opportunity to practice providing answers on the spot, a chance to determine how to sit comfortably yet professionally, and the opportunity to receive immediate feedback. Most mentors, supervisors, and professional staff in your functional areas of interest will be happy to do mock interviews with you. The career center on your campus might also offer interview practice sessions.

Follow-up

Immediately after an interview, take a few moments to reflect on it. Write some notes or impressions of the interview, including the position and institution, interviewers' names, and discussion points. At a placement conference—where you will meet many employers in a short time—these notes will be crucial for helping you remember each interview later.

The next step is the thank you. The choice of e-mail or handwritten note is still highly debated in the profession. A general rule of thumb is to send the note using the method by which the employer has conducted most communication with you. When in doubt, send a handwritten note.

Regardless of the method, always be gracious, whether or not you are interested in the position. Send a thank you note within 24 hours to the person or persons with whom you interviewed by telephone or on campus; at a placement conference, the thank you note should be sent within hours of the interview. Be sure to spell the name of the institution and the interviewer correctly. If you decide that you are not interested in the position, a simple thank you and a statement that you are no longer interested is sufficient (Placement Exchange, 2008). If you are sincerely interested in the position after an interview, your thank you note should express your appreciation for the interview; reiterate your interest in the institution and the position; note how your education, experience, and interest align with what the institution is seeking; and suggest some references who can speak of your qualifications for the position (The Placement Exchange, 2008).

The interviewing process does not end with the formal interview at a placement conference or scheduled meetings during a campus interview. You are being observed and evaluated throughout the placement conference and throughout the time you are visiting the campus. The way you interact with interviewers before and after the formal interview, and your behavior in general are being evaluated.

Be patient. The search process takes time. Different institutions and even different departments within institutions operate at a different pace. University calendars, commitments of search committee members, and availability of candidates all contribute to delays in hiring decisions. In addition, some institutions may require departments to seek approval from the HR or affirmative action office before they can offer a position. Sometimes a department is waiting for budget approval. It is appropriate to check with your contact at an institution about the status of your candidacy, but don't be a pest. As a general rule, contact the institution if you haven't heard anything in three weeks, unless you have been given a specific date or time frame by which you will be informed. Don't panic. In the end, you are very likely to find a position that you like.

> It would have been easy to jump on the first good fit that came along, but I had my heart set on a position. I stretched everyone's patience a little bit, but in the end I got what I wanted. (In Medias Res, 2007)

Evaluating an Offer

You receive a job offer from the institution of your dreams in a progressive department with a caring supervisor. What could be better? But before you say "yes," there are some practical things to consider. Assuming that housing is not provided, what is the cost of living in the city or town where the institution is located? A salary might sound great until you discover the cost of living in the area. (Salary comparison and cost of living sites are available on the Internet.) Also, consider the benefits package at the institution. What type of health insurance coverage is provided? Can you take free classes at the institution? What are the retirement benefits, and how long must you stay to be vested in the institution's contributions? What are the parking fees? Will you receive special rates on athletic tickets or tickets to entertainment on campus? Are funds available for traveling to professional conferences? Will your moving expenses be covered?

For entry-level positions, salaries often are not negotiable. Because an institution may be hiring several persons for entry-level positions with similar requirements for education and experience, salaries must be consistent. Also, supervisors are leery of offering a new hire a higher salary than that of someone who is already employed in a similar position. However, there may be some flexibility with perks. The institution may help with moving expenses or put you on payroll earlier to provide additional income. It may arrange for housing at a reasonable price in property owned by the institution. It may provide temporary housing until you find permanent living arrangements. It may be willing to provide additional funds for travel to conferences. Be creative in asking for perks, and note that a private institution likely will have more flexibility in this area. However, do not make a final decision on accepting a position based solely on perks.

You may receive an offer from an institution that is not your top choice. The institution may want an answer in 48 hours. What do you do? It is reasonable to ask for an extension. Institutions know that you probably have interviewed with more than one institution and usually are willing to grant a few more days. Contact your first choice institution and explain that you have an offer from another institution but you are still very interested and would appreciate knowing the expected time frame for them to make a hiring decision. Chances are, they will give you an honest answer concerning when you might hear about the position. If you are not being seriously considered, they will probably tell you.

But what if your first choice institution will not be making its decision for another two weeks? Do you accept the offer you have or turn it down and wait to hear from your first choice? The timing may make a difference. If it's April and you are still a serious candidate for several other positions, turning the offer down might be the right thing to do if you are not excited about the institution, the department, or the position. If it's July and you are not a candidate at other institutions, you should probably consider taking the offer, assuming the fit is strong enough.

Financial Issues

Searching for a job has financial implications. Be sure to save money for the semester in which you will be interviewing. You will need money for clothing, travel to placement conferences and interviews, moving expenses, and temporary housing. As a graduate student, you probably have a closet full of casual clothes, but you may not have suitable clothing for interviewing. Be prepared to buy some professional clothing.

Institutions handle travel arrangements for campus interviews differently. Some institutions make the arrangements and pay for your flights and hotel; some require you to pay for everything. Some institutions reimburse you for travel within institutional or state guidelines, possibly depending on whether you are offered a position and accept it. If you are interviewing at more than one institution over a three- or four-week period, your credit card may reach its limit while you are waiting for reimbursement. Even after you submit receipts, it often takes three or four weeks to receive a check from an institution. If finances are a concern, ask the potential employer how travel arrangements are paid.

The good news about being a poor graduate student is that you likely do not have a lot of furniture and belongings to move; the bad news is that it is still expensive to move. Unless you can fit everything you own into your vehicle, you will probably have to rent a moving trailer or truck to transport your belongings to the new location. Along the way, you will have fuel, food, and lodging costs. You may also have the cost of temporary housing, either in your current location or in the new community. Remember that moving also means deposits for an apartment, utilities, phone, cable, and so on. Rarely do you graduate and start your new job the next week. Many entry-level positions have start dates tied to the opening of residence halls, the start of the fall semester, or the beginning of a new fiscal year. You will need funds to make it through this transition period.

Finding Balance

Searching for a job can be very stressful. You may be finishing graduate work, leaving the comfort of a familiar institution, leaving friends, perhaps moving a spouse or partner or family, and heading off into the unknown. The search process is like a marathon; you need to pace yourself. There will be excitement one day and disappointment the next, and this pattern will be repeated throughout the process. You can do many things to prepare yourself for each step of the process, but it takes commitment to focus on a job search and not neglect yourself, those around you, or your responsibilities to work, school, and family.

Remember that you are still a graduate student. If you are in a student-affairs-orientated master's program, your faculty will understand that you will be interviewing in spring semester, but they will still expect you to attend class and complete assignments on time. Missing one class for an interview might be acceptable, but missing several classes in March and April (typical interview season) is unacceptable. Your graduate assistant supervisor will have similar expectations—you are still an employee with a job to do. All graduate assistants cannot be away from campus at the same time; someone has to be there to run the residence halls, implement programs, and provide services.

Pay attention to your family and friends. It is easy to become so wrapped up in your own situation that you forget about those who care about you. Find time to spend with family and friends. They are your support system, and you will likely need them as you face some difficult decisions during the search process.

Finally, take care of yourself—get enough sleep, eat right, and exercise regularly. This is easier said than done, but it has been proven over and over that regular exercise and a proper diet help reduce stress and lead to better sleep.

Other Search Issues

Disabilities

If you require an accommodation (e.g., captioning or wheelchair accessibility) during the interview or search process, do not hesitate to request assistance. For example, if you have a hearing impairment, placement conference interviewing may be a challenge because of the physical setup. Any reputable placement service will provide accommodation (e.g., a sign language interpreter or a different location for interviews) and should help you contact the employers with whom you are interviewing to communicate the details of the accommodation. If you are attending a placement conference or a campus interview, touch base with the staff or hiring entity in advance to explain your requests and ensure that your accommodation will be in place (C. Donahue, personal communication, September 10, 2008).

Gay, Lesbian, Bisexual, Transgender

For a candidate who identifies as gay, lesbian, bisexual, or transgender, environmental fit is especially important. You may want to determine whether the institution has nondiscrimination statements and policies that mention sexual orientation or gender identity, along with domestic partner benefits. You will also have to decide if and when to come out (e.g., during the interview or after you are in the position). This is also something you will need to consider and really depends on your comfort level in doing so.

Dual Career

Dual career couples are not uncommon in student affairs and other professions, but it does complicate the job search. Dual career couples face all the challenges and pressures of individuals involved in a job search, plus some additional challenges, including "whether, when, and how to reveal to prospective employers that your spouse [or partner] is also looking for a job; deciding whether (and for how long) you and your spouse [or partner] are willing to live apart for the sake of one or both careers; and even choosing how you (as a couple) will make choices" (Science Education Resource Center, n.d.).

The first step in determining your job search strategy is to identify what you value most in your life (e.g., family time, income, location) and what aspects of your job (e.g., salary, title, responsibilities, career opportunities) are most important. You should complete this step individually and then as a couple (University of Michigan, n.d.). Next, discuss possible models for dual careers: one primary career with a "trailing spouse" or partner, taking turns at beneficial career moves, two careers of equal importance, or "linking career decisions to the time line of the primary caretaker of children" (University of Michigan, n.d.).

> Not only did we talk openly about our frustrations and disappointments...we also had to develop a willingness to explain our parameters or limitations to each other. (Gardner & Woodsmall, 2004, p. 48)

Many institutions have departments or contract with firms to assist with relocation of dual career couples, but you really need to take charge of your own search. It is highly unlikely that you will find two dream jobs in the same geographic location. If you are conducting two job searches simultaneously, one person may receive an offer of a position while the other partner has no leads in that area.

Conclusion

Each year, hundreds of soon-to-be new professionals enter the job market, eager for their first interviews and the prospect of finding the job of their dreams. The job search process requires dedication and patience, as well as a sense of humor. Remember that many people have followed a similar process as they began their student affairs career. If you have prepared properly, you will be successful. And so your student affairs career begins.

References

American College Personnel Association (ACPA) Steering Committee on Professional Competencies. (2007). *Professional competencies.* Washington, DC: ACPA.

Cooper, D. L., Saunders, S. A., Winston, R. B., Jr., Hirt, J. B., Creamer, D. G., & Janosik, S. M. (2002). *Learning through supervised practice in student affairs.* New York: Routledge.

Gardner, K. & Woodsmall, C. (2004). The art of compromise and other secrets of the dual career job search. In P. M. Magola & J. S. Carnaghi (Eds.), *Job one*. Lanham, MD: University Press of America.

Hirt, J. B. (2006). *Where you work maters: Student affairs administration at different types of institutions*. Lanham, MD: University Press of America.

In Medias Res. (2007, May 26). All's well [msg. 26]. Message posted to http://studentaffairscom3.blogspot.com.

MacKinnon, F. (Ed.). (2004). Rentz's *Student affairs practice in higher education* (3rd ed.). Springfield, IL: Charles C. Thomas Publisher, Ltd.

Pick Me-Choose Me-Hire Me. (2007, April 9). Whirlwind adventure! [msg. 16]. Message posted to http://studentaffairscom3.blogspot.com.

Science Education Resource Center. (n.d.). Dual career couples: Preparing for academic careers in the geosciences. In *On the cutting edge—Professional development for geoscience faculty*. Retrieved September 6, 2008, from, http://serc.carleton.edu/NAGTWorkshops/careerprep/jobsearch/dualcareer.html.

The Placement Exchange. (2008). Candidate "how-to." Retrieved August 4, 2008, from, www.theplacementexchange.org/candidates/index.cfm.

University of Michigan Human Resources. (n.d.) Dual career couples and the job search. Retrieved December 30, 2008, from, http://www.hr.umich.edu/empserv/dual/DualCareerTips.pdf.

WORDS OF WISDOM

CHAPTER ELEVEN

Shannon E. Ellis

Y ou have chosen well. It does not matter whether you fell into the student affairs profession by accident or have methodically studied and planned your career. The exemplary senior student affairs officers who contributed their perspectives to this chapter have shaped successful careers from both origins. They would all concur with Cheo Torres, vice president for student affairs at the University of New Mexico, who has pursued a career both in and out of higher education. "All the years I have worked in student services have been the best years of my life."

Each senior administrator would agree that you are destined for a life full of fascinating people, provocative problems, global exploration, instigating change, deep sadness and high elation—all because you have the daily capacity to create a better world. We are fortunate to have found a career that offers such challenges and satisfaction. Our wisdom is intended to help you be the best you can be at the start of and throughout your career. We hope it will make your journey to becoming an exemplary student affairs professional all the more enjoyable and rewarding.

As you begin your career, we encourage you to start "where you are." You don't know everything and should continue to explore new information and different ways of thinking. In the beginning, you are likely to focus on what you don't know, but you'll see progress as you read, observe, reflect, and practice. As we share advice, remember that we are practitioners who have been doing this and learning, most of us for more than 30 years. We started with the same passion you have for helping students. Our objective is to help you coordinate your love of college students with strong organizational, administrative, and communication skills. As you practice the wisdom we share here, you will work with greater skill, effectiveness, confidence, and enthusiasm.

Be Values-Driven

This is a values-centered profession. "Knowing your values is a significant tool in becoming the professional you aspire to be," says Ed Whipple, vice president student affairs at Bowling Green State University. "It is never too early to start answering the question of where you want to go and how you can get there." Values are an important barometer for personal career paths as well as professional decisions. If you know what's important to you, you'll know your parameters and priorities. Rob Kelly, vice president for student development at Seattle University, says, "Your own values and beliefs will be tested throughout your career. Finding out what you believe in from time to time is a lifelong skill that will serve you well in providing direction on the journey." What to do when personal values and institutional values do not align? Larry Moneta, vice president of student affairs at Duke University, says, "Don't sacrifice your values, but don't stand on ceremony. Issues of institutional preference trump *your* preference. Try to fit."

Maintain Perspective

Kelly says, "Often, as a new professional, the smallest issue can seem like the biggest thing." Perspective colors how people look at a situation and their ability to handle it in the best way. Kelly warns, "Don't make any major decisions until you can really sit back and look at the situation." It's not uncommon for new professionals to take everything too seriously. Moneta says, "Stop taking yourself so seriously. If you haven't laughed during some part of each day, you've wasted the day. And make sure you go home for dinner."

As a new professional, "You want to develop a wider perspective on how things work," advises Deneece Huftalin, vice president of student services at Salt Lake Community College. This is the reason Whipple tells new professionals to "be involved in bigger campus initiatives, ask to be appointed to institution-wide committees, and volunteer for different opportunities." Moneta urges new professionals to be conversant on what is happening in the world as well as in our field and in higher education. "I'm a firm believer that smart people do very well. One indicator of this is to be conversant in world events."

Find Storytellers, Effectors, and Mentors

Campus storytellers provide the context and history to educate a new person quickly. "You'll learn the nuances of a place and how to get things done," Kelly says. Huftalin urges new professionals to identify the "effectors" at their institution: "Campus effectors are the people who get things done." Moneta warns against staying "nested": "A successful student affairs professional is multilingual. They listen to and talk with a cadre of folks, from the parking guard and mail carriers to parents and alumni."

Mentors focus on your success and provide you with opportunities to learn and grow by doing and observing. Les Cook, vice president for student affairs at Michigan Technological University, always looks for the "trusted sage" on campus. "They have your best interests in mind," he says. Huftalin looks for mentors on and off campus, in and out of student affairs: "Try to work for amazing supervisors. I've worked for some passionate, smart, and engaging people. They were not only great mentors but became good friends." Whipple encourages new professionals to spend time with the senior student affairs officer on campus: "If you ask, they'll help you identify your strengths and weaknesses, and advise you how to become the professional you want to become."

> Campus storytellers provide the context and history to educate a new person quickly.

Commit Yourself and Work Hard

Loving what you do for a living is a great way to spend your life. Don't shrink from the joy you find in pursuing your craft because other people do not feel the same way. There is no greater feeling than the flow of a productive work day, where aspirations are high and achievements are realized. The "good tired" that one feels at the end of such a day is the result of personal satisfaction in a job well done. While it is always nice to be recognized by others for doing a good job, learn not to expect or need it. A sure sign of professional maturity is to be self-motivated and satisfied without needing praise from others. Loving your work is nothing to be ashamed of; in fact, having a passion for your career is to be envied and shared.

Seek Out and Develop Relationships

Relationships are the way you build a career and get things done. Whipple advises new professionals to seek out and develop relationships with as many people as possible: "Do this with frequent conversations and shared experiences that lead to helpful and trusting partnerships." From the moment you meet another person, you are working on the "terms" of your relationship and your expectations of one another. Even though you may never discuss relationship-building directly, you are always deciding whose interests deserve attention, whose opinion matters, and how cooperative you will be.

> Loving what you do for a living is a great way to spend your life.

Cynthia Cherrey, vice president for student affairs and dean of students at Tulane University, says, "The most important relationships new professionals have are with their students. In order to do this well, they need to think strategically about where their work intersects with the needs and priorities of the institution." The best thing you can do to build a lasting relationship is to link your own interests to the other person's needs. Enhance this sense of connection by engaging in genuine dialogue while you make time to build relationships during your busy day.

Understand Campus Politics

Politics is about relationships with people. Many senior student affairs administrators express regret that, as new professionals, they did not understood this key to navigating politics on their campus. Moneta says, "The nature of politics means there are vested interests, and the nature of humans is competitive. The secret to success is through relationships and information." Student affairs professionals have the strong interpersonal skills necessary to be effective campus politicians.

Early in her career, Huftalin was a young woman in a big power structure dominated by men. She says, "Don't be afraid to navigate the political landscape with your interpersonal skills. It can only strengthen your role so you can be effective." She advises new professionals to immerse themselves in the entire campus culture, not just student affairs. "I had a lot of conversations with my new colleagues throughout the institution, especially academics. It was a great way to build allies around issues to move things forward. I also served on college-wide committees that exposed me to curricular and personnel issues, not just student issues." Cherrey says, "We can't do this work alone. We must work with our academic colleagues." She encourages new professionals to develop relationships with a minimum of five faculty members. "Really understand their role," she says. "Your work and their work don't have to intersect, but try to understand their work and build a relationship."

> **Relationships are the way you build a career and get things done.**

Be a Great Supervisor

Huftalin admits that she was nervous about her first job, where she would be supervising 20 people: "I was comfortable with my programming skills, but when I became a supervisor, all I could think was, 'I don't know how to do this.'" Everyone Rob Kelly supervised was older than he was; and he "was afraid they were going to find me out." Huftalin advises calling colleagues. "I called people and asked them to tell me about the best boss they ever had *and* the worst. I learned that it's important to develop the ability to lead and to coach so you don't kill your employees' spirit." Kelly overcame his fear by "just doing it" and accepting the fact that he would make mistakes. To his surprise, he says, "I also did some amazing things." Learn how to do things, like supervising, by doing them. Moneta stresses the need to "be clear about expectations and be okay about being wrong."

Be a Great Employee

What about the other side of the job—being an employee? "It's just as important to make sure you understand your boss's expectations. If they don't tell you, go ask," advises Juanita Chrysanthou, vice president for student services at Truckee Meadows Community College. Honest performance reviews are not only helpful in clarifying what you are supposed to do and how you are doing; they give you goals for learning and contributing. Chrysanthou says, "Remember that your boss also reports to somebody, and you need to support him or her in achieving that boss's goals."

Surprise Your Mother

Do the things you think you cannot do. "Surprising your mother" means taking the opportunity to be someone your mother doesn't know. If she sees you as meek and mild, be assertive and powerful. If she can't imagine you getting people to do things for you, become a supervisor of 20 people. If she thinks you can't balance your checkbook, get a job managing a $12 million budget. If she believes you would never leave the area where you grew up, apply for a job 1,000 miles away. Do things others do not expect of you. It's the same advice we give our students, just framed a different way: Unshackle yourself from the expectations of others—a boss, a partner, a faculty member, a colleague. Don't hold yourself back.

Don't Be Afraid

Because you are a new professional, some people at the institution will make you feel small and unimportant. Kelly recalls, "My ability to see myself as an educator went a long way in overcoming how other people made me feel about myself." Moneta observes, "Sometimes new professionals try to position themselves as equals to faculty and then take umbrage when they are not. Student affairs is critical but not comparable." Everything we do augments classroom education. Moneta adds, "Be okay with the role of enlivening your students' learning in and out of class."

Looking back on his own career, Cook says, "Don't be afraid to move around. New professionals shouldn't be afraid to go someplace for two or three years and then move on to someplace new." Occasionally, you can do this within your own institution, but Cook says, "Don't be afraid to look at different types of institutions. Expose yourself to a lot of different experiences." Whipple encourages new professionals to take advantage of the knowledge held by senior student affairs officers. "I wish I had overcome my intimidation to learn more from them." As the senior student affairs person on his campus, Whipple advises young professionals and graduate students "not to be afraid to try something new. And don't intellectualize too much. You don't always need a theory and a framework. Sometimes just go with your heart."

Have Broad Shoulders and Small Tear Ducts

There is no doubt about it: This can be a tough profession. As Kelly says, "You must have the stomach to do this job." Every day, the student affairs professional faces critics, controversy, public tensions, and endless problems to resolve. Perhaps that is exactly why we love this work—because of the opportunity to develop skills that allow us to lead the campus in creating a positive environment for student learning. Even the best student affairs professionals make mistakes, but they learn from their mistakes by reflecting, evaluating, and accepting constructive feedback and criticism from others. "Stop worrying about people liking you or your decisions," says Huftalin. Thick skin, a commitment to the bigger picture, and a self-assurance that allows for improvement will not only sustain a successful career in this field but ensure it.

Dick McKaig, vice president for student affairs at Indiana University-Bloomington, was right when he said, "Student affairs is not for the weak of heart or the insecure." He added that the one factor that makes all the difference for a fulfilling career in student affairs is "institutional fit."

Respect the Mission of the Institution

McKaig explains, "In student affairs, you can be a change agent, but you start in a context that is set by the history, tradition, and mission of the institution." Select an institution that is a good fit for you and one that you can fully embrace. Chrysanthou loves the values of community colleges: "The mission fits with my character—opportunities for everyone." Huftalin has worked at two- and four-year colleges as well as private and public institutions. She says, "The advice about understanding institutional mission transcends institution type. An understanding of politics, organizational dynamics, people, and problem solving are needed by student affairs professionals at all institutions." Cook says, "Students are students are students. The foundations are the same." Kelly suggests asking yourself, "Where do I feel I can be most effective?"

Don't try to make your institution be what it wasn't intended to be. Participate in and benefit from the best of what it is and accept the problems. Use language that is valued and understood by your on-campus audience and avoid student affairs jargon. Often this means learning the vocabulary of academicians.

Stay Learner Centered

This is the senior student affairs administrator's way of saying, be completely connected to the academic mission of your institution. Of her division's mission, Cherrey says, "We aspire to be student-centered and learning-focused in creating a distinctive experience. This means we are always thinking about how student affairs can help students map out a learning environment." Totally embrace the student services mission, which is to help students learn. Moneta observes that the term "learner-centered" can be cosmetic, a veneer, just words. "We are truly learner-centered when we develop our programs through the lens of the learner rather than that of the administrator." Cherrey adds, "We must be very intentional in our work. There is structure to a learning environment, and it is the questions we ask that help a student process through a new program or policy." Chrysanthou urges focus: "Everything you do is about helping students have the best educational experience possible."

Respect the Historical Perspective of Campus Colleagues

Art Costantino, vice president of student affairs at Evergreen State College, likens the arrival of new staff on campus to the tension between the enduring influence of past events on world events and U.S. foreign policy, which often seeks a "quick fix" to centuries-old disputes. He says, "An analogous situation occurs when a new staff member arrives on campus. The newcomer will be working with colleagues who remember events from the past and who have a long-term view of the college. It can be frustrating to be told that an idea will not work based on something that occurred 10 years ago; but to be successful, new staff members should convey a respect for the past and strive to understand the perspective of those who have a protracted view of time." If you are promoting an idea that has been tried before, you will not only have to be sensitive to the past, you will also need to be persuasive about why past conditions no longer apply.

Bend Rules and Get Rid of the Dumb Ones

It is a great joy to realize that because we make the policies and rules, we can change them. It is motivating to answer the question, "If we were truly student-centered, what would this campus be like?" with acts of real change led by speedy and strategic thinking. We are inspired by staff, faculty, and students who not only raise the question but bring answers, too.

Be a Student of Students

No one should know your students better than you. Your understanding of demographics, attitudes, trends, and pending changes, and your ability to make predictions for the campus will make you an invaluable asset to the institution. This is only true, however, if you share the results of your studies openly, regularly, and widely. Your ability to share knowledge about your students will greatly increase the impact of successful pedagogy, satisfaction with services, and student learning. Be sure to spend time with students, as opposed to merely assessing, developing, and analyzing. Kelly advises "Get a beat on what's going on."

Be a Problem Solver

Chrysanthou says that new professionals must never lose sight of the fact that their job is to resolve institutional issues and meet institutional needs, "not the other way around. Solve the problems we hope an organized community can solve on campus." Meaning is found in many parts of our work. The ability to bring people together to resolve issues is extremely satisfying. By sharing your knowledge about students, facilitating conversations among diverse campus constituencies, and listening to the wisdom of others, you can help the community become one that curbs substance abuse and violence, retains students, and makes them smarter as they learn more.

> **No one should know your students better than you.**

Advocate for Student Interests, Not Your Personal Agenda

Costantino says that student advocacy requires careful representation of the concerns of individual students and groups of students: "You should strive to make it clear whether you are trying to reflect what students are saying or whether you are talking about what you believe is in the best interest of students. Whatever you try, try not to project your beliefs or agenda onto students." McKaig adds, "The needs of students will change over your student affairs career. It is more important to know how to assess student needs and facilitate change than it is to understand what you and your peers wanted as students."

Join Professional Organizations

"NASPA taught me early on the value of getting to know other new professionals, both on my campus and off of it," says Kelly. Start your network now. Like all the senior student affairs officers who contributed their perspectives to this chapter, Huftalin's professional involvement has led to a personal network of hundreds of colleagues around the country who are valuable resources for advice and ideas on professional issues.

Don't consider professional activities as something extra that helps you get ahead. The myth still exists that you can get ahead simply by doing your job and that things like professional involvement are the cream. You want to be professionally active because that is HOW you can do your job well. Solutions to problems, development of new skills, forecasts of upcoming issues, job contacts, mentors, leadership opportunities, models of best practice, and much more await the student affairs professional who takes advantage of all that associations have to offer.

Review Professional Standards and Ethical Codes

Each fall, Costantino meets with new student affairs staff on his campus. As part of the process, they review codes of ethics and statements regarding good practice (the ACPA "Statement of Ethical Principles and Standards," NASPA's "Principles of Good Practice for Student Affairs," and the Council for the Advancement of Standards in Higher Education's Statement of Shared Ethics). Costantino says, "Become familiar with these documents. These writings reflect the judgment of experienced professionals and are helpful guidelines regarding best practices." The interplay of one's personal ethics with professional standards and principles is an important key to happiness and effectiveness in the job. Be clear with yourself about your unshakeable values and core beliefs. As you advance into jobs with greater responsibilities, your personal ethics will be a useful guide in your role as an exemplary student affairs professional.

Develop Professionally Throughout Your Career

Moneta advises new professionals to "take all you learned in graduate school and contextualize it with your first experiences, because the world is far more complicated." Professional development encompasses clear values, broad capabilities, and valuable work experiences. Senior student affairs officers stress the need to:

☞ Follow through on commitments.

☞ Avoid self-promotion. It gets old!

☞ Become a good writer by rewriting until it is right.

☞ Always arrive prepared.

☞ Think hard before saying "no" to a request or an assignment.

☞ Seize opportunities to learn and demonstrate new qualities.

☞ Learn from new professionals when you are no longer one yourself.

☞ Teach if you are qualified.

☞ Develop trust.

☞ Learn to distinguish the urgent from the important and the useful from the useless.

☞ Create a context for the work you are doing so you see its larger purpose.

All senior student affairs officers were new professionals once. While it was a long time ago, we all remember it as a time of great fun, when we knew everything and nothing, tried to listen and learn from those more senior while forging our way with new ideas and fresh approaches, read everything in the field and felt fortunate to attend student affairs institutes and conferences. We quickly learned that all the cutting-edge knowledge we had gained in our graduate programs (if we were in a college student development program) served us well for the next five years; after that, the learning cycle needed to be rejuvenated forever.

Many of us recall thinking that when we achieved a certain position in the field, we would change things. And many of us have.

Integrate Your Personal and Professional Life

Striving for balance between your personal and professional life is a losing battle. Try integrating all facets of your life so that there is no division, only complementary actions and thought. Personal and professional values are the same, as are constantly shifting priorities of family and staff, activity and reflection, managing and socializing. It doesn't have to be "either/ or" but rather "this, then that." Integrating still allows for boundaries and limits when it comes to personal relationships with students, and for modeling the responsible use of alcohol and the ethical use of money. When living "life as career" you are always on the job, because your personal behavior affects your professional reputation. Fair or not, it is a fact that how you are perceived on campus and in the town will enhance or diminish your ability to be an effective advocate for a student-centered campus.

New professionals fresh from graduate programs should recognize the differences and relish the complexity of the workplace. At some point we became aware of the difference between the classroom setting and work setting. Costantino reminds us that a classroom is not a workplace. "In a classroom, the participants come together for relatively short periods of time, arguments tend to be based on reason, and alternative courses of action can be contemplated without the pressure to make an actual decision. In a workplace, individuals have often worked together for years and developed fascinating patterns of influence and connection, the rational and irrational are mixed, and it is often necessary to quickly arrive at a single course of action."

Develop a Vision of the Possible

People enjoy being around those who are optimistic and positive in the face of realistic challenges and adversity. Become known as a person who acknowledges the problem but overcomes the negatives with creative thinking and new alternatives. Develop a vision of "the possible." Make this vision congruent with the vision of senior campus administrators. Infuse your vision with current and future thinking.

Your vision should take a long look into the future—the future of college students, of higher education, of the student affairs profession, and, most of all, of you. Create and promote this vision so that at first it becomes a possibility and eventually, a reality. Think of yourself and everyone else as a resource in developing competencies and personal influence. Adopt the right mindset, participate willingly, build success for others, and model personal and professional development by leading with integrity.

Paddle Faster Than the Current

Good student affairs professionals are not victims, swept away by powerful currents over which we can exercise little influence. At first it may seem as though we must either paddle upstream, battling all the way, or just go with the flow, hoping we can float along undisturbed. But skilled student affairs professionals, like skilled whitewater rafters, remind us that neither paddling against the current nor going with the flow is a productive tactic. The best way to get where you want to go when negotiating rapids in a fast-moving river is to paddle faster than the current. The best of us anticipate the trends and look far ahead for the issues. This allows us to capture energy and create initiatives, strategies, new rules and philosophies.

Conclusion

What kind of student affairs professional will you become? What values will you hold and act on in this profession as you compose yourself? This concluding chapter is meant to inspire you rather than intimidate you. Developing into a great student affairs professional takes patience and practice. We promise you'll get better as you acquire skills over time. Many of us wish we could relive our first years in the profession. It is a time of discovery, when you are aware of your commitment to students and seek to become more effective at your work as an administrator, educator, programmer, and counselor.

Don't forget your excitement and passion for the job. Chrysanthou observes, "As time goes by, you will have colleagues who are jaded. When *you* cross the line to that place, pull back and remember the time you received the phone call offer of your first job and how excited you were to come onto campus and do great things." Don't abandon ship psychologically while remaining physically.

We offer the following tips and challenges as you embark on a life in service to students, learning, and higher education:

☞ Look into a student's eyes when you are listening.

☞ Walk up and introduce yourself to the scariest faculty member on campus.

☞ Have the courage to challenge authority.

☞ Stop in the middle of the craziest part of the day and admire a piece of art.

☞ Find a handful of colleagues along the way to whom you can turn with your problems and worries for honest advice, sympathy, and friendship.

☞ Take risks, push the envelope a little more, make some mistakes.

☞ Change lives, lots of lives, every single day.

☞ Cry when a student is a heroin addict, a survivor of incest, or their partner is an abuser.

☞ Celebrate when a student is six months into recovery, getting a "B" in statistics, or has moved into a shelter.

☞ Change yourself because of their tragedies and achievements.

☞ Just as you develop a vision for your organization so should you craft a vision for your own personal and professional journey.

☞ Be funny...make people laugh, put them at ease.

☞ Read what your students are reading, listen to their music on the latest technology, and ask them about their hopes, dreams, and fears.

☞ Struggle with a real-life ethical dilemma at least once a day.

☞ View criticism and negative feedback as a gift.

☞ Be the one who always asks, "How is this best for our students?"

☞ Reflect once in a while.

☞ Travel to a foreign land every year to remember what it is like to be a new student on a strange campus.

☞ Remember birthdays.

☞ Go to funerals.

☞ Communicate in person more than in text.

☞ Help realize dreams

☞ ...especially your own.

The inspiration and advice shared by successful senior student affairs officers from a variety of institutions, backgrounds, and beliefs is given to you, the new professional, as a gift. The gift is to learn from our mistakes, be motivated by our insights, and fully embrace the wonderful life you have chosen as a student affairs professional. You will occasionally have your doubts, and you will most certainly know failure, conflict, and sadness. Be assured that these will be far outweighed by the triumphs, easy comfort of career fit, your personal commitment, and the realization of dreams, both yours and those of your students.

Welcome to the finest profession in the world.

Welcome to our world.

Professional Organizations in Student Affairs and Higher Education

American Association of Collegiate Registrars and Admissions Officers (AACRAO)

Category:	Admissions and Student Records/Registrars
National Headquarters:	One Dupont Circle N.W., Suite 520
	Washington, D.C., 20036-1171
	(202) 293-9161, FAX (202) 872-8857
E-mail:	info@aacrao.org
Website:	www.aacrao.org

American College Health Association (ACHA)

Category:	Student Health
National Headquarters:	P.O. Box 28937
	Baltimore, MD 21240-8937
	(410) 859-1500, FAX (410) 859-1510
E-mail:	contact@acha.org
Website:	www.acha.org

ACPA–College Student Educators International (ACPA)

Category:	General Student Affairs
National Headquarters:	One Dupont Circle, NW, Suite 300
	Washington D.C. 20036-1110
	(812) 855-8550, FAX (812) 855-0162
E-mail:	info@acpa.nche.edu
Website:	www.acpa.nche.edu

Association of College Unions International (ACUI)

Category:	Student Unions
National Headquarters:	One City Centre, Suite 200
	120 W. Seventh St.
	Bloomington, IN 47404
	(812) 245-2284, FAX (812) 245-6710
E-mail:	acui@acui.org
Website:	www.acui.org

Association of College and University Housing Officers–International (ACUHO–I)

Category:	Student Housing
National Headquarters:	941 Chatham Lane, Suite 318
	Columbus, OH 43201
	(614) 292-0099, FAX (614) 292-3205
E-mail:	office@acuho-i.org
Website:	www.acuho-i.org

Association of International Educators: NAFSA

Category:	International Students
National Headquarters:	1307 New York Avenue, NW, 8th Floor
	Washington, D.C. 20005
	(202) 737-3699, FAX (202) 737-3657
E-mail:	inbox@nafsa.org
Website:	www.nafsa.org

Association of Fraternal Advisors (AFA)

Category:	Greek Affairs
National Headquarters:	9640 North Augusta Drive, Suite 433
	Carmel, IN 46032
	(317) 876-1632, FAX (317) 879-6981
E-mail:	info@fraternityadvisors.org
Website:	www.fraternityadvisors.org

American Association for Employment in Education (AAEE)

Category:	Placement Services for Education Majors
National Headquarters:	3040 Riverside Drive, Suite 125
	Columbus, OH 43221
	(614) 485-1111, FAX (614) 485-9609
E-mail:	office@aaee.org
Website:	www.aaee.org

Association for the Study of Higher Education (ASHE)

Category:	Higher Education Faculty and Administrators
National Headquarters:	424 Erickson Hall
	East Lansing, MI 48824
	(517) 432-8805, FAX (517) 432-8806
E-mail:	ashemsu@msu.edu
Website:	www.ashe.ws

Association for Student Judicial Affairs (ASJA)

Category:	Student Judicial Affairs
National Headquarters:	P.O. Box 2237
	College Station, TX 77841-2237
	(979) 845-5262, FAX (979) 458-1714
E-mail:	asja@tamu.edu
Website:	www.asjaonline.org

National Academic Advising Association (NACADA)

Category:	Academic Advising
National Headquarters:	Kansas State University
	2323 Anderson Avenue, Suite 225
	Manhattan, KS 66502-2912
	(785) 532-5717, FAX (785) 532-7732
E-mail:	nacada@ksu.edu
Website:	www.nacada.ksu.edu

National Association for Campus Activities (NACA)

Category:	Student Activities
National Headquarters:	13 Harbison Way
	Columbia, SC 29212
	(803) 732-6222, FAX (803) 749-1047
E-mail:	info@naca.org
Website:	www.naca.org

National Association of College Admissions Counseling (NACAC)

Category:	Admissions
National Headquarters:	1631 Prince Street
	Alexandria, VA 22314
	(703) 836-2222, FAX (703) 836-8015
E-mail:	info@nacacnet.org
Website:	www.nacacnet.org

National Association of Colleges and Employers (NACE)

Category:	Placement
National Headquarters:	62 Highland Avenue
	Bethlehem, PA 18017
	(610) 868-1421, FAX (610) 868-0208
E-mail:	mmackes@naceweb.org
Website:	www.naceweb.org/default.asp

National Association of College Auxiliary Services (NACAS)

Category:	Auxiliary Services
National Headquarters:	P.O. Box 5546
	Charlottesville, VA 22903-4610
	(434) 245-8425, FAX (434) 245-8453
E-mail:	info@nacas.org
Website:	www.nacas.org

National Association of Student Financial Aid Administrators (NASFAA)

Category:	Financial Aid
National Headquarters:	1101 Connecticut Avenue, NW, Suite 1100
	Washington, DC 20036-4303
	(202) 785-0453, FAX (202) 785-1487
E-mail:	web@nasfaa.org
Website:	www.nasfaa.org

National Association of Student Personnel Administrators (NASPA)

Category:	General Student Affairs
National Headquarters:	1875 Connecticut Avenue, NW, Suite 418
	Washington, DC 20009
	(202) 265-7500, FAX (202) 797-1157
E-mail:	office@naspa.org
Website:	www.naspa.org

National Conference on Race and Ethnicity in American Higher Education (NCORE)

Category:	Multiculturalism and Diversity
National Headquarters:	3200 Marshall Avenue, Suite 290
	Norman, OK 73072
	(405) 325-3694
E-mail:	pnabavi@ou.edu
Website:	www.ncore.ou.edu

National Intramural-Recreational Sports Association (NIRSA)

Category:	Recreation Services
National Headquarters:	4185 SW Research Way
	Corvallis, OR 97333-1067
	(541) 766-8211, FAX (541) 766-8284
E-mail:	nirsa@nirsa.org
Website:	www.nirsa.org

National Orientation Directors Association (NODA)

Category:	Orientation Staff
National Headquarters:	1313 5th Street, SE, Suite 323A
	Minneapolis, MN 55414
	(612) 627-0150, FAX (612) 627-0153
E-mail:	noda@umn.edu
Website:	www.nodaweb.org

CONTRIBUTORS

MARILYN J. AMEY is professor of higher education and chair of the Department of Educational Administration at Michigan State University. Marilyn received her bachelor's degree in elementary and special education from Wittenberg University, a master's degree in college student personnel from Ohio State University, and a Ph.D. in higher education from Penn State University. Previously, she was a faculty member at the University of Kansas, and she has student affairs experience in residence life and student activities. She served two terms as a NASPA Faculty Fellow and has been a member and chair of the NASPA Dissertation of the Year Committee.

GRACE A. BAGUNU is currently the assistant director of Express to Success programs at the University of California, San Diego. She received her bachelor of arts degree in psychology and a master of arts degree in higher educational administration from the University of Missouri–Kansas City. She has worked in the areas of student activities, student organizations, leadership development, and orientation, and she is actively involved in NASPA at the regional and national levels.

KEVIN W. BAILEY is associate vice president for student affairs at Tulane University. He received his Ph.D. in higher education administration from Bowling Green State University and his bachelor's and master's degrees from Indiana University of Pennsylvania. He previously worked at Millersville University, Bowling Green State University, and the University of North Carolina at Charlotte.

JOY BLANCHARD received a Ph.D. in higher education from the Institute of Higher Education at the University of Georgia, focusing her research primarily on higher education law and institutional liability. She previously was assistant dean of students at the University of Louisiana at Lafayette and has worked in several areas of student affairs, including residence life, judicial affairs, service learning, and student activities. She holds a master's degree from Florida State University in higher education/student affairs and an honors baccalaureate in French education from the University of Louisiana at Lafayette.

CHRISTA COFFEY is an assistant director of student involvement at the University of Central Florida. She has a bachelor's degree in mathematics and a master's degree in educational administration from Texas A&M University, and is working on her doctorate in educational leadership. She served for six years on the NASPA Career Services Committee and as co-chair for the first NASPA/ACUHO-I Placement Exchange, held in 2008.

CAMILLE CONSOLVO is dean of student affairs at Eastern Oregon University. She received her Ph.D. in counseling psychology from Florida State University and her bachelor's and master's degrees from Missouri State University. Camille worked previously at Bowling Green State University, Washburn University, Kansas State University, and Missouri University of Science and Technology. She has worked in counseling, career services, residence life, orientation, judicial affairs, and disability services, and has held administrative positions in both student affairs and academic affairs.

MICHAEL DANNELLS is interim director of admissions at Eastern Oregon University. He received his Ph.D. in college student development and higher education from the University of Iowa and his bachelor's degree from Bradley University. Previously, he served as a professor in the Department of Higher Education and Student Affairs at Bowling Green State University and at Kansas State University. His practitioner experience includes student life, residence life, and new student programs.

KARI ELLINGSON is the associate vice president for student development at the University of Utah, where she has also served as director of the Counseling Center. She has faculty appointments in the departments of Educational Psychology and Educational Leadership and Policy. She earned a bachelor's degree in English from the University of Virginia, and a master's in counseling and a Ph.D. in counseling psychology from the University of North Carolina at Chapel Hill.

SHANNON E. ELLIS is vice president of student services at the University of Nevada, Reno. She received her Ph.D. in higher education from the University of Southern California, her master's in public administration from the University of Massachusetts-Amherst, and her bachelor of science in journalism from the University of Illinois-Champaign Urbana. Shannon is a past president of NASPA.

FLORENCE A. HAMRICK is associate professor of higher education at Iowa State University. She earned a bachelor's degree in English from the University of North Carolina at Chapel Hill, a master's degree in college student personnel from Ohio State University, and a Ph.D. in higher education from Indiana University. Before becoming a faculty member, she held professional positions in career planning and placement and residence life. She is past editor of the *Journal of College Student Development* and a former national chair of the NASPA New Professionals Network.

MELISSA HAZLEY is currently a resident director at Creighton University. She also advises several student organizations such as the Association of Multicultural Greek Organizations and the Inter Residence Hall Government. She has enjoyed working in areas such as student leadership and diversity training and awareness. Melissa is also a member of Delta Sigma Theta Sorority Incorporated. She received a bachelor of arts in American studies with a minor in political science and a master of arts in higher education administration from the University of Missouri–Kansas City.

BRIAN O. HEMPHILL is vice president for student affairs and associate professor at Northern Illinois University in DeKalb. He earned a B.A. in organizational communications at St. Augustine's College, an M.S. in journalism and mass communications at Iowa State University, and a Ph.D. in higher education administration at the University of Iowa. Brian previously worked at Iowa State University, Cornell College, and the University of North Carolina at Wilmington. He currently is co-chair of NASPA's Enough Is Enough campaign to address and stem the tide of violence on college and university campuses.

ERIC R. JESSUP-ANGER is a doctoral candidate in higher, adult, and lifelong education at Michigan State University. He received his bachelor's degree in English and an independent major of education from the University of Wisconsin–Madison; a master's degree in college student personnel from Bowling Green State University; and a graduate certificate in women's studies from Colorado State University. He previously served as a faculty member in the student affairs in higher education program at Colorado State University. He has administrative experience in residence life, student life, judicial affairs, and academic affairs.

CARLA R. MARTINEZ is coordinator of student leadership at Orange Coast College, a community college located in Orange County, California. She earned her bachelor's degree in business administration with a concentration in marketing from Cal Poly State University, San Luis Obispo, and a master's degree in counseling with a specialization in student development in higher education from California State University, Long Beach. Carla previously worked at California State University, Fullerton, and the University of California, Irvine. In addition, she recently served as the co-chair for the NASPA Southern California Professional Development Committee.

BRENT G. PATERSON is senior associate vice president for student affairs at Illinois State University. He earned a bachelor's degree in elementary education from Lambuth College, a master's degree in counseling and personnel services from Memphis State University, and a Ph.D. in higher education administration from the University of Denver. Brent formerly served as dean of student life at Texas A&M University. He has extensive experience with NASPA Career Services and chaired the 2001 and 2005 NASPA Conferences.

LORI M. REESOR is an associate vice provost for student success at the University of Kansas. Lori received her bachelor's degree from the University of Wisconsin–Whitewater, her master's in higher education from Iowa State University, and her doctorate in educational policy and leadership from the University of Kansas. She was dean of students at Wichita State University and worked at the University of Missouri-Kansas City. She is involved in NASPA, including having served as regional vice president for Region IV–West.

RANDI S. SCHNEIDER has a bachelor's degree in social work and a master's in counselor education from Illinois State University, and a doctorate from the University of Illinois at Urbana-Champaign. Currently, Randi is director of the Student Health Center at Indiana University of Pennsylvania. Her student affairs experience has been in residential life, health services, student activities, and student services.

RA SNYDER is vice president for student affairs at the University of received a bachelor's degree in home economics/speech communica-io State University, a master's degree in counseling from St. Cloud and a Ph.D. in higher education from Iowa State University.

Previously, she was vice chancellor for student affairs at the University of Nebraska at Kearney.

CONNIE TINGSON-GATUZ is the director of the Center for Personalized Instruction and project director for the Student Support Services TRIO Program at Madonna University. She has a bachelor's degree in political science and a master's degree in college and university administration from Michigan State University. She is a doctoral candidate in higher education administration. She has previously held positions in the areas of advising, grants administration, student leadership development, mentoring coordination, multicultural programming, residence life, and student life. Over the last decade, Connie has trained professional facilitators for a national student leadership development program, and served as a consultant for various national scholarship programs for college students.

DAWN WATKINS is vice president for student affairs and dean of students at Washington and Lee University. She earned her bachelor's degree in English and master's degree in student personnel services from Virginia Tech, and her Ph.D. in higher education administration with an emphasis in organizational behavior from the University of North Carolina at Greensboro. In addition to her work in student affairs, she is an adjunct faculty member in the School of Law at Washington and Lee.

EUGENE L. ZDZIARSKI II is vice president for student affairs and dean of students at Roanoke College. He holds a bachelor of science in business administration from Oklahoma State University, a master's degree in student personnel and higher education from the University of Tennessee at Knoxville, and a Ph.D. in educational administration from Texas A&M University. He is the former dean of students at the University of Florida and served as regional vice president for NASPA Region III.